Revolution in America

Don Higginbotham

Revolution in America

Considerations & Comparisons

UNIVERSITY OF VIRGINIA PRESS

Charlottesville & London

University of Virginia Press
© 2005 by the Rector and Visitors of the University of Virginia
All rights reserved
Printed in the United States of America on acid-free paper

First published 2005

9 8 7 6 5 4 3 2 1

Library of Congress Cataloging-in-Publication Data

Higginbotham, Don.
   Revolution in America : considerations and comparisons /
Don Higginbotham.
      p.   cm.
   Includes bibliographical references and index.
   ISBN 0-8139-2383-2 (cloth : acid-free paper) — ISBN 0-8139-
2384-0 (pbk. : acid-free paper)
   1. United States—History—Revolution, 1775-1783.
2. United States—History—Revolution, 1775-1783—
Biography. 3. Political leadership—United States—History.
4. Revolutions—History. 5. War and society. 6. State, The.
I. Title.
   E208.H58 2005
   973.3—dc22

                                        2005005033

For
Jim and Suzie
Dick and Leslie
Emory and Winifred

Contents

Acknowledgments

ONE ALWAYS RUNS THE RISK of leaving out of acknowledgments several people who in some important ways have contributed to a book in the making. This danger is particularly likely when the volume in question is made up of essays that were initially written over a considerable period of years—in this case going back to 1990 or so. In almost every case I profited from running most of these pieces by my graduate course on the American Revolution and my undergraduate seminar on the Two American Revolutions: 1776 and 1861. Needless to say, I also absorbed numerous insights from reading the research papers that came out of those courses, just as I widened my horizons from directing M.A. theses and Ph.D. dissertations during the last decade and a half, along with some written in earlier decades. Before enlarging my obligations outside the Research Triangle area, which embraces Chapel Hill, Raleigh, and Durham, I wish to thank the early American scholars who constitute the Colonial Seminar that has met monthly, except for the summers, for nearly a decade at the National Humanities Seminar in the Research Triangle Park. John Nelson, Robert Calhoon, Peter Wood, Elizabeth Fenn, and Holly Brewer, our coordinator, have been a part of our group from the very beginning and always add enormously to the intellectual content of our gatherings.

At the risk of omitting people deserving of thanks, I will mention Ira Gruber, Bill Freehling, Peter Coclanis, Robert M. S. McDonald, Stuart Leibiger, Brian Steele, Lacy Ford, Robert F. Jones, Philander D. Chase, Joseph J. Ellis, Rosalie Radcliffe, Linda Stephenson, Fred Anderson, Peter R. Henriques, John Kaminski, Jim Rees, Emory Evans, John Larson, Peter Onuf, and Michael McGiffert. Once again I was privileged to work with Dick Holway of the University of Virginia Press. My lovely wife, Kathy, has brought her talents as an English major at North Carolina to bear on still another book, which, whatever its faults, always owe its virtues in considerable part to her conceptual and literary talents.

Abbreviations

Frequently cited Washington primary sources are referred to by the following abbreviations:

GW: Writings   John C. Fitzpatrick, ed., *The Writings of George Washington from the Original Manuscript Sources,* 39 vols. (Washington, D.C., 1931–44)

PGW: W. W. Abbot et al., eds., *The Papers of George Washington,* in progress (Charlottesville, Va., 1983–), cited by series:

PGW: Col. Ser.   *Colonial Series* (10 vols., completed)

PGW: Rev. Ser.   *Revolutionary Series* (14 vols. published to date)

PGW: Conf. Ser.   *Confederation Series* (6 vols., completed)

PGW: Pres. Ser.   *Presidential Series* (12 vols. published to date)

PGW: Ret. Ser.   *Retirement Series* (4 vols., completed)

PGW: Diaries   Donald Jackson and Dorothy Twohig, eds., *The Diaries of George Washington,* 6 vols. (Charlottesville, Va., 1976–79)

Revolution in America

Introduction

A CONSTRUCTIVE CRITIC suggested that I ought to take this opportunity to reflect on my forty-year career as a scholar and teacher, to add something about what led me to history, and to include a few words about my approach to the subject. My interest in history seems to have been a part of me for as long as I can remember. My mother taught American history in the public schools when I was growing up, although it was probably for the best that I never took a course from her. So there was much talk about the American past in our home. My father, a successful businessman with only an eighth-grade education, could scarcely join comfortably in these conversations. But as secretary of the local school board, he acquired many complimentary books for me when he ordered textbooks for the schools. My mother put him up to these requests and always stipulated that he ask for any new volumes on the American experience. For a good many years the American Civil War was my intellectual passion, partly, I am sure, because I heard so much about it from my family. My mother's grandfather Jonas Myers served in the Confederate Army and was killed in northeastern Arkansas after the conflict ended while on his way home to Bollinger County in southeast Missouri. Some accounts say that he and several other local men on their return journey were robbed and then lined up and executed by so-called bushwhackers, lawless men who preyed on both sides. But the old tombstone, erected after their bodies were exhumed and returned home, says they were "murdered by Union soldiers." My mother recalled that his widow, a pioneer woman who spit on the floor and was illiterate, lived into her nineties and, as was customary with some war widows, always wore black. Whatever her limitations, she responded to the challenge of raising two sons who never remembered their father, and she encouraged them to obtain what would be the equivalent of a college education today. There were still a handful of people in our community who had lived through the Civil War, and I once interviewed one of them for a school project.

If my father, a World War I veteran, further amplified my historical imagination with stories of his own army experiences, World War II had a much more immediate impact on me. As early as age eight, in 1939, I began to follow the conflict in the newspapers, and I have been an avid reader of that media form ever since. Our elementary school principal insisted when I was about ten that I come into his eighth-grade history class once a week to report on the news from the battlefronts. I probably did not know what I was doing, but I remember I once drew a map on the blackboard of French Equatorial Africa while talking about General Charles de Gaulle and his Free French forces. In 1942 the Army Air Corps erected a base for training glider pilots just two miles north of our town, Malden, because of the low flat terrain in this delta area near the Mississippi River. Soon the small community of 2,000 souls seemed overwhelmed by a host of military personnel just outside our gates. I learned then what I have repeated countless times in writing history, that when you put soldiers and civilians in close proximity—even your own troops—the results are mixed at best. All kinds of people descended on Malden, not wholly unlike the camp followers that accompanied eighteenth-century armies. Subsequently, of course, I lived through other wars—Korea, Vietnam, and the Cold War. The male members of my family, at our frequent clan reunions in the late forties and fifties, predicted that an armed showdown with the Soviet Union was inevitable.

It is hard to escape the conclusion that these experiences led me as a historian to develop a specialty in war and war-related subjects. But even with my abiding interest in history, I regressed. An indifferent student in high school, I compiled a mediocre academic record because girls and athletics took priority. Much to my mother's dismay, I even toyed with contenting myself with a high school diploma and driving a family friend's oil truck to make a living. Except for my mother, a few teachers, and a remarkable city librarian, I did not find much to stretch my mind. I lived in a rural atmosphere, far removed from the closest urban centers, St. Louis and Memphis. Peer pressure, in the short run, was more formative in my teenage years than the really worthwhile people in my life. It was not fashionable in high school to study hard and make good grades. I believe no more than five out of a graduating class of fifty or so went directly to college (a few others went in later years, usually with the benefit of the GI Bill).

At Washington University in St. Louis, after giving up any pretensions to being a college football player and a future coach, I became a more serious student and began to consider the possibility of being a high school history teacher. As a junior I encountered a first-year faculty member, Frank E. Vandiver, who was no more than six or seven years older than I. He was one of the most dynamic, inspiring lecturers I have ever encountered. I fell under his spell, and he took a keen interest in me. He told me I could even call him by his first name, an unheard-of thing fifty years ago. His approach to history would now seem anti-quated to many of my colleagues. Much of what he taught in his Civil War and other courses dealt with what we now call human agency, narrative history that assigned responsibility for successes and failures to individuals—to Abraham Lincoln and Jefferson Davis, to U. S. Grant and Robert E. Lee. His classes were dramatic and exciting. He made little if any attempt to explain the outcome of momentous events in terms of determinism, of impersonal forces. I came to the conclusion that despite the overwhelming advantages that the North had over the South owing to population, industrial resources, and other things, as late as the election of 1864 the outcome of the conflict could have turned out quite dif-ferently.

I entered Vandiver's office in fear and trepidation near the end of the 1952 fall semester. I said that I knew what I came to discuss sounded pretentious, but I had decided I wanted to get a Ph.D. in history and teach in college. Didn't he think that such talk was premature and that I might not have the gray matter to reach such exalted academic heights? He laughed and said that I would have no problem. He had met few if any people of genius in the profession; lead in the seat of one's pants was paramount, for getting the doctorate was actually an endurance contest.

Once committed, I wasted no time. I carried twenty-one hours in the spring term of that junior year and picked up twelve more in the two summer sessions in 1953, finishing my undergraduate degree in three years. After returning for my fourth year in college, now a graduate student, I presented an M.A. thesis on a Civil War topic and fully intended to remain at Washington University for the Ph.D. But Vandiver had some concerns. He felt that the Civil War field was crowded and suggested I specialize instead in the American Revolution, my sec-ond area of interest. He doubted that I should earn three degrees from the same institution. He also believed that as a young academic himself, he might lack the visibility to place doctoral students in desirable positions at the college level.

Vandiver gave me sound advice, although his concern about congestion in Civil War studies may have been exaggerated, for the torrent of books on that struggle continued and remains unabated today. I applied to several prestigious graduate programs that had well-established programs in colonial and Revolu-tionary studies. The one school that offered me an attractive financial package was the University of Nebraska, which was hardly in the Ivy League but had a very sound history department. My mentors at Washington University offered me some advice that is still relevant. It went something like this: if you go to a second-level institution, you probably will do well enough later on in the job market provided you work under the direction of a scholar with national visibility and if that professor will make some effort to place you.

John R. Alden at Nebraska was such a man. Though still in his forties, he had already published four books on the Revolutionary era. He gained much additional visibility with that fourth book in 1954, the year I arrived at Nebraska. *The American Revolution, 1775–1783* became the first or second volume to appear in Harper's much-publicized New American Nation Series, edited by Henry Steele Commager and Richard B. Morris of Columbia University, which eventually came to approximately fifty volumes, the most ambitious effort ever made to embrace the latest scholarship in United States history. Alden's professional stock continued to rise. He began reviewing for the *New York Times Book Review* and contributed a volume in the Louisiana State University Press's History of the South Series. Published in 1957 as *The South in the American Revolution, 1763–1789,* that work was equally well received. These two books indicated one of Alden's virtues as a historian: his ability to synthesize copious amounts of material in a stylistic narrative. Alden's other strong suit was biography and monographic accounts of some phase of a man's public career. Over forty-five years he wrote monographs on John Stuart, the British Indian superintendent; General Thomas Gage, British commander in chief in North America; and Stephen Sayre, American Revolutionary diplomat and European soldier of fortune. Charles Lee and George Washington were the subjects of his biographies.

Alden attracted good students to Nebraska and later to Duke University, where he accepted a James B. Duke Professorship a year after I arrived in Lincoln. Three of his Nebraska students, Jack P. Greene, R. Kent Newmyer, and Don Gerlach, all published notable books in early American history. Alden had considerably more students at Duke, where he taught for nearly twenty years. Jack Greene and I elected to follow him to Duke because he generously convinced his new institution to admit us with financial aid. In some respects Vandiver and Alden were much alike as historians, both noted for biographical and synthetic approaches. Most of Alden's students at Duke wrote biographies of Revolutionary generals or other public figures of the time. We presented him with a festschrift in 1979, *The Revolutionary War in the South: Power, Conflict, and Leadership: Essays in Honor of John Richard Alden,* edited by W. Robert Higgins.

I too initially started with biography, a life of General Daniel Morgan, a frontiersman, Indian fighter, and leading authority on rifle and light infantry tactics in the Continental army. When Alden suggested Morgan, I admitted that I wasn't sure who Morgan was, but he said, "Well, go read about him. You need to write on something that will result in a book if you do a good job." That proved to be sound advice. Most dissertations, even some valuable ones, never see the light of day because no market exists for them. *Daniel Morgan: Revolutionary Rifleman* was published by the Institute of Early American History and Culture and the University of North Carolina Press in 1961 and is still available in paperback. Alden next advised me to start on a second book but to move away from war and things military for the time being at least because, he warned, "You don't want to be pegged as a military historian." There were minimal teaching opportunities for that specialty, though that field opened up to a limited degree in a decade or so. In fact, I have always thought of myself as more a historian of war than as a military historian. I started researching a biography of James Iredell, a North Carolina lawyer, Federalist leader, and United States Supreme Court justice; but the lure of a financially rewarding undertaking proved tempting to a man with a wife and three small children making about $7,000 a year at Louisiana State University.

So I put Iredell aside for the time being (never to write the biography, although I later edited two volumes of his letters and papers) and accepted an advance from Macmillan to produce a volume in that firm's Wars of the United States Series. I turned out to be, at age thirty-two, the youngest author with a contract in the series—and maybe the least qualified. Connections—politics?—count in the academic world as well as everywhere else, and in this case it was my Duke connections. Professor Theodore Ropp of Duke, one of the most eminent military historians in the country, recommended me to the Macmillan series editor, Professor Louis Morton of Dartmouth, another Duke graduate. I wanted to write a different kind of book on the Revolutionary War, one that looked broadly at war and society and minimized the treatment of battles and campaigns. The finished product received a good deal of attention and became a History Book Club selection. Today, given the growing interest in this approach to war, I would have a considerable body of rich secondary literature to draw upon, books and articles by John Shy, Fred Anderson, E. Wayne Carp, Charles Royster, Harry Ward, Judith Van Buskirk, Holly Mayer, and numerous others. I also expanded the chronology normally followed for writing about the war. Instead of focusing solely on the years 1775–83, I went back and began with the impact of the Seven Years' War on the colonies, including the stationing of British troops in America after 1763. I also advanced beyond the traditional 1783 ending date and described the movement for greater national consolidation between that year and the writing and ratification of the Constitution, a document that was both political and military in character.

My principal interests in the last thirty years have led to writing or editing three books on George Washington and publishing a spate of essays and articles, many of them on comparative revolution. Perhaps it is not surprising that a scholar who has devoted his professional life to the American Revolution would feel a need to come to grips with Washington, the human centerpiece of American nation making, and to look at our revolution in relation to such upheavals elsewhere in the world over the last two hundred years or more. My own training as a graduate student proved invaluable in trying to grasp the big picture of Washington and his revolution, to do so in a larger context by looking at other revolutionary chieftains and the movements they led. Professor William T. Laprade, who chaired the Duke Department of History for many years, had retired by the time I arrived in 1955, but his view that graduate students should be broadly trained still prevailed. My doctoral orals covered five fields: the United States, Britain since 1688, European diplomacy since 1815, all of Latin America, and political thought, the last-mentioned a required outside field in the Department of Political Science. My adviser also insisted, given my interest in the seventeenth and eighteenth centuries, that I should take a readings course on Europe from the Renaissance to the French Revolution. The Duke idea behind such an endurance contest was that American history graduate students should devote their time to acquiring breadth. Americanists, except for their dissertation field, could wait and learn United States history when they started teaching. (Indeed, the Duke system in those days required new faculty members in American history to spend their first two or three years teaching the European survey course in order for them subsequently to place the American story in a wider framework.) This strenuous undertaking served me well not only in the long term when I delved into Washington's generation but also in the short run, for during my first three years of full-time teaching—at Duke, the College of William and Mary, and Longwood College—I mainly offered sections of Western Civilization. Today, an American history doctoral student at the University of North Carolina must take only one six-hour field outside of United States history.

My earlier conviction that individuals—human agency—have often made a profound difference received reinforcement from this rigorous education. Certainly early modern thinkers and writers such as Hume, Voltaire, and Rousseau believed it to be the case, even if their great-man theories of history were sometimes overblown. It is probably true that a leader such as an American president can achieve greatness only if he encounters a crisis. James Monroe and Grover Cleveland never confronted the test. But there is no guarantee that a chief executive will rise to the occasion. President James Buchanan did not measure up during the secession turmoil, and President Herbert Hoover failed to do so in the Great Depression. What is so incredible about Washington, Lincoln, and Franklin Roosevelt is that all three dealt effectively with a succession of crises, with Washington's extending over twenty years and Roosevelt's over a dozen years. That sets the trio apart from other American notables, elevates them to the highest level of attainment.

Nothing does more to refute the notion that history is shaped by irreversible currents than the examination of wars and revolutions. The statement applies even to the most mundane kinds human behavior, where the lost dispatch, a shift in the wind, or a rivalry between two ranking generals—say, General John Burgoyne and Sir William Howe or Charles, Lord Cornwallis, and Sir Henry Clinton in our War of Independence—can generate wholly unforeseen consequences in a battle or campaign. Carl von Clausewitz, the preeminent military thinker of modern times, wrote in the aftermath of the Napoleonic struggles of war as being not unlike sitting down to a game of cards. How right these cautionary ideas were in terms of the War of Independence, which pitted the thirteen disunited colonies against Europe's foremost superpower after 1763. And yet I know of no well-respected historian who even ventured the suggestion that the odds might have been against Britain's subduing its wayward provinces in 1775—that is, not before France and America suffered catastrophes in Southeast Asia in the 1950s and 1960s. Vietnam is only one of countless instances where comparative history can be illuminating. Things do not have to follow a set scenario. Sometimes there are anywhere between a handful and an infinite number of variations that might have brought different results.

That is why I believe that counterfactual history can be rewarding. What if Washington, hardly a part of the leadership of the Virginia House of Burgesses, had not been elected to the Continental Congress? He would hardly have been that body's choice for commander in chief of the Continental army. What if Virginia had not ratified the federal Constitution, an uphill fight in the state convention in 1788; then, with Washington ineligible, who would have been elected president of the United States? America's war in Iraq that began in 2003 provides further grist for the mill of legitimate counterfactual history. Two instances concerning loyalists during the American Revolution illustrate the point. What if Britain had made great efforts to win over neutralists and skeptical loyalists by promptly creating legitimate civilian governments in areas occupied by royal armies in the half-dozen years after 1775? And what if the London ministry had refused to buy uncritically the claims of departed crown administrators and loyalists exiles from the Carolinas that redcoats would be greeted as heroes if they invaded the southern states in the late 1770s? Recently one United States Army officer, mindful of misinformation that partly at least drove the war in Iraq, referred to these Pollyannaish loyalist exiles as "Chalabis."

Civil War scholars ponder the possible consequences for Lincoln's presidential ambitions in 1860 had he not given his Cooper Union speech in New York City in February of that year. On the subject of the Constitution and slavery, it was masterful in content, electrifying his audience. New York was the media capital of America. The soon-to-be-famous photographer Mathew Brady clicked his shutter on the tall midwesterner, whose national political career had been limited to a single term in the House of Representatives more than a decade earlier. Lincoln's address appeared the next day in its entirety in four of the city's newspapers. The Battle of Gettysburg also has elicited "what ifs." For example, the second day of fighting found Colonel Joshua L. Chamberlain and his 20th Maine Regiment protecting the Federal left flank from their position on the rocky elevation called Little Round Top. The battle's outcome may have been decided when Chamberlain, his ammunition exhausted, charged with fixed bayonets the on-coming Alabamians, driving them back and preventing the entire Union left from exposure to Confederate fire had he given up Little Round Top.

In every one of these examples, one's thinking is challenged to explain why certain things did not happen. Then, having done that, we can more successfully account for what did happen. But "what ifs" are useful only when they are plausible, when there is solid historical evidence that different results were quite possible and not merely "parlor games." Comparative and counterfactual history do not always enlighten us, but they are often worth a try. When a certain distinguished historian of the American Civil War advised President Lyndon Johnson to stay the course in Vietnam, as Lincoln had done in the midst of severe criticism in 1864, the historian and the president were guilty of a grievous mistake.

The eight essays in this volume were all written since 1990. Some were initially talks or lectures, including two presidential addresses to historical organizations. Only chapter 1 has never been previously published. Each chapter begins with a short introduction designed specifically for this volume, explaining how I happened to write it and how it fits into a larger historical context. They are excursions into comparative history and revolutionary history. Although counterfactual questions invariably inform my own thinking, I do not in every case specifically present the reader with "what if" alternatives. I agree with the notion that historians always think somewhat in counterfactual terms as they work toward conclusions, even when they are unaware of the concept itself.

These offerings are also linked by the fact that they deal with events that lead to wars or that occurred in wartime. Let me explain briefly. I am in varying degrees comparing my subjects with other peoples, places, and time frames. Some examples illustrate the approach. In the first section, I compare George Washington and Thomas Jefferson and their fellow members of the Virginia dynasty with other political leaders of their generation, both in terms of their rise to leadership positions (chapter 1) and in terms of their disagreements, which in three instances led to estrangements within the Old Dominion's hierarchy (chapter 2). Washington's relationship with three women reveals how each, in her own way, affected his life in general and his public career as well (chapter 3). In the second section I compare the process of state formation in early modern Europe and eighteenth-century America (chapter 4), and I similarly look at how the Federalists and Antifederalists during the ratification debates in 1787–88 clashed on the subject of controlling the state militias (chapter 5). This section also examines the connection between European and American military education (chapter 6). Both essays in the third section (chapters 7–8) endeavor to distinguish between northern and southern regional thinking and behavior about war and martial ardor. And in various ways all eight pieces are about people who engaged in revolution, but only the last two focus on both the American revolutions of 1776 and 1861. In *War and Society in Revolutionary America,* a collection of essays published in 1988, I made some earlier forays into comparative history along with some more focused pieces on the American Revolution.

Statesmen in War and Peace

1 | *Washington's Remarkable Generation*

THIS UNDERTAKING ORIGINATED as a keynote address at a conference for Jefferson interpreters sponsored by Monticello's Thomas Jefferson Research Center in Charlottesville, Virginia, on September 24, 1998. The numerous attendees came from such diverse places as National Park Service sites, including Independence Hall and the Jefferson Memorial, and privately operated institutions, including the Missouri Historical Society, Colonial Williamsburg, and Poplar Forest, Jefferson's vacation home near Lynchburg. One thing, if not others, all conference participants could agree on: the challenge of presenting Jefferson fairly and accurately to the public had increased significantly in the 1990s because of the growing literature that limned dark images of the Master of Monticello, especially over slavery. Before my visit to the research center, the heaviest body blows that decade had come from books that had appeared the previous year: Joseph J. Ellis's *American Sphinx: The Character of Thomas Jefferson* and Annette Gordon-Reed's *Thomas Jefferson and Sally Hemings: An American Controversy.* The interpreters reported that they had been criticized for doing either too little or too much with those persons whom Jefferson preferred to call his servants, whose quarters were known as Mulberry Row. One interpreter reported that a visitor to Monticello expressed the view of many others when he complained that he had come to see Jefferson's house with its marvelous inventions and not to hear staff members give him a guilt trip about the peculiar institution. The release of the now much publicized DNA report just a few weeks after my presentation led to the Thomas Jefferson Memorial Foundation's appointing a committee of experts from various disciplines to examine all forms of existing evidence on the Jefferson-Hemings relationship. The result was that the Monticello Web site now states that Thomas Jefferson "most likely was the father of all six of Sally Hemings' children" (http://Monticello.org/plantation/hemingscontro/dnareport6.html).

Washington, the other principal Founder covered in this essay, thus far has escaped most of the criticism on slavery that now engulfs Jefferson, partly at least because Washington's slaves received their freedom in accordance with the provisions of his will, whereas Jefferson manumitted only the Hemings children. Although rumors have circulated of Washington's having had sexual dalliances with his bond servants, they have been traced to British sources in the Revolutionary War or to his later political enemies. More recently, descendants of Wes Ford, a bondsman of Washington's brother John Augustine, have claimed that family oral tradition traces Ford's paternity to Washington. Henry Wiencek, in his recent *An Imperfect God: George Washington, His Slaves, and the Creation of America,* seems intrigued with that possibility but draws back from making that assertion. Even so, Wiencek's book goes too far. No evidence at this point places Washington as ever having been in the presence of Wes Ford's mother. Washington, of course, appears never to have fathered any children; he confessed it was a sad dimension of his otherwise rewarding marriage. If any comparison between Jefferson and Washington is worth making, it is that as the years passed Jefferson grew more unwilling to express concerns about human bondage. Washington, by contrast, steadily became more openly opposed to its continuation in America.

———— • • • ————

MY GRAND STRATEGY IS to advance the argument that the great-man idea, woven into the fabric of the eighteenth century, served Revolutionary America well, that it seemed to have disappeared in a generation or so, but that it continues to hover in our psyche in some form. It lingers because few leaders have measured up to the Founders. That itself suggests a difficult truism to admit: namely, as Freud put it, we need fathers not only in our personal lives but also on a higher level, whether our political system is elitist or democratic. The faces enshrined on Mount Rushmore are political giants, not our renowned scientists or literary lights. If the Founders are down today, particularly in certain academic circles, they are not down for the count; they will come back.[1]

This treatment of the subject takes as its eighteenth-century examples Washington and Jefferson because they stand out above all others for their accomplishments and because they draw attention to Virginia, which led the way in producing eminent men in the Revolutionary years. In the nation's capital we have the Washington Monument and the Jefferson Memorial. Owing to constraints of space my undertaking neglects the four other great men of that era: Franklin, Madison, Hamilton, and John Adams. They have also been neglected in the sense that they are not memorialized in the District of Columbia with pantheons like those we have erected for Washington and Jefferson. Perhaps all six should be so recognized. Many scholars have maintained that these half-dozen worthies deserve to be in a class by themselves for their astounding accomplishments in a lifetime of public service. The late Richard B. Morris, in his *Seven Who Shaped Our Destiny,* conducted a less than successful campaign to add John Jay to this list.[2] Hamilton and Adams in their own day suffered from quirky personalities and perceptions about their alleged monarchical tendencies.

Madison, who had the finest political mind of the group, stood out in the movement for the writing and ratification of the Constitution and in the initial term of Washington's presidency; but later he encountered his own image problem—that of being retiring and nonassertive and being simply another Jefferson. Indeed, Madison faced serious competition for the presidential nomination of his own party in 1808. And his presidency foundered on the War of 1812. Even so, his stature rose during his retirement years after he became a national treasure as "the last of the fathers." It would not be until after World War II, however, that Madison approached equal billing with Washington, Jefferson, and Franklin in the historians' guild.[3]

By the conclusion of the Founding era, these three men—Washington, Jefferson, and Franklin—had captured the bulk of the national acclaim. The last-named never became highly controversial, although Franklin had his critics, especially in Congress, because as a diplomat he was not a hardliner in dealing with France.[4] Franklin might have been tarnished by the party battles of the 1790s, but he perhaps luckily departed from the stage before the fallout from the French Revolution. On the other hand, had the lives of Washington and Jefferson been cut drastically short, Franklin might have been heralded as the foremost Revolutionary American, as he was in 1776. At that time, of course, his worldwide reputation rested on his accomplishments as a scientist.

Recall the excitement when Franklin and Voltaire both appeared at the Academy of Science in Paris in 1778 amid exclamations that they were the two most illustrious notables of a century noted for its Enlightenment immortals. When the members cried out that the savants should do more than bow and extend hands, that they should embrace in the French manner, the two geriatric performers hugged and exchanged kisses on the cheek. In the same year the renowned sculptor Jean-Antoine Houdon chiseled his marble likeness of Franklin.[5]

Controversies of the post-Constitution decade permanently ruptured the Washington-Jefferson relationship, but Jefferson in after years would draw the best overall assessment we have of Washington's strengths and weaknesses.[6] Would Washington have shown equal generosity to Jefferson had he survived beyond 1799? Maybe not, for he rarely displayed a forgiving side. Generals Adam Stephen, Charles Lee, and Horatio Gates, Secretary of State Edmund

Randolph, and George Mason, his old friend and neighbor, would attest to that if they were still around. Washington's hard edge may explain why some of his biographers have had trouble taking seriously Jefferson's political concerns about certain measures of the Washington administration.

Now, however much our eighteenth-century stars may have had their own political and personal rivalries, the idea of a great-man theory of history hardly disappeared during the Revolution. That is perhaps ironic, for it was a republican revolution, or it became that by 1776 when Americans crafted constitutions in the name of the people, eschewing monarchy and other aristocratic institutions. Yet deference remained powerful and seductive. Americans continued to elect their betters to office. Some of Washington's countrymen, however, did not rest easy with the adulation heaped on the Virginian during the Revolution and afterward. The language used to extol him—"God Save Great Washington," for example—troubled John Adams during the war. He did not wish to trade George III for George I, although his wife Abigail opined that the American George looked more like a king than the British George. John Adams, perhaps more conservative in later years, did something of a switch. He offended Congress and embarrassed Washington when as vice president he proposed a pompous title for the first president. And some of his other utterances and writings in the postwar years kept him in hot water. Few prominent men of the Revolution would have been uncomfortable with Adams's contention that the electorate should elevate to office those most conspicuous for their experience, fortune, and family. But by that time it invited retribution to express such notions.[7]

In fact, one historian maintains persuasively that the first six American presidents, from Washington through John Quincy Adams, were expected to behave according to the prescription embodied in Henry St. John Bolingbroke's well-known 1730s essay *The Patriot King,* which encouraged Crown Prince Frederick, on succeeding George II as George III, to dismiss Prime Minister Robert Walpole and to turn kingship in a positive direction. British monarchs should rise above the political infighting, commercialism, and corruption of Walpolian England and reign for the good of the nation. They should be wise and just, staying above factions and schisms, and act in disinterested fashion for the people. Such ideas had been around since classical times, emphasizing additionally that disinterestedness and independence not only characterized the right kind of magistrate but also the right kind of citizen, notwithstanding countervailing forces of narrow private interests.[8]

Such thinking appears not wholly naive, even from our angle of vision. Chief executives still assert that they are president of all the people. Leaders do have the opportunity to set a moral tone and provide a sense of purpose. No doubt that is why we continue to quote President John F. Kennedy's inspiring first inaugural plea that we "ask not what your country can do for you but what you can do for your country." I agree with Columbia University historian Allan Nevins, who, in a lecture at Charlottesville, Virginia, in the 1950s, stated that "under our American system, the President always gives tone, character, and tendency to the government. An able, resourceful, farsighted President multiplies the faculties of even the ablest subordinate, as a weak president paralyzes their powers. An idealistic President does something to uplift his nation, and a vulgar President to vulgarize it."[9]

The creation of the presidency itself offers further evidence that the authors of the Constitution believed that their system of selecting leaders, whatever its definition, would continue to elevate men of great virtue, experience, and ability to the highest political stations. Therefore, the presidency, a post of unprecedented power and influence, would be in the hands of responsible and respected leaders. Hence, the president might be reelected more than once, and he received the veto authority. That the office might ever become a popularity contest would have been unthinkable. After all, the electoral college would pick the president, not the general public.

Another irony about the continuation of great-man thinking stems from America's birth in the Age of the Enlightenment when countless forms of conventional wisdom received slings and arrows. Superstitions, dogmas, and tradition encountered withering criticisms in the salons of the philosophes. America after 1776 beckoned as a laboratory where ideas and theories about how things ought to be were finally put to the test: freedom of speech, religion, separation of powers, and federalism drew particular attention in the Age of Reason. Even so, some, but not all, positive historical change could be explained by the performance of a single individual. Francis Bacon, still influential in the mid-eighteenth century, placed at the top of his list of public benefactors "founders of states and commonwealths."[10]

David Hume, who prided himself on his realism, displayed a divided mind on the subject. Though distrustful of the wielders of power, he conceded in the *Ideal of a Perfect Commonwealth,* published in 1752, that it was not inevitable that the imposing leader, the symbol of force and unity in empire building, succumb to the temptations of the sword and become an absolute monarch. A modern leader might someday reveal the wisdom and virtue of a Solon or a Lycurgus and fashion a new state in an expansive domain to promote the happiness and liberty of future generations. Hume died in 1776, before he could follow the campaign of a tidewater planter in quest of such an objective. Voltaire, for all his withering fire at the machinery of the old regime, still embraced the great-man theory, although he thought that sometimes official honorifics were bestowed prematurely, as in the case of Louis XIV. The acts of great men deserve the attention of all time because they can instruct the young, inculcate virtue, and instill devotion to the fatherland. His own frequent correspondents included Catherine the Great and Frederick the Great.

How did Washington and Jefferson acquire their talents and secure the opportunity to use those talents—to do the things outside Virginia that made them great men? One finds no more intriguing questions about the Founding Fathers than these, along with a corollary question about Virginia. Did Virginia breed more talent than any other colony-state? Not only did Virginians command the Continental army and write the Declaration of Independence, but stalwarts from the Old Dominion served as president of the Continental Congress, principal author of the Constitution, first distinguished chief justice, and president of the United States from 1789 to 1825, except for John Adams's single term.

Let us put off the most difficult question for a moment—how they acquired their talents—and address why so many of them obtained their opportunities to operate on what became in the Revolution a continental and then a national stage. Their opportunities came in part from being Virginians, hailing from a populous, powerful, and geographically strategic colony-state. The Continental Congress recognized advantages in Virginia's leadership; indeed, eventually it became the leader, even eclipsing Massachusetts, exercising a role that could hardly have been assumed by smaller states such as New Hampshire or Delaware or larger states with internal divisions such as New York or Pennsylvania. We will never be sure, but men from Georgia or Connecticut might have equaled the Virginians' accomplishments had they received the opportunities. So assuming that the Virginians had the talents, and they did, it made eminent sense for the Old Dominion to lead in severing the ties with Britain, winning independence, ceding the western lands during the Confederation, bringing about the Constitution, and launching the federal government. In short, Virginians got a careful look because they were Virginians, and American dignitaries elsewhere liked what they saw.

In all probability Virginians attained high station in their province for reasons special to their own immediate surroundings and for other reasons in common with elites throughout America and possibly elsewhere. In the early modern period, landed gentry in the Western world constituted the primary source of direction. One examines the backgrounds of veteran members of the Virginia House of Burgesses and its chieftains and finds a high percentage of them to have been from old, well-established planter families from long-settled areas, Anglican, and British in origin. Half of the members in the leadership category received some college or university education. Jefferson studied at the College of William and Mary; Washington, whose father died when the boy turned eleven, failed to receive the British education that his older brothers Lawrence and Augustine had enjoyed.[11]

Charles Sydnor saw in the making of this leadership a pathway to power. First, a man proved himself by the successful management of his estate, and then he advanced through a succession of offices to the Burgesses and finally to its inner circle.[12] Clans that had consistently contributed to the gentry tradition of personal sacrifice and public engagement expected their offspring and, in turn, their children's sons to do no less. In theory, at least, they reluctantly, or generously, but never eagerly, stood a poll; they did not campaign or give speeches (and we know that Jefferson and Washington possessed modest forensic skills). In all this, the office sought the man; the man did not seek the office. Littleton Waller Tazewell told of a gathering of York County freeholders who showed displeasure with two speakers offering themselves for election to the state's constitutional ratifying convention in 1788. A freeholder got up and announced that they could do better. The assemblage concluded that George Wythe and John Blair ranked head and shoulders above the announced candidates. When the crowd proceeded to Wythe's house—he was not present at the meeting or in search of office—it chanted, "Will you serve? Will you serve?" Wythe lacked a choice; he could not refuse.[13]

Edmund S. Morgan has raised the disturbing suggestion that the Virginians' achievements owed much to slavery. If their wealth and plantation management skills cannot be disconnected from the peculiar institution, slavery per se was not essential to the formation of an elite class there or in other places—not to European agrarian elites, or Hudson Valley patroons, or the nonrural leadership of Massachusetts, which, more than any other colony-state, rivaled Virginia in the quantity and quality of its luminaries. However Virginia's first families amassed their wealth, they would have found common cause with the yeomanry because of universal desires to advance tobacco cultivation, inland transportation, and westward expansion.[14]

A more demonstrable point, in acknowledging that we savor too much moonlight and roses in this class as we traipse through their surviving mansions, is this: the opportunity to advance because of their pedigrees provided no guarantees. Not every planter measured up to a Washington or a Jefferson. Some, like William Byrd III, Robert Wormeley Carter, Charles Carter Jr., and Richard Bland Jr., fell short. And, for all their Revolutionary accomplishments, neither Washington nor Jefferson relished the legislative arena, where they performed as constructive representatives, not emulating enthusiastic workmen like Richard Henry Lee and Edmund Pendleton.[15] Even so, they reaped incalculable benefits from their apprenticeship in this particular forum, which proved effective and harmonious and expanded its power in the eighteenth century at the expense of its royal governors, all the while maintaining civil and usually cordial relations with most of those executives prior to the imperial crisis.

Even though they hardly enjoyed the daily grind of drafting bills and resolutions, both Washington and Jefferson must have displayed intangible qualities that make for leadership: acumen, sagacity, and the ability to deal with men. Their particular talents suitable to the defense of American liberties vaulted them to the top of the leadership ladder in 1774. Washington, because of his military background and intercolonial visibility, and Jefferson, because of his grasp of constitutional issues and literary skills, helped frame Virginia's response at home and represented it in the Continental Congress.

Now for the other part of our effort to fathom the special preparation of these Virginians: the things they shared with other Americans such as John Adams, Alexander Hamilton, Benjamin Franklin, and an impressive array of other worthies who fall in a slightly secondary category, including John Hancock, John Jay, John Dickinson, James Wilson, James Iredell, and the Morrises, Rutledges, and Pinckneys. Just as the argument thus far has been that special things about Virginia cast light on leadership in the Old Dominion, unique things about the American experience and the Western heritage help account for the remarkable galaxy of men who secured independence and created a nation.

First, Revolutionary leaders had time to practice statecraft because they encountered severely limited career opportunities, not only by the standards of the next century, which saw unlimited professional choices resulting from liberal capital formation and its link to the transportation and industrial revolutions, but also by European career choices in their own century. In Hanoverian England a combination of family and abilities (often the former proved enough) provided entry to the navy, army, and established church or to a scholar's life at a venerable university. America, by contrast, remained overwhelmingly rural and agrarian, with a handful of small, commercially oriented cities and a sprinkling of tiny, struggling colleges.

Second, there was, however, one new career opportunity, which became closely linked to public service, the way the ownership of landed estates had been and continued to be. Many of the finest minds in the colonies—here Washington was an exception—turned to the law and away from the clergy, the earlier magnet for prominent young men of intellect and ambition.[16] Edmund Burke underscored this development in his 1775 speech in the House of Commons urging conciliation with the colonies. "In no country . . . is the law so general a study," he proclaimed. American legal authorities had from their studies become "acute, inquisitive, dexterous, prompt in attack, ready in defence, full of resources. . . . They augur misgovernment at a distance; and sniff the approach of tyranny in every tainted breeze." It is no exaggeration that ours was a lawyers' revolution, and that was fortunate since the colonists needed men schooled in law and constitutionalism to defend American rights within the empire and later to write constitutions at the state and national level.[17]

Third, for another generation or more, they normally could concentrate on statecraft without newspaper intrusions into their private lives and without engaging in overt partisanship or political party activity. To be sure, exceptions to every generalization are part of history. But if Jefferson's enemies excoriated him on trumped-up charges of atheism in the 1790s, Richmond publisher James Callender's accusations about the president and Sally Hemings produced only short-lived reverberations and hardly received mention in Jefferson's smashing reelection victory in 1804.[18] And as for party, even Jefferson, who behind the scenes guided his followers in Congress, never bought the idea of party as desirable and refused to accept the label as head of the Republicans.

The fourth factor is partly intangible, impossible to quantify or define precisely. Arnold Toynbee helps us with his challenge and response theory: the idea that there are those historical moments when men have risen above themselves, so to speak, invigorated and inspired to do momentous things because of difficult if not seemingly impossible tasks that their generation cannot escape confronting. And what challenges could have been more imposing than those faced by American leaders between 1763 and 1800 or so? They not only brought to these challenges their commitment to public life, their political experience, and their legal background, but they also drew on the Enlightenment, with its emphasis on the restoration of the classics, the reading of history, and the idea of progress.

Never have Americans employed history in their national discourse as fully as did the Revolutionaries. Madison's *Notes on Debates* at the federal Convention and the *Federalist Papers* are among the prime examples of the vitality of the past for men who wanted to put their human engineering into context and perspective. History inspired them just as it cautioned them to make their own

experience the guide as to what to do.[19] They could not and should not replicate the past. America was different, with wonderful possibilities. They could
make a new and better America, which could become a beacon to the world.
That was all pretty heady stuff. Jefferson can be quoted endlessly on these hopes
and possibilities. And we do not need to leave out Washington, with his limited
formal education, who wrote nothing like the Declaration of Independence or
Notes on Virginia. But he had a library of 900 or so volumes. Jefferson considered him reasonably well read in history, and he seems to have been a voracious
consumer of newspapers.[20] His Circular to the States in 1783 shows his vision—
infected with the challenge and response idea—and his sense of Enlightenment
possibilities. America's birth, he proclaimed, came in an age when the rights of
men and the principles of government were better understood than ever before.
So if Americans faltered at nation making after the War of Independence, if they
failed to emerge from "their political probation," they could blame only themselves. With "the eyes of the whole World . . . turned upon them," they would,
by their success or failure, determine "whether the Revolution must ultimately
be considered as a blessing or a curse: . . . not to the present age alone, for with
our fate will the destiny of unborn Millions be involved."[21]

Here we have a generation that had no doubt of the justice of its mission of
nation making and its implications for humankind. One is struck by how often
our forefathers used the word *posterity.* They were thinking ahead of the implications of their deeds for the present and for the future. In all this we find a distinction between a leader and a statesman. After all, a leader may get society to
do his bidding, but his goals may not be beneficial, may even be disastrous, ex-
emplified by a Napoleon or a Hitler. A statesman leads his countrymen in di-
rections that prove positive in the long term. He has a sense of history, of the
direction human tides are moving. Robert Penn Warren observed with a literary
man's sensitivity that the Revolution's giants look serene and confident in their
portraits. They felt good about what they were doing, whereas most major characters of the Civil War era look drawn and pensive in their photographs.[22]

None of the Founders were more focused than Washington and Jefferson.
That explains to some degree at least why they were the most formidable figures
of their age. Washington's eye always steadied on strengthening the Union and
forging bonds of nationality. Jefferson's vision focused consistently on expand-
ing the boundaries of liberty. When we think of union and nationality, we visual-
ize Washington, and when we talk of liberty, we go back to Jefferson.[23]

It is hardly surprising that ideas about great-man history would not long survive
the American Revolution in the New World and would come under assault in

much of the Old World after the French Revolution. Their demise sprang from the very nature of the American Revolution, although their implications did not become fully apparent until the rise of Jacksonianism in the 1820s. Patrician and participatory politics coexisted for a time. The changes occurred gradually. In Virginia, for example, by 1800 the freeholders expected candidates to give speeches and even to debate each other. And yet, as Daniel P. Jordan notes, the composition of the state's congressional delegation continued into the early nineteenth century to show little variance from the profile of the membership of the House of Burgesses on eve of the Revolution.[24] No doubt the generation born after the Revolution found it relatively easy to discard elitist values. Trends similar to changing political ideas and practices manifested themselves in the military, the church, and the professions. Indeed, as Joyce Appleby explains, innovation and opportunity became American gospel.[25]

Alexis de Tocqueville, visiting America in 1831, observed, as did countless others at home and from abroad, the leveling taking place in the fledgling nation. He said that European states still possessed a well-defined social base from which to draw their leadership in contrast to America, where no recognized pool of talent resided in a given place. Elected leaders were "absolutely on the same footing as the rest of the citizens. They are dressed the same, stay at the same inn when away from home, are accessible at every moment, and shake everybody by the hand. They exercise a certain power defined by the law; beyond that they are not at all above the rest." Madison, among others, worried in his retirement years that learned men of reasonable instincts and deliberate actions now seemed to lose out to political opportunists, who pandered to the public with simple solutions and false promises. If his judgments sound harsh, they hardly lacked verisimilitude. Davy Crockett, defeated for reelection to Congress, spoke caustically about electioneering. To win, one made promises, promises, promises—everything people wanted and more if one could think of anything. Promises cost nothing![26]

In democracies, it seems, the price for their political forms is a lowering of the talent level. In his first inaugural address, President Andrew Jackson lectured his audience on the new day in American politics. Offices existed for the benefit of the people, and therefore public positions should be open to people of all backgrounds. Their duties were plain and easy to comprehend.[27] It is no accident that in 1824, during the early upsurge of Jacksonian Democracy, the first of what would subsequently be an endless outpouring of campaign biographies appeared. That genre of political literature has stressed that our presidential candidates are like us, not different from us, not superior in any way.[28] (Such biographies, however, no longer claim that the subjects have log-cabin origins, although they sometimes come close. For example, Hubert Humphrey, the 1968 Democratic nominee, said that he was born in a small apartment above his father's drugstore since log cabins were in short supply at the time!) John Quincy Adams, the last president of the old school, who refused to campaign for reelection or reward his followers with public offices, lost to Andrew Jackson, the embodiment of the emerging political age, in 1828. The influential commentator Walter Lippmann, in the *Public Philosophy,* claimed that since the early nineteenth century in the Western world, men of substance have hesitated to stand for office because people would no longer let their leaders lead.[29] In his classic examination of American political life and institutions, James Bryce, a frequent visitor to this country and British ambassador in Washington in the early twentieth century, echoed views expressed earlier by Jefferson and later by Lippmann. Bryce's *American Commonwealth* devoted chapters to "Why Great Men Are Not Chosen President" and "Why the Best Men Do Not Go into Politics."[30] I had an elderly Socratic political science professor in graduate school who mused that we would be fortunate to elect as our presidents the very best second-raters available.

Jefferson, of course, hoped we would not have to pay such a price. The answer for him meant no more political upstarts like Andrew Jackson, whom he considered unfit and ill-tempered. Although he trusted that our future leadership cohort would not have to come from a landed gentry such as the one he knew in Virginia, he did favor the creation of an elite achieved through education, as did Washington. In this regard Jefferson's views during the Revolution on the role of a three-tiered educational system for his own state and his later paternity of the University of Virginia are well known. And Jefferson created the United States Military Academy in 1802 largely as a way of breaking the grip of the aristocratic Federalists on the army's officer corps.[31] Jefferson himself may well have unwittingly contributed to the rise of Jacksonian Democracy by his attacks on the Federalists. He discouraged all forms of pretentiousness such as public celebrations of his birthday and formal entertaining. His rank-and-file followers hailed him as a "man of the people." Therefore, toasts were not to him per se but made in the context of Jefferson's representing "the people." His small-town admirers in Connecticut presented him with an enormous cheese, hardly the kind of gift that Washington ever received.

If the concerns of men from Jefferson to Tocqueville to Lippmann have merit, they may illuminate why we have had only two presidents since the Founding era that seem to rival our preeminent Revolutionary worthies: Abraham Lincoln and Franklin D. Roosevelt. Neither looked grandly promising on entering the

White House. Lincoln lacked formal education and social status, and he had held national office for only two years as a member of the House of Representatives. One is tempted to see Lincoln as evidence for those who argue for nature over nurture in that long-running and endless debate among geneticists, psychologists, and other scholars in nonhistorical disciplines.

In any event, we may not want to dismiss out of hand the contention the French military expert Marshal Maurice de Saxe, made two centuries ago, that leaders are born and not made.[32] As for Roosevelt, he did have family, education, and experience, and yet he gave no sign of greatness when he ran against President Herbert Hoover in 1932. Lippmann complained of his vague and at times contradictory speeches and described him as a pleasant man but almost too eager to be president. Haynes Johnson, the columnist, speaking on C-Span illustrated the difficulty of predicting distinction in rising political figures. He once asked Averell Harriman, the adviser of presidents and a veteran diplomat, what to look for that might be harbingers of greatness. Harriman's response showed the pitfalls in the question, recalling his own two polar-opposite assessments of Franklin Roosevelt. When he met Roosevelt in the middle 1920s, Harriman saw a lightweight. Ten years later, he continued, he thought FDR a great man.[33] Even those men who on paper resemble the Founders in terms of their backgrounds usually have fallen far short of them. Take, for instance, Jefferson Davis, the Confederate president—a West Point graduate, Mexican War colonel, senator, and secretary of war, who had it all over Lincoln except for the latter's political shrewdness, eloquence, and sense of history.[34]

For all the reasons thus far mentioned, we will not recapture the phenomenal combination of ingredients that produced a generation of world-class leaders. Let us accept the reality of that and pray for admirable second-raters and the occasional miracle of a Lincoln or FDR. Not only are we without great leaders save for rare moments, those of the Founding era are somewhat out of favor with much of the historical guild today. Two things explain this situation, both a reflection of current preoccupations.

First is the matter of racial problems that remain unresolved in America life, even though a half century has passed since the Supreme Court, in *Brown v. Board of Education,* struck down the separate but equal doctrine. The Founders did not abolish slavery and often talked out of both sides of their mouths about the peculiar institution. Jefferson, because of his oft-expressed belief in liberty and the evils of human bondage, comes across as the preeminent culprit. Some scholars appear obsessed with Jefferson's failings in this area, as well as with some other perceived character problems, such as Jefferson's compartmentaliz-ing his life and shrinking from hard truths of any nature, be they about slavery or anything else.[35] Merrill Peterson proved to be wrong when he declared in 1960 that Jefferson no longer generated controversy, that he now resided securely in the American pantheon. By then some southern segregationists had already em-braced Jefferson for his states' rights views, and some civil rights champions be-gan a retreat from Monticello.[36] More recently, the long-simmering allegations about Jefferson's relationship with his slave Sally Hemings received widespread attention as a result of the work of novelists, historians, filmmakers, and DNA researchers. Even before the DNA study, a reviewer of a book of Jefferson essays that originated in a conference at the University of Virginia speculated that the contributors had come "to bury Jefferson, not to praise him."[37]

A second explanation for this revisionist scholarship is that it mirrors recent trends in the discipline that zero in on social history broadly defined, including studies of working classes, family, gender, and ethnicity. The age-old staples of academic history, especially political and constitutional approaches, often have been shunted to the rear. The pursuit of great white men is at best irrelevant. The evidence is overwhelming, as one can see from examining the structure of textbooks, collateral readings, collections of documents, and the subjects of doc-toral dissertations and monographs.

There is every reason to think the old historical approaches will come back. The nature of historiography is that what goes around comes around. Only so much can be said about race and the Founding Fathers. Advocates of the new histories, some of whom are quite combative, will rest easier once their special-ties are more comfortably in the mainstream. The old approaches will revive, additionally, because they have never lost out completely, for politics and state-craft remain the vital center of public life. And in some countries individuals still occasionally make a profound difference for human betterment. Mikhail Gor-bachev, Nelson Mandela, Václav Havel, and Lech Walesa reveal proof of that. In the case of Washington and Jefferson, whatever their elitism and racism by our standards, their faults fail to dent their long record of successful public service over four decades or so. Finally, the historians may not know as much as the public, whose opinions of these worthies, however naive at times, continues to be positive. As Fawn Brodie warned some years ago, historians cannot ignore Americans' interests and psychic needs. Moreover, Brodie contended, political heroes are essential to "the emotional health of the nation." In evaluating our leaders, "we do not have to choose between the clinic and the shrine. We do not have to worship without reservation or discard great achievement because it was accompanied by flaws."[38]

Perhaps because there have been so few statesmen since 1800, Americans will continue to measure our magistrates by their images of Washington and Jefferson. I conclude with an anecdote that makes this point. In the midst of the Watergate hearings, a couple visited a famous art museum in the company of the curator. The official pointed to one portrait and said, "This is the Father of our Country." He then looked at one on the opposite wall and said, "This is the Godfather of our Country."

Notes

1. This is hardly a first or a particularly original attempt to address the subject. It is one, however, that has interested me for many years. For my earlier explorations of leadership, see "Military Leadership in the American Revolution," in Library of Congress, *Leadership in the American Revolution* (Washington, D.C., 1974), 91–111, and *George Washington and the American Military Tradition* (Athens, Ga., 1985). The subject is addressed by numerous authors in various disciplines. I found the following most useful: Henry Steele Commager, "Leadership in Eighteenth-Century America and Today," *Daedalus* 90 (1961): 652–73; Alfred H. Kelly, "American Political Leadership: The Optimistic Ethical World View and the Jeffersonian Synthesis," in Library of Congress, *Leadership in the American Revolution*, 7–39; Richard D. Brown, "Where Have All the Great Men Gone?" in *Major Problems in the Era of the American Revolution: Documents and Essays*, ed. Brown (Lexington, Mass., 1992), 610–20.

2. Richard B. Morris, *Seven Who Shaped Our Destiny: The Founding Fathers as Revolutionaries* (New York, 1973).

3. Drew R. McCoy, *The Last of the Fathers: James Madison and the Republican Legacy* (Cambridge, Eng., and New York, 1989).

4. Prior to independence Franklin surely had his critics, both in Pennsylvania and in Britain. For his role in provincial and imperial politics, see David T. Morgan, *The Devious Dr. Franklin: Benjamin Franklin's Years in London* (Macon, Ga., 1996), and Robert Middlekauff, *Benjamin Franklin and His Enemies* (Berkeley, Calif., 1996).

5. L. H. Butterfield et al., eds., *The Diary and Autobiography of John Adams*, 4 vols. (Cambridge, Mass., 1961), 4:80–81.

6. Jefferson to Walter Jones, Jan. 2, 1814, in Paul L. Ford, ed., *The Works of Thomas Jefferson*, 10 vols. (New York, 1892–99), 9:446–51.

7. Peter Shaw, *The Character of John Adams* (Chapel Hill, N.C., 1976), deals at length with Adams's controversial views on mixed government and human nature. See also John R. Howe Jr., *The Political Thought of John Adams* (Princeton, N.J., 1966).

8. Ralph Ketcham, *Presidents above Party: The First American Presidency, 1789–1829* (Chapel Hill, N.C., 1984).

9. Allan Nevins, *The Statesmanship of the Civil War* (Charlottesville, Va., 1955), 40.

10. Francis Bacon, *The Essays*, ed. John Pitcher (1625; rpt. New York, 1985), 219.

11. Jack P. Greene, "Foundations of Political Power in the Virginia House of Burgesses, 1720–1776," *William and Mary Quarterly,* 3d ser., 16 (1959): 485–506.

12. Charles S. Sydnor, *Gentleman Freeholders: Political Practices in Washington's Virginia* (Chapel Hill, N.C., 1953).

13. Daniel P. Jordan, *Political Leadership in Jefferson's Virginia* (Charlottesville, Va., 1983), 219–20.

14. Edmund S. Morgan, *American Slavery, American Freedom* (New York, 1976), chap. 18.

15. Jack P. Greene, "Character, Persona, and Authority: A Study of Alternative Styles of Political Leadership in Revolutionary Virginia," in *The Revolutionary War in the South: Power, Conflict, and Leadership: Essays in Honor of John Richard Alden,* ed. Robert W. Higgins (Durham, N.C., 1979), 3–42.

16. The switch from the clergy to the legal profession, with its implications for the American Revolution, is the theme of Edmund S. Morgan, "The American Revolution Considered as an Intellectual Movement," in *The Challenge of the American Revolution* (New York, 1976), chap. 3. Although many if not most Virginia lawyers doubled as planters, the former constituted the most significant occupational group in the House of Burgesses after 1750. During that time lawyers held thirty of sixty-seven committee chairmanships. Lucille Griffith, *The Virginia House of Burgesses* (Tuscaloosa, Ala., 1969).

17. Edmund Burke, *Speeches and Letters on America* (1908; rpt. London, 1961), 94–95. Twenty-five of fifty-six signers of the Declaration of Independence and thirty-one of fifty-five signers of the Constitution were lawyers.

18. Robert M. S. McDonald, "Race, Sex, and Reputation: Thomas Jefferson and the Sally Hemings Story," *Southern Cultures* 4 (1998): 46–63, and "Was There a Religious Revolution in 1800?" in *The Revolution of 1800: Democracy, Race, and the New Republic,* ed. James Horn, Jan Ellen Lewis, and Peter S. Onuf (Charlottesville, Va., 2002), 187–91.

19. There is no better place to begin the study of the Founders and their use of history than Douglass Adair, *Fame and the Founding Fathers,* ed. Trevor Colbourn (New York, 1974), esp. chap. 5.

20. Paul K. Longmore, *The Invention of George Washington* (Berkeley, Calif., 1988), appendix: "The Foundations of Useful Knowledge," 213–26.

21. *GW: Writings* 26:483.

22. Robert Penn Warren, *The Legacy of the Civil War: Meditations on the Centennial* (New York, 1961).

23. I have elaborated on Washington's vision in *George Washington: Uniting a Nation* (Lanham, Md., 2002).

24. Jordan, *Political Leadership.* Men continued to serve "in the personal terms of prestige, patriotism, and noblesse oblige—all traditions of the Virginia gentry." Ibid., 84.

25. Joyce Appleby, *Inheriting the Revolution: The First Generation of Americans* (Cambridge, Mass., 2000). See also Gordon Wood, *The Radicalism of the American Revolution* (New York, 1992), esp. chaps. 13–19.

26. James T. Schleifer, *The Making of Tocqueville's Democracy in America* (Chapel Hill, N.C., 1980), 143; McCoy, *Last of the Fathers,* esp. chaps. 1–3; Davy Crockett, "How to Win an Election," *American Heritage* 9 (1958): 112.

27. James D. Richardson, ed., *A Compilation of Messages and Papers of the Presidents,* 10 vols. (Washington, D.C., 1896–99), 2:449.

28. W. Burlie Brown, *The People's Choice: The Presidential Image in the Campaign Biography* (Baton Rouge, La., 1960).

29. Walter Lippmann, *The Public Philosophy* (New York, 1955).

30. James Brice, *The American Commonwealth,* 2 vols. (1888; rpt. New York, 1916).

31. Theodore J. Crackel, *Mr. Jefferson's Army: Political and Social Reform of the Military Establishment, 1801–1805* (New York, 1987), chap. 3, and *West Point: A Bicentennial History* (Lawrence, Kan., 2002), chap. 2.

32. Maurice de Saxe, *My Reveries upon the Art of War,* trans. T. R. Phillips (Harrisburg, Pa., 1955), 297.

33. Haynes Johnson, "America in the Next Century," Sept. 6, 1998, C-Span.

34. See the explicit comparison between Davis and Lincoln in Nevins, *Statesmanship of the Civil War,* chaps. 2–3.

35. See especially on Jefferson's inconsistencies and compartmentalizations, Joseph J. Ellis, *American Sphinx: The Character of Thomas Jefferson* (New York, 1997).

36. Merrill D. Peterson, *The Jeffersonian Image in the American Mind* (New York and Oxford, Eng., 1960); Robert Glen Parkinson, "A Founder Held Hostage: The Image of Thomas Jefferson in the Civil Rights Movement, 1954–1968" (M.A. thesis, Univ. of Tennessee, Knoxville, 1998).

37. Joseph J. Ellis's review of Peter S. Onuf, ed., *Jeffersonian Legacies* (Charlottesville, Va., 1993), in *Journal of the Early Republic* 13 (1993): 556–57. Since the publication of Annette Gordon-Reed's *Thomas Jefferson and Sally Hemings: An American Controversy* (Charlottesville, Va., 1997), strongly suggesting a sexual relationship, resulting in children, between Jefferson and his bondswoman, the literature on this subject and on Jefferson and slavery in general threatens to overwhelm us. For an introduction to this bibliography, see Alexander O. Boulton, "The Monticello Mystery—Case Continued," *William and Mary Quarterly,* 3d ser., 58 (2001): 1039–46.

38. Fawn Brodie, "The Political Hero in America: His Fate and His Future," *Virginia Quarterly Review* 46 (1970): 46–60, quotations on pp. 48, 56.

2 ❖ *Virginia's Trinity of Immortals*

AN INVITATION FROM Jon Kukla, director of the Patrick Henry Memorial Association, led to my speaking on the relationship between Patrick Henry and George Washington at Charlotte Court House, in Southside Virginia, on April 22, 2001. Prior to my address, two professional actors reenacted the debate that had taken place there in 1799 between Henry, a recent convert to the Federalist political cause, and John Randolph of Roanoke, who campaigned as a Republican and follower of Jefferson. Henry, though elderly and in bad health, had heeded Washington's plea to return to public life and seek a seat in the Virginia House of Delegates, which had fallen under Republican control. Here, in an earlier wooden courthouse, the old warhorse and the rising young Jeffersonian star debated before a crowd of the freeholders of Charlotte County, where Henry had recently moved and established his home, which he called Red Hill (now the headquarters of the Patrick Henry Memorial Association). The actors were superb as they contended over the meaning of the XYZ affair with France, the Federalist Congress's Alien and Sedition Acts, and Madison and Jefferson's responses in their Virginia and Kentucky Resolutions. Henry won the election, only to die before he could occupy his seat in the legislature. The day following my appearance at Charlotte Court House, I repeated the lecture in Richmond at the Library of Virginia, a wonderfully new, state-of-the-art archival agency. I could not help recalling the summers of 1955 and 1956 when I did research across the street in the old facility, known as the Virginia State Library, on General Daniel Morgan, who hailed from Winchester in the Shenandoah Valley, the subject of my doctoral dissertation at Duke University.

When James Horn, then the director of the Thomas Jefferson Research Center at Charlottesville, asked me to give a lecture on the relationship between Jefferson and Washington, I countered with a proposal he generously accepted: that I broaden the topic to include material from my lecture on Washington and Henry. It seemed a defensible proposition because all three of these men were reasonably close to one another, but in time they all had a parting of the ways.

Jefferson and Henry split over state issues, and Washington broke with both Jefferson and Henry over national issues. Only Washington and Henry ever reconciled. To some degree, this pattern of political divisions occurred in all the states. The issues were never exactly the same, and personalities and ambitions figured in numerous ruptures. Even so, we can say that, broadly speaking, the problems stemmed from internal state issues, or from attitudes about ratifying the Constitution of 1787, or from national issues that led to the formation of political parties in the 1790s. Perhaps nowhere were the fissures as deep and bitter as in Virginia, nor did they divide the most popular and influential men of any state in quite the way events occurred in the Old Dominion. Owing to scheduling difficulties, I delayed giving my lecture on the three Virginians at the research center until February 10, 2004. It recently appeared in the *Journal of the Early Republic* 23 (Winter 2003): 22–44, from which it is reprinted by permission of the coeditors.

THE PUBLIC CAREERS OF George Washington, Thomas Jefferson, and Patrick Henry overlapped for over three decades—in the Virginia resistance movement before 1776, in the Continental Congress, in General Washington's pleas to Governors Henry and Jefferson for men and supplies during the Revolutionary War, in the fight over the ratification of the Constitution, and in the events of Washington's presidency and the politics of the 1790s. Eventually, these relationships unraveled. First Henry and Jefferson became estranged. Then the same thing happened between Henry and Washington and, finally, between Washington and Jefferson. Only one reconciliation took place between any of these pairs: Washington and Henry, both of whom died in 1799. As has often been true in American politics, political disagreements took on personal dimensions, and the combination of the two ended friendships and generated bitterness and estrangements. Even so, the three Virginians dealt with their conflicts by peaceful means. That fact alone tells us something important about the American Revolution and the future character of American politics.

Over the years the intense fascination for the trio fed partly on myth, which always enlarges the accomplishments of heroes who stand tall even without embellishment. That explains the late Bernard Mayo's title for a slim volume called *Myths and Men: Patrick Henry, George Washington, Thomas Jefferson.* Mayo begins his masterly surgery on the layers of exaggeration by re-creating a cold February 1858 scene in Richmond's Capitol Square when Washington's equestrian statute was unveiled, with figures of Jefferson and Henry standing beside him. Panegyrists hailed them as "The Sword, The Pen, and the Trumpet of the Revolution."[1]

Washington's role in the American founding took place on the colonial and national scene, as was the case with Jefferson's, whereas Henry's participation in that same process happened almost exclusively at the local level, a career that was Virginia-centered. Prior to Henry's departure from the Second Continental Congress in August 1775, however, he had inspired and energized Americans with his vigorous speeches and calls to action in defense of their liberties. Washington, on the other hand, consistently thought and acted from a high ground, in continental terms. Jefferson too knew how to view things in a national context, but he did not do so with Washington's consistency. Certainly Washington's critics rarely described him as preoccupied with Virginia and the South; he was a statesman who ranks as the most consistent and influential nationalist of his generation. Fair or not, Henry's detractors eventually did see him as a particularist, and, to a somewhat lesser extent, so did Jefferson's.

There is no evidence to suggest any friction or dislike between Washington, Jefferson, and Henry for some years after their acquaintance began. All came from gentry families. All served in the House of Burgesses, entering that body shortly before or during the early years of the imperial crisis: in 1758 (Washington), 1765 (Henry), and 1769 (Jefferson). Henry's entry in 1765 found Jefferson still in the capital after attending the College of William and Mary and then staying on to read law under George Wythe. Jefferson's extramural political education received a shot of adrenaline in May 1765, as he stood at the back of the House chamber and heard the freshman legislator Henry attack the Stamp Act. As an old man Jefferson still remembered vividly "the splendid display of Mr. Henry's talents as a popular orator . . . such as I have never heard from any other man." He spoke "as Homer wrote."[2] Jefferson was never silver-tongued and never claimed to be. If he envied Henry in that respect, he denigrated his talents as a lawyer. Both were part of what Merrill Peterson calls "a new generation of professional lawyers." In Jefferson's eyes Henry was intellectually lazy. No doubt it irritated Jefferson that Henry "came to the bar after six weeks of desultory reading," whereas Jefferson devoted several years to "exhaustive preparation."[3]

The trio all advocated resolute steps to defend American rights against British taxation and other London incursions on colonial liberties. Jefferson claimed in his autobiography that he and Henry, along with the Lee brothers, Richard Henry and Francis Lightfoot, took the lead in urging strong retaliatory measures in the early 1770s. That is likely true, although Washington could not have been far behind. He had been outspoken in 1769-70 against the Townshend duties, and he was equally forceful, if not even more so, in condemning the Coercive Acts—or Intolerable Acts, as Americans labeled them. In fact, the three could hardly have been more tough-minded, short of calling for an immediate armed response and possibly independence. Washington chaired the meeting in his county that brought forth the stern Fairfax Resolves, unsurpassed, possibly unequaled, among similar documents from local bodies in its condemnation of the mother country, a document that soon became well known throughout the colonies. Both Thomas Lynch of South Carolina and Silas Deane of Connecticut reported that prior to Washington's attendance at the First Continental Congress, he had inspired his fellow Virginians on the subject of the imperial crisis with an eloquent speech in which he promised to raise a thousand men at his own expense and lead them to the relief of the Bostonians if necessary.[4] Jefferson wrote his *Summary View* essay, which suggested a commonwealth conception of the British Empire, and Washington contributed money for its publication. Henry, of course, gave his immortal "Liberty or Death" speech to the second Virginia convention meeting in Richmond in March 1775, and just over a month later he threatened to march his Hanover County militiamen on Williamsburg to seize from Governor Dunmore the colony's munitions that had been taken illegally from the public magazine. Washington and Henry were among the top vote getters when Virginia chose its delegation to the First Continental Congress, and Jefferson joined them as members of the Second Continental Congress.

Given his energetic role in the Virginia resistance, it may have surprised some delegates to find that Henry's participation in the Congress seems to have been marginal. To be sure, he made some of his fiery, inspirational speeches in the First Congress in 1774. Washington, a strong, silent type, contributed more substantially, becoming that body's unofficial authority on how armed resistance might work if that recourse became necessary. Jefferson probably accurately assessed Henry's place in the Second Continental Congress, which convened in the late spring of 1775, just after fighting erupted at Lexington and Concord. It was a time for new ideas and long, tedious committee work, and now Henry was out of his element, and he knew it. He displayed "good sense to perceive" that great oratory no longer had its place there. "He ceased therefore, in great measure," declared Jefferson, "to take part in the business."[5] When Henry wisely retired from Congress, he unwisely acquired for himself the position of commander of Virginia's military forces. But he soon recognized that he was no potential Marlborough or Wolfe, and he resigned, much to the relief of Washington, who correctly opined that the Virginia political scene was the natural habitat for a Patrick Henry. Washington and Jefferson were in the forefront of those in favor of independence in early 1776. Interestingly enough, Henry, for a time that spring, favored putting off secession from the empire until one or more foreign alliances could be secured in Europe; but after sensing the mood of the majority at the Virginia convention, he vigorously seconded the motion that instructed the Virginia congressional delegation to introduce a resolution for separation.[6]

When do signs of strains appear in the relationship between the three great Virginia chieftains? They were slow in coming, especially in terms of Washington's links with Henry and Jefferson. Washington sought Henry's advice about his duties as commander in chief, considered Henry one of the most supportive of the state governors during the latter's three years in office, appreciated his defense of the commander in chief against his wartime critics (allegedly members of a so-called Conway Cabal), and approved Washington's recommendations for improving the militia in the immediate postwar years. Jefferson and Washington also saw eye-to-eye on efforts to win independence and, in general at least, on the need to invigorate the government under the Articles of Confederation.

Jefferson and Henry were both back in Virginia for the better part of the remainder of the Revolutionary War. Henry served three consecutive one-year terms as governor, from 1776 to 1779, followed by Jefferson, who held the executive office from 1779 to 1781. If both were committed to the war, domestic issues brought cracks in their earlier wall of unity forged on resistance to Britain and independence. Henry's previously well-earned reputation as a radical no longer characterized his political science. He displayed no more interest in a revolution for liberal reform than his old conservative antagonist Edmund Pendleton. As governor, Henry, like almost all state governors at the time, had no veto over legislative acts, which therefore became law on passage. But there is little if any evidence that he showed enthusiasm for what amounted to Jefferson's package of reforms, including state-supported education, abolishing primogeniture and entail, and assaulting cruel and unusual punishments. The one best-remembered today because of Jefferson and Madison's success and its critical significance was what we have come to call separation of church and state. As Peterson says, "The contending principles and measures were identified with the two giants of Virginia politics, Jefferson and Henry."[7] With independence, it was impossible to argue effectively for continuing the old church arrangement.

Anglicanism as the state religion could not survive, but conservative Christians, led by Henry, fought a rearguard action for nearly a decade.

Let the state support all Protestant denominations; that became the conservative strategy. Matters came to a head in 1785 when Henry's forces failed to push through the legislature a bill to provide taxes for the support of "teachers of the Christian religion." The following year Madison, in the absence of Jefferson, now minister to France, secured the Act for Establishing Religious Freedom, one of the great documents of the American Revolution. Washington, who never returned to the legislature after the war, stayed out of the battle, but his respect for all churches, including Catholic and Jewish denominations, was well known. As president, he often publicly expressed such views and played a critical part in assisting Madison in the adoption of a bill of rights.[8]

Jefferson's victory over Henry on the disestablishment issue must have been doubly satisfying, for it amounted to a kind of payback for efforts in the legislature to investigate Jefferson's conduct as governor in the months just before he left office in June 1781, a grim period in the Old Dominion as British raiding parties ravaged much of the state. Jefferson believed that the legislative inquiry into the conduct of the executive—it eventually was dropped with a resolution of support for the now ex-governor—was instigated by Henry. The evidence remains cloudy, but Jefferson also felt that Henry's "hand" lay behind a resolution during the war crisis to appoint a dictator of the state and that some of Henry's friends, possibly Henry as well, had the orator politician in mind for the job.[9] Working on his *Notes on Virginia* after his governorship, Jefferson included an angry response to such machinations. He never forgot the 1781 crisis and what he thought to be Henry's part in bringing on his miseries.[10] Quite possibly Jefferson took some consolation from Washington's warm expression of appreciation when he left the governorship. The commander in chief spoke of "the readiness and Zeal" with which Jefferson had responded to his recommendations for assisting the Continental army. "I shall esteem myself honored by a continuation of your friendship and corrispondence shou'd your country permit you to remain in the private walk of life."[11]

Still other issues further widened the gulf between Jefferson and Henry. Jefferson, who drafted a new constitution for Virginia, never saw it seriously considered as a replacement for the original instrument of 1776 that now seemed so inadequate to him. Jefferson had favored a state convention to address his ideas and other suggestions that might be presented on the subject. But when the legislature failed to call such a gathering, Jefferson concluded it was probably just as well. As he explained to Madison, "*While Mr. Henry lives* another bad constitution would be formed, and saddled forever on us. What we have to do I think is *devoutly to pray for his death*."[12] It would be hard to find such a harsh wish about any other human being in Jefferson's correspondence, even at the height of the political wars of the next decade when his party feared extinction after passage of the Alien and Sedition Acts.

Not surprisingly, an examination of the Boyd edition of *The Papers of Thomas Jefferson* reveals a lack of warmth and cordiality in the letters that Henry and Jefferson exchanged after Henry returned to the governorship in the years 1784–86 and after Jefferson became American minister to France in 1784. Their epistles, usually official and businesslike, focused on such matters as the Virginia assembly's desire to have Houdon, the eminent sculptor, craft statues of Washington and Lafayette for the state. On one occasion in 1785 Henry seemingly suggested to Jefferson that they broaden the nature of their correspondence to other subjects; if so, Jefferson declined to take up the offer.[13]

If the Henry-Jefferson relationship steadily deteriorated during the Revolutionary War and afterward, Washington maintained his cordial ties with these old Virginia comrades. And yet Washington sensed in the 1780s that Henry was ambivalent at best about what became the master of Mount Vernon's campaign to strengthen the Union. They exchanged numerous friendly epistles, replete with compliments to each other and devoted to business and local affairs. When the legislature picked its delegation to what became the Constitutional Convention in Philadelphia in 1787, Washington received a unanimous vote, followed by Henry in second place. (It is worth recalling that Washington and Henry, in that order, had been near the top in Virginia's balloting in 1774 and 1775 for the First and Second Continental Congresses.) Henry rejected the appointment, allegedly saying that he "smelt a rat." While Jefferson deplored the secrecy of the Constitutional Convention, he nonetheless dispatched encouraging words to Washington, the presiding officer. As an often-frustrated diplomat in Europe, Jefferson declared that the new instrument should "make our states one as to all foreign concerns" and provide "the federal head . . . their just authority, to organise that head into Legislative, Executive, & Judiciary departments."[14]

When Washington sent Henry a copy of the Constitution, with a cover letter, he knew that Henry would be a tough sell. So Henry's politely negative response hardly created shock waves. Thanking Washington for his efforts in Philadelphia, he voiced his "unalterable Regard & Atachment" for Washington but warned that the "proposed Constitution" generated "Concern . . . greater than I am able to express."[15] Washington encouraged his friends to use his name freely in the Virginia ratification convention. The Virginia Federalists needed Washington to counter the formidable oratory of Henry, a colossus on the convention floor. Lance Banning writes that Henry sometimes resorted to "verbal terrorism." A man would be a "lunatic," Henry thundered, to adopt a defective government in hopes of improving it later. The Constitution was "the most fatal plan that could possibly be conceived to enslave a free people."[16]

Twice at the Richmond gathering Madison invoked Washington's sentiments. In responding to Henry's claim that Jefferson sought amendments before Virginia should ratify, Madison countered with a reference to Washington's advocacy of immediate approval. "After this exchange," writes Stuart Leibiger, "Henry did not cite Jefferson again."[17] And in fact, Jefferson rather quickly came around to an acceptance of the Constitution, although his change of heart regarding immediate ratification caused Madison and other Federalists some embarrassment since his alteration of views was not known before Virginia acted. In any case, James Monroe said Washington's views made the difference in the Old Dominion, where ratification squeaked by 89 to 79.[18]

As the nation's first president, Washington recognized the need of winning over the Antifederalists to accept the verdict. In various ways he held out the hand of reconciliation to his former opponents, even Governor George Clinton of New York, who had fought the Constitution as tenaciously as Henry and George Mason, his longtime friend and neighbor.[19] Washington displayed a different attitude toward some of the Virginia Antifederalists. Perhaps in the case of men like Henry and Mason, Washington's reluctance to bury the past stemmed from the closeness of their former close ties. Moreover, he may have felt that Virginia's narrow vote constituted a near repudiation of him. Mason died in 1792, disappointed that he and Washington remained estranged.[20]

Washington and Jefferson, the latter back from France and now Washington's secretary of state, saw Henry's opposition to the new government in much the same way. Washington complained that Henry dominated the state legislature; the "Edicts of Mr H" brought no more opposition than those of "the Grand Monarch" of France. Henry had "only to say let this be Law—and it is Law."[21] Henry not only labored to elect Antifederalists but prevailed on both the ratifying convention and the legislature to advocate amendments and later to get the legislature to endorse a second constitutional convention.

Jefferson too expressed dismay that "Antifederalism is not yet dead in this country." Henry, the "avowed foe" of the Constitution, was the ringleader in keeping the spirit "of malevolence towards the new government" alive. "He stands higher in public estimation than he ever did." Nearly a year later, in November 1791, Jefferson suggested that Hamilton's financial system, which he considered especially unpopular in Virginia, was "harped on by many to mask their disaffection to the government on other grounds." Speaking of Henry, whom he did not identify by name, he continued: the "great foe is an implacable one. He avows it himself, but does not avow all his motives for it."[22] Jefferson elaborated on this theme to Washington in May 1792. Again he named no names, but Henry had to be in mind. The former Antifederalists believed that their worst fears about the Constitution were confirmed by Hamiltonian financial schemes. When they assaulted such new federal laws, it was their way of attacking and undermining the Constitution itself.[23] Jefferson, of course, was already drawing away from Hamilton and, in time, from the Washington administration itself, in which he would continue to serve owing to the president's urging until the end of 1793. Before long, Jefferson and Madison would be accused of similar behavior, of opposing the Federalist-controlled government because they were at heart Antifederalists out to wreck the Constitution. We know that Jefferson and his Republicans would come to see the Federalists in an unholy alliance with former Antifederalists, with the latter intent on reversing the ratification of the 1787 political engineering and the former set on gradually transforming it into a monarchy. In short, both sides accused the other of using subterfuge and indirection to destroy the work of the Philadelphia convention.[24]

It may not have been transparent to either man, but the early 1790s found Jefferson and Henry slowly exchanging positions on the political continuum. Henry hardly savored his successes for long. He refused to accept appointment to the Senate on the death of William Grayson, and he talked at various times of moving either to Georgia or to North Carolina. Historians disagree about his motives, but his attitude changed to one of giving the new government a chance to make the Constitution work. He sensed that most Virginians now seemed ready to accept the reality of the political system crafted in Philadelphia. As he wrote to Monroe in 1791, "we are one & all imbarked" together. Although the Constitution may have been "a crazy Machine," Americans should care for it as long as they had it. While he had no love for Madison and Jefferson, it is doubtful he would have changed horses in the middle of the stream simply to avoid being allied with his inveterate enemies who emerged as leaders of the Republican faction. There was more to it than that, especially after the French Revolution created divisions in foreign policy, which, in Henry's view, threatened the American union.[25]

Contributing to Henry's change of heart was his rapprochement with influential Virginia Federalists and with Washington as well. It seems unlikely that Henry ever lost his respect for Washington. At any rate, no record exists of his engaging in open criticism of the president.[26] Because Washington's public career had been outside of Virginia beginning in 1775, he and Henry had never been rivals on the local scene, unlike Henry's relations with Madison and Jefferson. One can reasonably speculate that John Marshall may well have had some part in bringing the two aging Virginia titans together. Although Henry and Marshall had sharply opposed each other at the Virginia ratifying convention, they found common cause in the years thereafter, performing as a legal team on behalf of Virginians who were fighting their British prewar creditors in the courts. Marshall revered Washington and always endeavored to bring the president's critics in Virginia over to the side of the administration. It is hard to imagine that Marshall and Henry, both affable and outgoing, failed to talk about Washington and state and national politics during the many hours they spent together riding from one court to another and probably sharing quarters in local taverns. If, as Henry said later, he came to love Marshall ("Tell Marshall I love him"), there was room for a reconciliation with Washington.[27]

Not only had Henry mended fences with Marshall, but he also did so with an ardent ally of the latter at the Virginia ratifying convention: Henry ("Light-Horse Harry") Lee, who now served as governor of the Old Dominion, and who at the convention in Richmond had cast sly aspersions on Henry's never having served in the Continental army ("It was my fortune to be a soldier of my country").[28] By some early date in 1793 Lee and Henry had cleared the air, and Lee hoped to see the same thing happen between Henry and Washington. It is not apparent whether the idea originated with Lee or with Washington. But by the opening of 1793 Washington and Lee were thinking along the same lines, including the possibility of a federal appointment such as a Supreme Court seat for Henry.[29] Lee, after subsequent conversations with Henry, saw the aging patriot as a man who might well become "one of the most active supporters of your administration." Possibly Marshall had been endeavoring to bring Henry around to such a position, although Marshall's part cannot be documented until sometime later. In any event, one problem still stood in the way. Lee described Henry as "deeply and sorely effected" by an unknown informant who declared that Washington considered Henry to be a "factious seditious character."[30]

Washington hastened to disavow the allegations. Although he and Henry had had their differences over the Constitution, and no doubt that remained true, he had "never expressed such sentiments of that Gentleman." Indeed, "I have always respected and esteemed him." Henry had never better demonstrated his loyalty to Washington than during the dark days of late 1777, the time of the Conway Cabal, when the governor had alerted him to "insidious writings" designed to undermine his reputation with Congress and the army. Washington knew from Congressman Isaac Coles, a friend of both Henry and Washington, that Henry had said he would honor the authority "of a government which had been chosen by a majority of the people"—or "words to that effect."[31]

Although Henry expressed great pleasure in learning of the chief executive's high opinion of him, he declined Washington's offer to be secretary of state, which was communicated to Henry at the same time he received encouragement from Henry Lee and John Marshall to accept it. Even though such matters as age and financial responsibilities kept Henry from considering national office, he assured Washington that he had long ago "bid adieu to the distinction of federal and anti-federal" and had "expressed my fears of disunion . . . from the baneful effects of faction."[32] Washington's pursuit of Henry shows that the president at times had remarkably good political instincts. Henry's name and influence transcended his stand on the issues of the day: the 1790s saw the old Revolutionary twice turn down offers of a United States Senate seat and decline to accept election to a sixth term as governor. The Virginia Federalists, led by Marshall, faced a growing tide of antiadministration sentiment in the Old Dominion, which received a boost from the increasing opposition of Jefferson and Madison to measures that Washington supported, even if he did not always initiate them. If Henry subsequently declined Washington's efforts to persuade him to take other federal positions—a seat on the Supreme Court and ministerial posts abroad—the result nonetheless solidified a growing bond between the former governor and the president, to say nothing of energizing Virginia Federalists as Henry leaned in their direction.[33] Indeed, Marshall and Lee and some national Federalist leaders such as Fisher Ames, Rufus King, and Alexander Hamilton, fearful that Jefferson would defeat John Adams in the presidential election, talked of the possibility of putting Henry at the head of their party's ticket, but Henry rejected all suggestions that he seek the presidency.[34]

That bond revealed itself for the final time when ex-president Washington, disturbed over Republican control of the Virginia legislature and the state's congressional delegation, urged Henry to take the lead in combating the heresies of Jefferson's political allies. Washington believed that they had relentlessly attacked the administration of John Adams, the Federalist president, with venom and lies. They had shown by their words and deeds no respect for the federal government and constituted a threat to the Union itself. They had slavishly committed to France in the war then raging in Europe and had contended that the Adams administration worshipped Britain and seemed intent on leading America toward monarchy. Because Washington had reason to believe that Henry had come to share his political mind-set, he urged Henry to return to public life—to seek election to the legislature and lead the fight to restore the dignity and integrity of Virginia, which seemed to Washington to have become the most radical of all the states to fall to the control of the Republicans, whose "principle leaders . . . dwell in it." Washington shrewdly made his appeal more in terms of what was happening to Virginia than to the condition of the nation as a whole.[35] As Richard Beeman has observed, Henry might at times be politically inconsistent, and notwithstanding occasional rhetoric to the contrary about being foremost an American, Henry was a localist. He defined "his country" as Virginia.[36]

If Washington knew Henry quite well, employing language that would resonate with the great orator, he was asking a lot of a man in his sixties with serious infirmities. But the ex-president was beside himself, seething with rage in his long, 1,200-word missive to the old patriot. Washington half expected Henry to decline, for he was a man who, besides considerations of mortality, had numerous properties, had fathered seventeen children, and had a relatively young wife to be concerned about.[37]

Henry, often unpredictable, could not have responded more fully to Washington's satisfaction. "My children would blush to know, that you & their Father were Co[n]temporarys, & that when you asked him to throw in his Mite for the public Happiness, he refused to do it. . . . I have declared myself a Candidate for this County at the next Election." He agreed "with every Sentiment you expressed to me." He closed by voicing his "reverential Regard & sincere Attachment" to Washington, signing himself "your affectionate humble Servant."[38] Archibald Blair, clerk of the Virginia Council of State, informed Washington that Henry had said that he "*loved* you" and Marshall.[39] In their effusiveness both sexagenarians exaggerated the continuity of their warm relationship. Curiously, the two men, in letters to others, used Henry's support of Washington at the time of the Conway Cabal during the Revolutionary War as proof of their uninterrupted mutual admiration, omitting their sharp differences over the Constitution and Henry's concerns about some aspects of the Washington presidency.[40]

Because they needed each other out of fear for the future of Virginia and the nation, it was just as well that Washington and Henry erased some recent history. But neither would fight the political battles that lay ahead. Henry died in June 1799, after being elected to the legislature, and Washington expired that December. Perhaps it was for the best that they had not remained around to witness subsequent developments as Virginia fell ever more completely under the Republican thumb and as Jefferson defeated Adams for the presidency the following year. Neither man could have accepted comfortably what Jefferson called "the revolution of 1800."[41]

Washington's break with Jefferson evolved over several years. In 1792, even as Jefferson voiced his concerns about Henry as a negative influence on the nation, he was also, in his conversations and correspondence with Washington, much more apprehensive about Hamilton's aims and objectives. Try as he might to determine his secretaries' conflicting views and adjudicate their differences, the chief executive could never bring the feuding department heads in line.[42] What had been a kind of coalition administration ended with Jefferson's resignation in December 1793, but both Washington and Jefferson, whether the latter was delusional or not, expressed warm feelings for each other on parting.[43]

Why, then, did a complete rupture occur in the next few years? To some extent, the answer is found in their competing visions of America—or what the American Revolution was to be all about. Washington's vision was hardly new, most obviously evident in his commitment to a cohesive union and a strongly centralized, proactive government, which found reflection in Hamilton's policy at the Treasury, but Jefferson had not faced up to that reality. To Jefferson, Washington now embraced ideas and practices reminiscent of the corrupting ties between the ministry and the moneyed interests in Walpolian England several decades earlier. And Jefferson, the champion of individual self-reliance, states' rights, and agrarian values, rejected things British to the point that his critics, then and now, have seen him as Anglophobic. In any case, it might be said that for Jefferson the goal of the American Revolution included not only political independence from the mother country but also escape from British ways, political and economic.

More concretely, the explanation for their rupture resides in Jefferson's growing conviction that Washington had become a hapless tool of a political party. Evidence of his negative perception of the president begins to emerge in the winter of 1794–95, a year or so after Jefferson stepped down as secretary of state. First, according to Jefferson, Washington had engaged in overkill when he personally rode at the head of a 13,000-man militia army that put down the Whiskey Rebellion in western Pennsylvania, a protest by people who suffered from a discriminatory Hamiltonian excise. Second, the president openly castigated the Democratic Societies, forty or more in number, throughout the country, which supported the French Revolution and the emerging Republican Party in America; it was a sad day when "the President should have permitted himself to be the organ of such an attack on the freedom of discussion."[44] Third, and most disturbing, Washington had put his weight behind the Jay Treaty with Britain, which in Jefferson's eyes gained a pittance for America and failed to elicit a promise from Britain to cease its seizing of cargoes and impressing of seamen from United States merchant vessels. Although Washington's behavior could be attributed to "honesty" and "political errors," his support of the Jay Treaty had severely damaged the nation. Another misjudgment of such magnitude would provide a further "occasion to exclaim 'curse on his virtues, they've undone his country.'"[45]

If these are harsh judgments, they are nonetheless consistent with pointed fears that Jefferson had expressed about the Constitution in the months before the completion of the ratification process in 1788. After much reflection on that parchment, Jefferson had reduced his reservations to two in number: the absence of a bill of rights and the failure to provide for rotation in office. His remarks on the latter may well help explain his criticisms of Washington—not only about term limits per se ("most of all" for the "Presidency") but about how the first elected chief executive might unintentionally do the country great harm. His comments in a letter to fellow Virginian Edward Carrington suggest that he already anticipated Washington's election as the first president. What should be Americans' sensitivity about presidential power and its misuse, whether intentional or not, was currently "put to sleep by the unlimited confidence we all repose in the person to whom we all look as our president. After him inferior characters may perhaps succeed [to the presidency] and awaken us to the danger which his merit has led us into."[46]

In any case, Jefferson shrank from terminating a thirty-year relationship with Washington. The two men had exchanged only occasional letters on nonpolitical subjects after Jefferson left the president's cabinet. Then Jefferson wrote to Washington in June 1796 to assure him that specific aspersions against the president published in Benjamin Franklin Bache's Philadelphia *Aurora* had not come from his hand, as was rumored. Washington's response, outwardly at least, sounded gracious. To that report and similar ones, Washington seemingly sought to put his former cabinet officer at ease. Although on some occasions "your conduct has been represented as derogating from that opinion I had conceived you entertained of me," he declared, Washington knew that Jefferson must have recognized that the president's motives had always been honorable and that "I was no believer in the infallibility of the politics, or measures of *any man living*"—in short, Washington was no puppet of Hamilton. "But enough of this," asserted Washington, shifting the ground to their shared passion for agriculture and discoursing on clover, field peas, and threshing machines.[47]

It is possible, however, to read Washington's reply differently—to see it as Washington's saying to Jefferson, in so many words, "I am on to your machinations. I don't believe you, but I am going to hold my temper and behave as a gentlemen, notwithstanding all the provocation from you and your political lieutenants." And if that was the real message to Jefferson, was Washington wrong?[48] Nearly two months before Jefferson's professions of innocence to Washington, he had dispatched his so-called Mazzei letter, which most historians have interpreted as containing what were probably the most severe strictures he ever delivered against Washington.

The following year, the public exposure of Jefferson's letter to his former Albemarle neighbor Philip Mazzei, who had returned to his native Italy, was the final incident to sever forever the bonds connecting these two Virginia patriarchs. Jefferson spoke of "an Anglican, monarchical and aristocratical party" intent on establishing the characteristics "of the British government" in the United States. As for "apostates" who now embraced these foreign "heresies," they included "men who were Sampsons in the field and Solomons in the council, but who have had their heads shorn by the harlot England." The epistle to Mazzei found its way into print in France and then in America, first appearing in Noah Webster's New York *Minerva* in May 1797.[49] Both Washington and Jefferson avoided public comment about the document. Years later Jefferson declared that "there never passed a word . . . between Genl. Washington and myself, on the subject of that letter." Moreover, he contended that Washington would never "have degraded himself so far as to take to himself the imputation in that letter on the 'Sampsons in combat.'"[50] Jefferson was both naive and self-serving. The reference to his former chief executive was obvious. At the time the controversy erupted, Washington had already been receiving a steady diet of reports that Jefferson had done his best to block passage of the Jay Treaty and had now openly assumed leadership of the Republican Party. Because of Jefferson's close association with Madison, who was leading the fight against appropriations for implementing the terms with England, Washington's once-intimate friendship with Madison became another permanent casualty of the political cockpit of the mid-1790s.[51] As for Jefferson's contention that he and Washington never discussed the letter, no doubt that was a fact. But the core point is this: they never discussed anything, because they never corresponded again, as Jefferson subsequently acknowledged.[52]

Another development surely indicates that Washington believed the "Sampson in combat" metaphor targeted him. John Nicholas of Charlottesville, a Federalist, clerk of Albemarle County Court, endeavored during the feverish aftermath of the Mazzei affair to prove to Washington that a letter to the former president, designed to prompt a reply that would bristle with harsh criticisms of Jefferson, was actually a setup, designed by Washington's enemies in Charlottesville, who were out "to intrap you." Nicholas claimed that one John Langhorne, its alleged author, was a fictitious name; that this piece of mail really came from the pen of Peter Carr, "a favorite nephew of your very *Sincere* friend Mr. Jefferson," a young man reared and educated by Jefferson and "a constant dependent & resident in his house." Nicholas, who claimed to know Jefferson quite well, condemned him as "one of the most artful, intriguing, industrious and double-faced politicians in all America." One cannot be certain of Nicholas's own veracity, but he correctly asserted that James Monroe, whom Washington had removed from his position as minister to France, had received assistance from Jefferson in writing *A View of the Conduct of the Executive in the Foreign Affairs of the United States,* a lengthy defense of his own diplomatic conduct and a strident condemnation of the Washington administration.[53]

Although Washington not infrequently showed a kind of outward resignation toward his reputed enemies, that was not always so. In this instance he not only encouraged Nicholas to document the source of the Langhorne letter and any accomplices that resided on a mountain near Charlottesville, but he also enlisted in the aid of Nicholas his nephew Bushrod Washington. If Nicholas and Bushrod could prove Jefferson's involvement in any way, they should do so. Dumas Malone, the distinguished author of a six-volume biography of Jefferson, contends that the Langhorne letter resulted in "the full alienation of the two men." It is more likely that Washington's intense effort to pin Jefferson to the wall here demonstrated that the relationship was previously broken beyond repair.[54]

Neither Washington nor his wife Martha ever give the slightest hint of mellowing toward the squire of Monticello. Tobias Lear, his secretary, noted that the night Washington came down with his fatal illness, before going to bed, he read aloud news from a Richmond gazette about the doings in Virginia politics of Jefferson's two chief henchmen, Madison and Monroe. Madison had nominated Monroe for governor of Virginia, and the Federalists saw his decisive victory as a slap at Washington in view of Monroe's apparent hostility toward the president who had removed him from his diplomatic post. Lear reported that Washington "appeared much affected and spoke with some degree of asperity on the subject."[55]

Given the traditional bias of biographers, Washington scholars understandably have not been kind to Jefferson. A personal anecdote illustrates the observation. Years ago as a graduate student researching in Richmond, I met Dr. Gertrude Richards, the senior member of Douglas S. Freeman's research team when he wrote his monumental seven-volume life of Washington. She informed me that she and Dr. Freeman had concluded that Jefferson was little short of being a fiend. Dr. Freeman, she added, had hoped to live to complete biographies of the three greatest Virginians of all time: Robert E. Lee, George Washington, and Woodrow Wilson![56]

One of our trio would have the last word about his fellow Revolutionaries—Jefferson, who outlived Henry and Washington by more than a quarter of a century. On various occasions Jefferson made reflective remarks about Henry that would eventually find their way into print. Most noteworthy were Jefferson's comments on William Wirt's efforts to produce a highly laudatory biography of Henry, which finally appeared in 1817, especially in his autobiography and in lengthy conversation in 1824 with Daniel Webster, the rising New England political star. Except for contending that Henry was the preeminent catalyst of revolution in pre-1776 Virginia and generally agreeable in daily conversation, Jefferson found Henry an unattractive human being—intellectually limited in his ability to read and write, his marvelous oratorical pronouncements inspiring but lacking content. "Neither in politics nor in his profession was he a man of business," Jefferson informed Webster. Henry "was a man for debate only." Wirt's biography of Henry, he continued, could be described as a "panegyric" rather than as "history."[57] Jefferson seems to have been remarkably consistent— and therefore mainly negative—in his assessments of Henry after the latter's death, beginning at least as early as 1805 when he responded to the first of numerous inquires from Wirt, who was then in the initial stages of his research on Henry.[58] Jefferson, who admitted he had not conversed with Henry or even seen him in person since the Revolutionary War, had added a new grievance to his list of pre-1783 negatives about his inveterate political nemesis: Henry, in seemingly going over to the Federalists during Washington's presidency, had betrayed holy republican political principles.[59]

As for Washington, Jefferson needed time to process the first president's character and his place in American history after his death in 1799. Besides, Jefferson eschewed public pronouncements; it was not his way. (Jefferson's chief standard-bearer, Madison, showed no such reluctance.)[60] And any laudatory words at that moment would have appeared insincere when the impact of the letter to Mazzei still generated fireworks, owing to its having been turned into a campaign issue by the Federalist press. Although there is no record of Jefferson's ever having expressed a wish for Washington's demise, he would have been embarrassed had word gotten out that he had on one occasion stated to Benjamin Rush, the illustrious Philadelphia physician, that so long as Washington lived the enemies of republicanism would use the great man as a weapon against them. In effect, then, the Father of His Country had become a threat to the American experiment in republican government.[61] Even so, Jefferson made a brief appearance at Mount Vernon on January 3, 1801, to pay his respects to Martha Washington. It must have been an awkward moment for both, although he divulged nothing of substance about their meeting in a letter addressed the next day to his daughter Maria Eppes. A man who disliked personal confrontation or candid admissions, he contented himself to inform Maria that his hostess "asked very kindly after you."[62] By contrast, Mrs. Washington supposedly said later "that, next to the loss of her husband," Jefferson's appearance there was "the most painful occurrence of her life."[63] She was obviously not impressed by President Jefferson's tribute to her marital companion in his first inaugural address. Whatever his lingering doubts about Washington, Jefferson's praise could understandably have been prompted by his desire to bring Americans together after the heated political campaign of 1800, which resulted in the first change in party control of the national government. His best-remembered expression is "We are all republicans, we are all federalists." In the same conciliatory tone, he acknowledged that he did not deserve "that high confidence you reposed in our first and greatest revolutionary character, whose preeminent services had entitled him to the first place in his country's love and destined for him the fairest page in . . . history."[64] Shortly before Martha's death in 1802, the Reverend Manasseh Cutler, a guest at Mount Vernon, recorded in his diary that Mrs. Washington was delighted that he and her other visitors that day were Federalists. Her political comments were "sometimes very sarcastic. . . . She spoke of the election of Mr. Jefferson, whom she considered as one of the most detestable of mankind, as the greatest misfortune our country had ever experienced."[65]

With the passing years Jefferson found it possible to soften his rhetoric toward some of his political adversaries of the turbulent 1790s when the political bloodletting seems to have been as harsh and shrill as at any time in our history, perhaps only equaled or exceeded in its extremes by the polarization of the 1850s and the secession crisis.[66] His positive expressions about Washington were quite honestly felt once his own political hyperventilating subsided. After all, he had only very infrequently criticized Washington by name. If there were momentary lapses by this man noted for his flights of hyperbolic rhetoric, he probably had never fully questioned Washington's own personal commitment to republicanism, nor had he deep-down doubted the first president's rectitude and probity, only his undue reliance on Hamilton and other Federalists in his thinking and decision making during his second term. He expressed enthusiasm for the inclusion in the curriculum for law students at the University of Virginia of Washington's first inaugural speech and his Farewell Address. If the idea for assigning them had come from Madison, Jefferson admonished himself for not thinking of doing so himself.[67]

Although Jefferson hardly stood alone against the tide of Washington hagiography from the pens of Mason Locke ("Parson") Weems and Chief Justice John Marshall, keeping company with Federalists such as John and Abigail Adams, the sage of Monticello provided the most balanced assessment of the Father of His Country to come from a contemporary (and a political opponent at that) of the first president. Jefferson's critics, who are numerous at the opening of the twenty-first century, may express skepticism. It is true that the tide of recent scholarship on Jefferson has somewhat dimmed his historical image. There is some basis for the contentions that he was often less than forthright and sometimes extremely inconsistent in his behavior, tending to compartmentalize his life and thought and to ignore his inconsistencies. Moreover, the third president, who said that posterity alone should fix his place in history, actually worked to craft his future image.[68] Being remembered as an enemy of Washington would threaten his place in the American pantheon. On the other hand, if Jefferson had been insincere in his final lengthy word portrait of the preeminent leader of the Revolution, it is unlikely that his undertaking would have stood the test of time.

His evaluation of Washington is worth quoting at some length.

> His mind was great and powerful, without being of the very first order; his penetration strong, though not so acute as that of a Newton, Bacon, or Locke; and as far as he saw, no judgment was ever sounder. . . . Perhaps the strongest feature in his character was prudence, never acting until every circumstance, every consideration, was maturely weighed; refraining if he saw a doubt, but, when once decided, going through with his purpose whatever obstacles opposed. His integrity was most pure, his justice the most inflexible . . . no motives of interest or consanguinity, or friendship or hatred, being able to bias his decision. He was, indeed, in every sense of the words, a wise, a good, and a great man. . . . his was the singular destiny and merit of leading the armies of his country successfully through an arduous war for the establishment of its independence; of conducting its councils through the birth of a government, new in its forms and principles, until it had settled down into a quiet and

orderly train; and of scrupulously obeying the laws through the whole of his career, civil and military, of which the history of the world furnishes no other example.[69]

Washington, of course, did obey the laws, but so did Jefferson and Henry. Unlike so many revolutions since 1776 that have not been resolved at the ballot box, the major transformations in America were peaceful in the postwar years, although the issues that divided the trio were profound, involving the constitutional configuration of the new nation and its political, economic, and social structure. It tells us worlds about the American Revolution to recall that our famous Revolutionaries did not die at the end of a rope or on a guillotine. They died in their beds, even if they were not in bed with each other politically.[70]

Notes

1. Bernard Mayo, *Myths and Men: Patrick Henry, George Washington, Thomas Jefferson* (Athens, Ga., 1959), 13.
2. *Autobiography of Thomas Jefferson,* intro. Dumas Malone (New York, 1962), 22.
3. Merrill D. Peterson, *Thomas Jefferson and the New Nation* (London and New York, 1970), 13, says five years, but David Konig, who is working on a legal biography of Jefferson, contends that three years is closer to the truth.
4. The details of the Washington speech are likely apocryphal, but the tale captures his well-known determination to stand firm for American rights. A fascinating and hitherto neglected part of the story is that it appears to have been a subject of conversation for two months or so. Paul H. Smith, ed., *Letters of Delegates to Congress,* 26 vols. (Washington, D.C., 1976–99), 1:5, 62, 247.
5. Jefferson to William Wirt, Aug. 4, 1805, *Pennsylvania Magazine of History and Biography* 34 (1910): 393.
6. Edmund Randolph, *History of Virginia,* ed. Arthur H. Shaffer (Charlottesville, Va., 1970), 250. Emory Evans clarifies Henry's position on independence in the spring of 1776 in *Thomas Nelson of Yorktown: Revolutionary Virginian* (Williamsburg, Va., 1975), 56–57, 169–70.
7. Peterson, *Jefferson and the New Nation,* 140.
8. Paul Boller, *Washington and Religion* (Dallas, 1963). A splendid new study of the Church of England in the Old Dominion is John K. Nelson, *A Blessed Company: Parishes, Parsons, and Parishioners in Anglican Virginia, 1690–1776* (Chapel Hill, N.C., 2001), with an epilogue on the fall of the establishment during the Revolution.
9. Jefferson to Isaac Zane, Dec. 24, 1781, in Julian P. Boyd et al., eds., *The Papers of Thomas Jefferson,* 31 vols. (Princeton, N.J., 1950–), 6:143–44.
10. Thomas Jefferson, *Notes on the State of Virginia,* ed. William Peden (Chapel Hill, N.C., 1955), 126–29, 284–85. For documents and editorial notes on the Virginia crisis in 1781, see Boyd, *Papers of Jefferson* 6:85–86, 88, 89, 106–9, 133–37.

11. Washington to Jefferson, June 8, 1781, in Boyd, *Papers of Jefferson* 6:83.

12. Jefferson to Madison, Dec. 8, 1784, in James Morton Smith, ed., *The Republic of Letters: The Correspondence between Jefferson and Madison, 1776–1826,* 3 vols. (New York, 1995), 1:353–54. Jefferson recorded these italicized words about Henry in code.

13. Madison, whose opinions of Henry were hardly more favorable than those of his mentor, fed Jefferson in Paris an additional diet of negatives about their political enemy. Madison informed Jefferson that the legislature returned Henry to the governorship "without competition or opposition." An act creating courts of assize would surely have failed except for the fact that Governor Henry was absent from Richmond at the time, and therefore the opposition lacked "both a mouth and a head." Ibid., 363, 355.

14. Jefferson to Washington, Aug. 14[–15], 1787, *PGW: Conf. Ser.* 5:291.

15. Henry to Washington, Oct. 19, 1787, ibid., 384. Washington's letter and copy no longer survive, but he sent identical documents to others that still exist; see Washington to Benjamin Harrison, Sept. 24, 1787, ibid., 339–40.

16. Lance Banning, *The Sacred Fire of Liberty: James Madison and the Founding of the Federal Republic* (Ithaca, N.Y., 1995), 240; Merrill Jensen, John Kaminski, and Gaspare J. Saladino, eds., *The Documentary History of the Ratification of the Constitution,* 17 vols. to date, not numbered consecutively (Madison, Wis., 1976–), 9:1072.

17. Stuart Leibiger, *Founding Friendship: George Washington, James Madison, and the Creation of the American Republic* (Charlottesville, Va., 1999), 94–95.

18. James Monroe to Thomas Jefferson, July 12, 1788, in Stanislaus M. Hamilton, ed., *The Writings of James Monroe . . . ,* 7 vols. (New York, 1898–1903), 1:186.

19. John P. Kaminski, *George Clinton: Yeoman Politician of the New Republic* (Madison, Wis., 1993), chap. 4.

20. Peter R. Henriques, "An Uneven Friendship: The Relationship between George Washington and George Mason," *Virginia Magazine of History and Biography* 97 (1989): 185–204.

21. Washington to Madison, Nov. 17, 1788, *PGW: Pres. Ser.* 1:115.

22. Jefferson to William Short, Dec. 14, 1789, Jefferson to Gouverneur Morris, Nov. 26, 1790, in Boyd, *Papers of Jefferson* 16:24–28, 18:82.

23. Jefferson to Washington, May 23, 1792, ibid., 23:538–39.

24. For both sides claiming to be defenders of the Constitution, see Lance Banning, *The Jeffersonian Persuasion: Evolution of a Party Ideology* (Ithaca, N.Y., 1978).

25. Richard R. Beeman, *Patrick Henry: A Biography* (New York, 1974), 165–76; Robert Douthat Meade, *Patrick Henry,* 2 vols. (Philadelphia and New York, 1957–69), 2:384–97; William Wirt Henry, *Patrick Henry: Life, Correspondence, and Speeches,* 3 vols. (New York, 1981), 2:459–62, quotation on p. 460.

26. There were complaints that President Washington's social events were stilted and formal, smacking of European royal courts. Dr. David Stuart, Washington's friend and confidant, informed the chief executive in 1790 that critics of the administration had made "some extraordinary representations" to Henry about "the Etiquette established at your levees." But neither Stuart nor Henry's recent biographers pro-

vided evidence of Henry's reaction. Stuart to Washington, June 2, 1790, *PGW: Pres. Ser.* 5:462.

27. R. Kent Newmyer, *John Marshall and the Heroic Age of the Supreme Court* (Baton Rouge, La., 2001), 96–100, 126–28, quotation on p. 127; Jean Edward Smith, *John Marshall: Definer of a Nation* (New York, 1996), 4, 148, 150, 156–57, 328, 329; John Marshall, *An Autobiographical Sketch,* ed. John Stokes Adams (Ann Arbor, Mich., 1937); Herbert Johnson et al., eds., *The Papers of John Marshall,* 10 vols. to date (Chapel Hill, N.C., 1974–), 1:113.

28. Jenson, *Documentary History of Ratification* 9:1073.

29. Henry Lee to Washington, Aug. 17, 1794, Washington to Henry Lee, Aug. 26, 1794, *GW: Writings* 33:476–77 and n.

30. Henry Lee to Washington, Aug. 17, 1794, ibid., 476–77n.

31. Washington to Henry Lee, Aug. 26, 1794, ibid., 476–77.

32. Washington to Henry, Oct. 9, 1795, ibid., 34:334–35; Henry to Washington, Oct. 16, 1795, in Henry, *Patrick Henry* 2:558–59; Meade, *Patrick Henry* 2:433, 443; Smith, *John Marshall,* 178–79.

33. Richard R. Beeman, *The Old Dominion and the New Nation, 1788–1801* (Lexington, Ky., 1972), chap. 5; Meade, *Patrick Henry,* 2:425–26.

34. Johnson, *Papers of Marshall* 3:21–22, 28; Harold C. Syrett, ed., *The Papers of Alexander Hamilton,* 27 vols. (New York, 1961–87), 20:151–59; Winifred E. A. Bernhard, *Fisher Ames: Federalist and Statesman, 1758–1808* (Chapel Hill, N.C., 1965), 278; Robert Ernst, *Rufus King: American Federalist* (Chapel Hill, N.C., 1968), 214–15.

35. Washington to Henry, Jan. 15, 1799, *PGW: Ret. Ser.* 3:317–20, quotation on p. 317.

36. Beeman, *Patrick Henry,* 122.

37. *PGW: Ret. Ser.* 3:317–20.

38. Patrick Henry to Washington, Feb. 12, 1799, ibid., 370–72.

39. Archibald Blair to Washington, June 19, 1999, ibid., 4:136.

40. Henry confided to his daughter Elizabeth Aylett on Aug. 20, 1796, that because of the great achievements of "our old commander-in-chief," Washington should be forgiven "for his mistakes in an office to which he was totally unaccustomed." He regretted Washington's having accepted the presidency, with all "its attendant difficulties." Henry, *Patrick Henry* 2:568–71.

41. Beeman, *Old Dominion,* chaps. 7–9.

42. See, for example, Jefferson to Washington, May 23, 1792, in Boyd, *Writings of Jefferson* 23:535–40; Washington to Hamilton, July 29, 1792, Hamilton to Washington, Aug. 18, 1792, in Syrett, *Papers of Hamilton* 12:129–34, 228–58.

43. Jefferson to Washington, Dec. 31, 1793, in Boyd, *Writings of Jefferson* 27:656; Washington to Jefferson, Jan. 1, 1794, *GW: Writings* 33:231.

44. Jefferson to Madison, Dec. 28, 1794, in Smith, *Republic of Letters* 2:867. Madison complained that Washington's lashing out at the Democratic Societies was "the greatest error of his political life." Madison to James Monroe, Dec. 4, 1794, quoted in ibid., 851.

45. Jefferson to Madison, March 27, 1796, in Boyd, *Papers of Jefferson* 29:51.

46. Jefferson to Edward Carrington, May 27, 1788, in Jensen, *Documentary History of Ratification* 18:81; also in Boyd, *Papers of Jefferson* 13:208–9.

47. Jefferson to Washington, June 19, 1796, Washington to Jefferson, July 6, 1796, in Boyd, *Papers of Jefferson* 29:127–29, 141–43, quotation on p. 142. Jefferson believed that at this time Governor Henry Lee of Virginia was the principal culprit in endeavoring to spread lies about him. Dumas Malone, *Jefferson and His Time,* 6 vols. (Boston, 1948–77), 3:269–72.

48. Joseph J. Ellis, *Founding Brothers: The Revolutionary Generation* (New York, 2000), 144, makes a strong case for the latter interpretation—that Washington believed Jefferson was duplicitous.

49. Jefferson to Mazzei, April 24, 1796. The various European and American forms of Jefferson's letter were altered to include passages and words not in the original to Mazzei; but the substance was largely the same, containing the obvious allusion to Washington. Four versions, including Jefferson's original and the *Minerva* rendition, with useful editorial notes, are in Boyd, *Papers of Jefferson* 29:73–89, quotations from Jefferson's original missive, p. 82.

50. Jefferson to Martin Van Buren, June 29, 1824, ibid., 29:77–78n.

51. Leibiger, *Founding Friendship,* chaps. 8, 9, Epilogue.

52. Jefferson to Madison, [1808], in Smith, *Republic of Letters* 3:1558.

53. The Washington-Nicholas correspondence, along with documents on the Langhorne affair, is in *PGW: Ret. Ser.* 1:475–77, 373–75, 409, 491–92, 509–11, 2:99–102, 127–29, 514–15, 546–47, quotations in 1:476, 510, 2:101. According to Dumas Malone, Jefferson offered advice only on direct questions raised by Monroe. Malone does concede that Jefferson always spoke highly of the work after it appeared in print. Malone, *Jefferson and His Time* 3:338.

54. *PGW: Ret. Ser.* 2:129–31, 514–15, 546–47; Malone, *Jefferson and His Time* 3:308–11, quotation on p. 308.

55. Leibiger, *Founding Friendship,* 220–21; *PGW: Ret. Ser.* 4:547.

56. David E. Johnson, *Douglas Southall Freeman* (Gretna, La., 2002), 279, 299, 331, 340–41, discusses Richards's work as Freeman's first full-time assistant, carrying the title chief research associate. Freeman died before writing volume 7 of his Washington biography. His treatment of both Jefferson and Hamilton is evenhanded in vol. 6, which concludes with the end of the president's first term. Volume 7 was written by two of Freeman's other assistants, John Alexander Carroll and Mary Wells Ashworth.

57. "Notes on Mr. Jefferson's Conversation 1824 at Monticello," in Charles M. Wiltse and Harold D. Moser, eds., *The Papers of Daniel Webster,* 7 vols. (Hanover, N.H., 1974–86), 1:371–73.

58. "Jefferson's Recollections of Patrick Henry," *Pennsylvania Magazine of History and Biography* 34 (1910): 386–418, which contains seven letters to Wirt. There were other opportunities for Jefferson to record some more positive evaluations of Henry. But two excellent published collections of his correspondence contain no efforts by him to do so. See Smith, *The Republic of Letters,* and Lester J. Cappon,

The Adams-Jefferson Letters: The Complete Correspondence between Thomas Jefferson and Abigail and John Adams, 2 vols. (Chapel Hill, N.C., 1959).

59. Malone, *Jefferson and His Time* 6:226.

60. Addressing the Virginia legislature, Madison paid handsome tribute to Washington, and that body passed unanimously his motion to wear mourning badges for the remainder of the session. In contrast, the legislature had rejected by a decisive vote a resolution honoring the memory of Patrick Henry. Leibiger, *Founding Friendship,* 221–22; Beeman, *Old Dominion,* 216.

61. On March 12, 1801, Rush reminded Jefferson of the latter's remark in the late 1790s about the Federalists' use of Washington's name as a political weapon. Lyman H. Butterfield, ed., *Letters of Benjamin Rush,* 2 vols. (Princeton, N.J., 1951), 2:832, 833; Malone, *Jefferson and His Time* 3:443–44. Jefferson, of course, was right about the Federalists' tactics. See Simon P. Newman, "Principles or Men? George Washington and the Political Culture of National Leadership, 1776–1801," *Journal of the Early Republic* 12 (1992): 477–507.

62. Paul L. Ford, ed., *Writings of Thomas Jefferson,* 10 vols. (New York, 1892–99), 7:478.

63. Malone, *Jefferson and His Time* 3:442–44; John Cotton Smith, *The Correspondence and Miscellanies . . .* (New York, 1847), 224–25.

64. Merrill D. Peterson, ed., *Thomas Jefferson: Writings* (New York, 1984), 493, 495.

65. William Parker Cutler and Julia Perkins Cutler, *Life, Journals, and Correspondence of Rev. Manasseh Cutler,* 2 vols. (Cincinnati, 1888), 2:56–57.

66. For a strong and generally persuasive argument for this interpretation, see James Roger Sharp, *American Politics in the Early Republic: The New Nation in Crisis* (New Haven, 1993), especially his contention that "historians have minimized the anxiety most Americans felt at the outset about the tenuousness and fragility of the union and the Constitution" and that for that reason "they have not fully understood the political developments of the 1790s" (p. 6).

67. Madison to Jefferson, Feb. 8, 1825, Jefferson to Madison, Feb. 12, 1825, in Smith, *Republic of Letters* 3:1925–26; Malone, *Jefferson and His Time* 6:417–18.

68. Joseph J. Ellis, *American Sphinx: The Character of Thomas Jefferson* (New York, 1996); Peter S. Onuf, ed., *Jeffersonian Legacies* (Charlottesville, Va., 1993); Robert M. S. McDonald, "Thomas Jefferson and Historical Self-Construction: The Earth Belongs to the Living?" *Historian* 62 (1999): 289–310.

69. Jefferson to Walter Jones, Jan. 2, 1814, in Ford, *Writings of Jefferson* 9:448–49. Four years after delineating these characteristics of Washington, Jefferson added some further reflections on Washington in the introduction to what is called his Anas, three manuscript volumes of notes and documents drawn mostly from the political battles of the 1790s. The Anas, an effort to set the political record straight, criticized Marshall's five-volume *Life of Washington* as a highly partisan enterprise that castigated those who disagreed with Washington's actions as president and that extolled the virtues of the Federalist Party. Noting that Marshall had access to Washington's papers at Mount Vernon, Jefferson asserted that Marshall had distorted their con-

tents and that had Washington employed them to write a history of his presidency, his account would have been far more balanced and objective. Jefferson, however, went on to claim his differences with Washington during the president's second term and after Jefferson left the cabinet stemmed in part from Washington's declining mental powers, which left him more vulnerable to Federalist manipulation: "His memory was already sensibly impaired by age, the firm tone of mind for which he had been remarkable, was beginning to relax, it's energy was abated; a listlessness of labor, a desire for tranquillity had crept on him, and a willingness to let others act and even think for him." Peterson, *Jefferson: Writings,* 661, 662, quotation on p. 673.

70. Joseph J. Ellis states admirably the challenge of all successful revolutionaries: "Bound together in solidarity against the imperialistic enemy, the leadership fragments when the common enemy disappears and the different agenda for the new nation must confront its differences. Securing a revolution has proven to be a much more daunting assignment than winning one." Ellis, *Founding Brothers,* 78.

3 ┆ *George Washington and Three Women*

I COMPOSED THE FOLLOWING PIECE as a modest contribution to the commemoration of the bicentennial of Washington's death in 1999. Americans observed the event in various ways, most notably with Washington exhibits that took places around the country, including the New-York Historical Society, the Virginia Historical Society in Richmond, and the Henry E. Huntington Library and Art Gallery in San Marino, California. The Mount Vernon Ladies' Association and the New-York Historical Society sponsored the most imposing and elaborate undertaking, called "Treasures from Mount Vernon: George Washington Revealed." In addition to displaying letters and documents, the exhibit featured personal effects from Mount Vernon, paraphernalia from his military service, materials from the presidency, and the original key to the Bastille. Shortly after this Washington commemoration opened at the New-York Historical Society, I took my American Revolution class at the United States Military Academy at West Point to see it. As one who saw "Treasures" several other times in New York City and elsewhere as it later made its way around the country, I got the impression from talking to numerous visitors that the president's set of dentures—a combination of cows' teeth, wooden teeth, several teeth purchased from his own slaves, and so on—attracted viewers in record numbers, as did a more serious and informative display: a highly detailed replica of his Mount Vernon home, with every room filled with models of the actual furniture in the house itself. It took several years, at a cost of five million dollars, to build to scale a miniature Mount Vernon, which could be operated electronically to give one a close-up look at different parts of the house.

Bicentennial observations also involved conferences, symposia, and special lectures on Washington and his times. I gave my "George Washington and Three Women" on several such occasions, beginning with a Washington conference at the University of Southern Mississippi at Hattiesburg on October 28–29, 1999. I had always felt that Washington's relations with his family and friends had been neglected and that, in fact, his domestic life held a partial explanation at least of why he was a safe man to lead a revolution. He entertained no grand ambitions for himself, and he never, unlike so many later revolutionaries in history, came to see himself and the American Revolution as one and inseparable. As has often been said, his willingness, even eagerness, to give up power, both that of military commander in chief and president of the United States, made him all the more revered by his countrymen. My contention here is that his relationship with these three women demonstrates his healthy commitment to family and friends—and, in a larger sense, to Mount Vernon and Virginia. I also wished to show that all three of these important women in his life have been somewhat misunderstood. My paper along with the others at the conference appeared in Tamara Harvey and Greg O'Brien, eds., *George Washington's South* (Gainesville: University of Florida Press, 2004), 121–42, and is reprinted with the permission of the publisher.

FOR SOME YEARS NOW, as I worked on a study of Washington as a Revolutionary leader, it became apparent that more could be said about his family relationships in understanding his later years on the national stage. If his early biographers largely ignored his private life save for extolling his character and physical prowess, his twentieth-century chroniclers have zeroed in on his life outside the public arena, with uneven or mixed results.

Once I decided to look at Washington's relationship with certain women, it soon became clear that he liked the opposite sex. That is hardly a profound statement, but it might have been said, if the evidence warranted it, that he was uncomfortable in the presence of women or generally displayed a cold or distant attitude toward them. We know that he has often been described, both by contemporaries and historians, as reserved and aloof, and the statement contains much truth concerning men he did not know well or did not particularly care for. Women, however, usually found Washington polite, attentive, and at ease in their presence. He frequently bantered with them, not averse to using occasional sexual innuendos in doing so, and he occasionally engaged them in discussions of public affairs.

By contrast, some historians such as Kenneth Lockridge, Joseph Ellis, Winthrop Jordan, and Jack McLaughlin find Thomas Jefferson usually distant and uneasy with the opposite sex but nonetheless as a widower playful in a romantically suggestive way in Paris with beauties such as Maria Cosway and Angelica Schuyler Church. Lockridge's study of Jefferson's commonplace book, his jottings from literature, contends that Jefferson was a misogynist, at best quite ambivalent toward women as a young man, and generally resentful toward his mother. Yet he deeply loved his wife, a passive woman in no way threatening to him. And as president he disbanded Martha Washington's republican court, a regular social gathering designed to get men and women of different parties and from various regions together to foster sociability and diffuse national tensions.[1]

This particular undertaking owes a large debt to Douglas L. Wilson's *Honor's Voice: The Transformation of Abraham Lincoln* (New York, 1998), a study of the young Lincoln's first decade or so in Illinois. Wilson gives special attention to Lincoln's relationship with three women who significantly influenced his life. It seems that three women also stand out in Washington's life before the Revolution: his mother, Mary Ball Washington; his friend and neighbor Sally Cary Fairfax; and his wife, Martha Dandridge Custis Washington.[2]

His relationship with all three needs reassessment. This venture is undoubtedly only a first step in that process. New Washington scholarship not only should set the record straight but also should cast aside stereotypical notions of these women. Consciously or not, some historians have pictured them in their relations with Washington in the rigid gender images that prevailed in history and fiction through the 1950s and sometimes later. They have hardly been portrayed as complex individuals whose ties to Washington were multidimensional. Instead, we have descriptions of Mary Ball Washington as the shrewish mother, Sally Fairfax as the flirtatious wife, and Martha Washington as the "Plain Jane."[3] After briefly looking at each relationship, this essay will contend that what we might call the family factor throws light on why Washington was a safe man to lead a revolution devoted to freedom and liberty.

Because Mary Ball Washington outlived her husband—he died when George was eleven—and even survived into George's presidency, there have been repeated attempts to measure her influence on Washington. The results have scarcely been fruitful for his formative years. Acolytes of the demigod cult depicted her as "Mary the Mother of Washington," a saintly Roman matron type. If hagiographers pictured her as faultless, as a profoundly positive influence upon a messianic son,[4] Douglas Southall Freeman in the late 1940s set the image of her that prevails to this day—a selfish, overbearing, and domineering parent. Freeman's view is that George survived and matured in spite of her, not because of her.[5] Freeman's characterization of Mary Ball received powerful reinforcement from James Thomas Flexner, author of what has long been recognized as the second most influential multivolume biography of Washington, which began appearing in the 1960s. (In fact, a recent poll of historians elevated it above Freeman's work, voting it the most valuable of the ten best books on Washington.) Flexner goes so far as to employ the word "Termagant" for Mary Ball in the title of a chapter about her.[6] Recent popular publications have joined in the unflattering delineation of Washington's mother. A piece in *American History Illustrated* repeats the standard barbs and adds one other that is said to be the key to Washington's lack of warm feeling for his mother: based on a single source, it is said that she supported Britain, not America, in the Revolution. A French officer, visiting in her hometown of Fredericksburg, reported that he was told that this "lady, who must be over seventy, is one of the most rabid Tories." And on the eve of the bicentennial of Washington's death, an issue of *Mount Vernon: Yesterday, Today, Tomorrow* asked, with reference to the "rocky relationship" between mother and son, "Did His Heart Belong to Mother?"[7]

Although Washington found Mary Ball to be a difficult person many years later, that was not necessarily the case during his youth. Only six of his letters to her are extant; five for the 1750s, then none at all for the next thirty years, after which, if not before, she suffered from breast cancer—a condition which may account for her preoccupation with her own welfare.[8] She displayed behavior that mortified her distinguished son when in 1781 she complained indirectly to the Virginia legislature of her impoverishment and seems to have sought a pension or some other form of financial relief. She also, according to Washington, spoke to friends and acquaintances of being neglected by her own family.[9]

And yet she genuinely cared for George. Three and a half years into the war, Mary Ball had asserted that because of his long absence from Mount Vernon, "poor George will be ruined" should anything happen to his overseer. The general had planned to visit his mother in Fredericksburg after the victory at Yorktown, but the illness and death of his stepson, Jacky Custis, and other matters delayed his arrival. Unaware of his new plans, Mary Ball was not home when her son arrived. Her letter to Washington, the only one to survive, hardly exposes the ever-present hard edge invariably attributed to her (although she continued to voice her fear of the future): "I was truly un[ea]sy My Not being at ho[me] when you went throu fredirecksburg[.] it was an unlucky thing for me now I am afraid I Never Shall have that pleasure agin[.] I am Soe very unwell & this trip over the Mountins has almost kill'd me[.] I gott the 20 five ginnes you was Soe kind to Send me & am greatly abliged to you for it. . . . pray give my kind Love to Mrs Washington & am My Dear George yo[ur] Loveing and affectinat Mother[.]" Two years later a planned excursion to her Fredericksburg home suffered a delay because, as Washington wrote, "we have been so fast locked in Snow & Ice since Christmas" that all travel had "been suspended." By January 22, 1784, conditions had improved. He expressed eagerness "to discharge that duty" to his mother "on which nature & inclination have a call." On February 14 of that year, while Washington was in Fredericksburg visiting "his ancient and amiable parent," the town fathers honored him with a dinner. He then thanked his hosts for their courteous favors and for their kind words about his "revered Mother." For it was by her "Maternal hand (early deprived of a Father) I was led to Manhood."[10]

Her detractors invariably make the point that Washington did not visit her often, and we have no record of her spending time at Mount Vernon. But Washington also saw his brothers and sister infrequently, even though evidence shows a good deal of closeness and a sense of responsibility for one another within the family, one example being Washington's positive involvement in the lives of his nieces and nephews. Moreover, Mary Ball lived quite near her daughter, Betty Lewis, who undoubtedly could watch over her and care for her immediate needs.

Washington, although he was once again involved on the national political scene, took time to see his mother three times during her last two years. Just before departing for the Constitutional Convention in Philadelphia, Washington, on hearing that Mary Ball was "in the agonies of death," hurried to Fredericksburg. He found her condition "better than I expected," but she appeared thin and weak, with "little hope of her recovery."[11] The following year he returned to see her, accompanied by his wife, at a time when he was much preoccupied with the fate of the Constitution in the Virginia ratifying convention and in state conventions elsewhere. Shortly before Washington left for New York to assume the presidency in 1789, he specifically traveled to Fredericksburg to say farewell to his mother, spending a weekend there. He acknowledged that it would surely be the last time he would ever see her. Since Washington preceded his wife Martha to New York City for the presidential inauguration, Mary Ball offered to lend Martha her coach for the trip, but she chose instead to turn to a man who rented horses and carriages for private journeys.[12]

According to Mary Ball's critics, she first displayed selfish behavior that can be documented decades earlier in turning thumbs down on her stepson Lawrence's proposal that George, then fourteen, seek a career in the Royal Navy because she desired her firstborn to stay at home to look after her and her business affairs. It is said that George subsequently sought to escape her clutches by staying away from Ferry Farm as much as possible, visiting Lawrence's plantation, working as a surveyor, and later serving as a provincial soldier. Some investigators even speculate that Washington's unhappiness with her treatment of him spawned several of his unfavorable characteristics that were so noticeable at the time of the French and Indian War.

The surviving evidence does not convict Mary Ball on these counts. She was a woman who hardly had an easy life when widowed in her middle thirties with five children under the age of twelve. It scarcely takes great effort to imagine the devastation she and her children felt. And Augustine's death occurred when George approached the age of establishing his own identity and some measure of personal independence. Evidently Mary Ball held her family together under her own roof, no small accomplishment in itself. She might have done otherwise. "Even when one parent survived," observes Patricia Brady, "children were often parceled out because the financial or emotional burden was too great for one parent alone."[13] Years later George and Martha Washington adopted two of Jacky and Nelly Custis's children after Jacky's death.

As for George's going to sea, Mary Ball took more than a year to make her decision, fluctuating in her attitude and voicing concerns, as a family friend put it, that "mothers naturally suggest."[14] At length, she put the question to her half brother Joseph Ball in England, who replied that George as a provincial would never have the connections to achieve "any considerable preferment in the Navy." Even a captain of a merchant vessel, he opined, would not live as well as a Virginia planter with "three or four hundred acres of land and three or four slaves."[15]

It is true that Washington himself as a Virginia military officer in his twenties comes across to us as quarrelsome, sensitive to slights, and extremely ambitious; in short, hardly a completely appealing figure. But the roots of aggressive behavior are not always easy to determine. Domineering mothers—if that is what Mary Ball Washington was—may generate visible aggressions in their sons (or daughters), or they are just as likely to leave their children timid or straitlaced. Conceivably, too, Washington, were he severely damaged by his mother's influence, might have become effeminate when in truth we know that he was ardently attached to the opposite sex, far more comfortable in the presence of women than Lincoln.

It is arguable that Mary Ball Washington contributed positively to the aspirations of George and her other sons. If the Washingtons were solidly anchored in the gentry, the same could be said of Mary Ball's father and her guardian, George Eskridge, both highly visible in local affairs, the latter a successful lawyer and a member of the House of Burgesses for nearly thirty years.[16] Consequently, it is hard to understand why some authorities have contended that Washington's father Augustine married somewhat below his station in selecting Mary Ball as his second wife. The assertion often appears in the context of stating that Mary Ball was orphaned at age twelve. Yet the Eskridges were at least the social equals of the Balls, and Augustine Washington was well acquainted with the

Eskridges; his first wife, Jane Butler, was a sister-in-law of George Eskridge. A few years ago I serendipitously discovered the burial site of one of Eskridge's daughters in the Yeocomico Church cemetery, which is in Westmoreland County in the Northern Neck; her casket-length gravestone appeared to be the largest one there. Mary Ball quite likely considered her life with the Eskridges in positive terms. Her own mother spoke of a loving relationship between her daughter and herself and George Eskridge.[17] It seems significant, in terms of Mary Ball's views of her own family experience and her ambitions for her first son, that she named him George, undoubtedly after George Eskridge. Her second and third children, Betty and Samuel, also bore names related to the Eskridges. In doing so, she had eschewed the name John, which, along with Lawrence and Augustine, had appeared in the Washington family with generational regularity since the 1650s. (Only the name John was available since her husband Augustine had already named his sons by his first wife Lawrence and Augustine. Mary Ball and her husband would later use the name John Augustine for their fourth child.)[18]

Finally, Mary Ball, in addition to holding up her own Ball and Eskridge families as worthy of emulation, may have had another positive influence on George: heredity. A determined, strong-willed woman, she withstood the pressures of three formidable men in deciding against George's setting out before the mast: Lawrence Washington, Colonel William Fairfax, and Robert Jackson, who seems to have been close to both of the other two advocates, as well as having been something of a friend and unofficial adviser to George's mother. She also showed her independence in 1787 when, despite her advanced age and severe illness, she rejected her son George's arguments that she live with one of her children. She must have passed on these firm, unflinching aspects of her nature to her oldest son. Assuredly, they were components of his own makeup, essential ones for any successful revolutionary.[19] But they no doubt at times led to tension and friction between a strong-minded, independent mother and a son who shared her characteristics. Given all that Washington had done for his mother, it was not surprising or improper that she left the lion's share of her estate to him. He seemed deeply touched by certain specific personal items that she bequeathed him. He referred to them as "mementos of parental affection," bestowed "in the last solemn act of life." He valued "them much beyond their intrinsic worth."[20]

Serious historians, popularizers, and novelists have all found more interesting, often downright titillating, Washington's relationship with Sarah ("Sally") Cary Fairfax, the wife of his close friend and nearby neighbor at Belvoir, George William Fairfax. Colonel William Fairfax, George William's father, held a seat on the royal council, serving for a time as its president. His relative Thomas, Lord Fairfax, the only British nobleman to make his permanent home in the colonies, held proprietary rights to the vast Northern Neck of Virginia. The Carys, who lived at Cellys, near Hampton in Elizabeth City County, were politically influential and highly cultivated, with deep roots in the Old Dominion. Sally had turned eighteen, two years older than George Washington, when she gave her hand to George William Fairfax and came to live at Belvoir, one of the great houses of the day, where gracious entertainment characterized life within its walls. Young Washington, often a visitor at his brother Lawrence's Mount Vernon, delighted in his many four-mile trips to Belvoir. He enjoyed the banter with other young people, the dancing and card playing, and the other pleasures of mingling with a family noted for its charm, manners, and intellect.[21]

We know that in September 1758 Washington and Sally Fairfax exchanged playful, some authors say flirtatious, letters, just a few months before he married Martha Dandridge Custis, a twenty-seven-year-old widow about his own age. The marriage is often described as one of convenience.[22] With his colonial military career nearing an end, he needed a mistress for Mount Vernon, which he had acquired after Lawrence's death, and she sought a manager for her extensive financial resources and a stepfather for her two young children.

The weight of scholarly opinion now holds that Washington had fallen in love with his friend's wife and that he had hardly put his feelings for Sally to rest when he took the widow Custis to Mount Vernon as his wife.[23] Evidently it was a short courtship. And did any lack of instant ardor on his part have something to do with her allegedly being only modestly attractive physically?

Some writers have gone so far as to say that Washington fell in love with Sally the first time he saw her, that she eventually reciprocated his feelings, that they undoubtedly exchanged numerous secret letters, and that they likely met for assignations. Not surprisingly, popularizers and novelists have been particularly bold and provocative. One recent, generally competent study of Colonel Washington in the French and Indian War maintains that from first acquaintance with the new Mrs. George William Fairfax, he "never afterward would be able to think of her without choking up."[24] Most youths in their late teenager years get over such hormonal surges, especially if directed at the wife of a well-connected friend. But not so Washington. Indeed, when George William and Sally Fairfax moved to England in 1773, never to return to Virginia, Washington bought numerous items from their estate, including an elegant mahogany double chest of drawers that had been in Sally's bedchamber (it must have once held her daintiest garments). This prized piece subsequently resided in the sleeping quarters of George and Martha Washington. It has been suggested that Washington received some sentimental, if not sensual, pleasure from having it there. The "romantics," if that is the proper term for such writers,[25] have seemingly been unaware that another furniture item in the Washington bedchamber, a small bureau, came from Martha's boudoir during her first marriage to Daniel Parke Custis. One hazards to guess whether there is meaning in their standing on opposite sides of the bedroom![26]

Looking at the record afresh, one finds problems with this portrayal of Washington's attitude toward both Sally Fairfax and Martha Custis on the eve of matrimony. The evidence quantitatively is slight if intriguing about Washington and Sally. They wrote two letters to each other in September 1758, by which time— if not as early as March of that year—he and Martha Custis probably were engaged.[27] Surely he wrote admiringly to Sally statements that could have been interpreted at the time as improper, whatever their exact meaning. Judging from Washington's end of the correspondence—Sally's missives have not survived— she teased him about the meaning of part of his first letter. His behavior—to some degree possibly reciprocated by her—hardly seems out of character for the age when men and women engaged in such banter replete with suggestive implications.

Examples abound. The intellectual historian Peter Gay writes of "hyperbolic language" in a "hyperbolic century." Certain effusions of the age have to be discounted, he maintains. Writers "peppered their letters with exaggerations that seem cloying today, but were ritual formulas then."[28] The most careful scholars of Benjamin Franklin's years as a diplomat in Paris likewise assert that his interest in French women has been torn from its context: he reveled in their embraces, banter, and confidences, but the evidence stops short of the boudoir. He never credited himself with seductions, nor do the numerous diaries and journals of elite Parisians record such tales. In fact, "there is no shred of evidence" that he had "affairs with French women."[29] The same might be said of Jefferson, who succeeded Franklin as an American diplomat in Paris. He relished metaphors and literary allusions charged with sexual implications in letters to Angelica Church and Maria Cosway, both married women whom Jefferson invited to visit Monticello. But complicating explication of Jefferson's famous Head and Heart Letter to Maria Cosway is that he addressed it to her husband as well. Even his correspondence with Abigail Adams is not without flirtatious metaphors, and when Jefferson visited England in 1786, he and Abigail took several sightseeing jaunts together to some of the kingdom's most celebrated houses and gardens.[30]

Men too could engage each other in correspondence that suggested deep emotional, possibly erotic, ties. The late Richard Showman, editor of *The Papers of Nathanael Greene,* asked me, as a consultant on the project, to read the eighteen letters that Nathanael Greene wrote Samuel Ward Jr. between 1770 and 1774. At first, Showman wondered if this flowery, effusive exchange might reveal more than an emotional link between Greene, still single in his late twenties, and a teenage boy. Eventually, we concluded that it did not.[31]

If, for a time at least, Washington's choice of language clouded his good judgment, the best evidence for it appears in his first September letter to Sally, which turned up a century ago, only to disappear again until 1958 when Harvard University acquired it. It reads in part: "You have drawn me my dear Madam, or rather have I drawn myself into an honest confession of a Simple Fact—misconstrue not my meaning—'tis obvious—doubt in [it?] not, nor expose it,—the World has no business to know the object of my Love,—declared in this manner to—you when I want to conceal it." Sally's response, which no longer exists, must have teased the young man with the remark that she found his meaning unclear. For he took up his pen to respond: "I cannot speak plainer without—but I'll say no more, and leave you to guess the rest." It is possible that in this missive he clumsily sought to conceal his intentions regarding Martha Custis, for his own reasons or possibly for reasons of Martha's. But Washington also expressed his frustrations with the military campaign, asserting that he could spend his time more agreeably playing Juba, with Sally taking the part of Marcia in Joseph Addison's *Cato,* a tragedy in which the two romantic characters never address openly their love for each other.

In the letters that historians have found so intriguing, both Washington and Sally make it clear that others knew of their correspondence, and both convey greetings from those members of their circle. Both of Washington's so-called amorous messages to Sally Fairfax—married for ten years—were written on the same days that he also addressed mail to her husband George William. And on each occasion the Washington letters (dashed off to the Fairfaxes while campaigning with General John Forbes against Fort Duquesne in Pennsylvania) traveled by the hand of the same dispatch rider. The Fairfaxes received their first letters from Washington at Belvoir and their second missives from him at the home of Sally's parents in Elizabeth City County. To put the matter more bluntly, Washington did not send secret epistles to Sally by some trusted messenger. The letters were carried to their destination over many miles to the Fairfaxes, both of whom were together on their arrival. The ones to George William concerned, among other things, Fairfax's careful, time-consuming efforts to oversee extensive renovations then being undertaken by Washington at Mount Vernon.[32] A probable link between Washington's correspondence with both Sally and George William was his forthcoming marriage to Martha Custis, an event that called for making Mount Vernon larger and more respectable in appearance.

Other surviving evidence about Washington's relationship with Sally Fairfax hardly arouses suspicion, especially in the context of the times. Both of them, several years earlier, at the beginning of Washington's military service on the frontier, had expressed a desire to maintain a correspondence. Sarah Fairfax Carlyle, daughter of Colonel William Fairfax, had also requested an epistolary connection with Washington. But few such exchanges appear to have taken place between Washington and either woman. Washington expressed disappointment about not hearing more often from the ladies of Belvoir, who undoubtedly learned a good deal about his activities from Colonel William Fairfax and his son George William, both of whom maintained regular contact with the young colonel and shared their information within the family. There is no evidence of any letters between Washington and his female friends, except for one perfunctory note from Washington to Sally, for more than two years prior to November 1757.[33]

One might think that any serious feelings of the heart might have deepened in the months between November 1757 and early March 1758, a time when Washington left his command and returned to Mount Vernon in an effort to recover from severe diarrhea and a nagging cough. During that same span Mrs. Fairfax's husband visited England on business. The three surviving letters from Washington to Sally during his convalescence contain none of the suggestive or ambiguous language that he employed in his messages of September 1758. All are brief and formal. His first letter, dated November 17, 1757, requested Sally's assistance in procuring and preparing certain medicinal food and drink. He assumed that she had known little if anything about his doings or health for some months. A Washington letter, composed February 13, 1758, implied that it had been some time since his neighbor had visited Mount Vernon. It would have been understandable had Sally traveled to see him in view of their long friendship and his ill health, but there is no evidence that she actually did so.[34]

If Washington ever committed romantic improprieties—or even considered such behavior—with Sally Fairfax, it would have been particularly painful to both families. Highly publicized reports some years earlier of an episode involving accusations of sexual wrongdoing probably had deepened the Washington-Fairfax family ties and made such behavior all the more offensive to both clans.

The matter involved Lawrence Washington's charge that their parish rector, Charles Green, had tried to seduce his wife-to-be Ann Fairfax just before their marriage. This sensational episode, which drew press attention even in Pennsylvania, found an out-of-court resolution and still remains murky in fact.[35] But another family sex scandal, this time involving yet another Fairfax woman, with George Washington as culprit, would have been unthinkable. Moreover, what would have been the risks for George in terms of his engagement to Martha Custis, a strong, capable woman, of very substantial resources, the wealthiest widow in the Old Dominion, had she been embarrassed by reports of loose talk about unfaithful conduct on the part of her suitor?

Yet the claim has often been made that Washington's loss of Sally, his greatest love, became the emotional crux of his life. Page Smith, a distinguished historian, asserts that in acknowledging that Mrs. Fairfax could not be his, Washington learned a painful lesson about suffering and adversity that would serve him well in the Revolution's trials: "A man who has given up what is for him the dearest thing in life has always thereafter a certain aloofness, a certain detachment; having survived the keenest anguish of all, he knows himself superior to most of the tribulations that the world can place before him. Having denied him what he most wished, the world had lost, to a substantial degree, the power to wound or dismay him further."[36] (Though Douglas Wilson joins those who accept the truth of the Lincoln–Ann Rutledge romance, he scarcely makes Lincoln's loss at her death a defining moment in his life but rather sees such a contention as "simplistic and hopelessly overdrawn.")[37]

How is the Sally Fairfax story relevant to Washington's future public life? In this case, unlike those of his mother and his wife, it is not, except in one respect. He undoubtedly learned a great deal about interacting with the fairer sex, including the social graces, from Sally Fairfax and the other women of Belvoir. If there is one constant refrain about Washington and women during his generalship and his presidency, it is, as I have observed, that he was ever comfortable, often charming, in their presence. Even Abigail Adams, capable as her husband John of biting assessments of luminaries of the day, admitted to being charmed beyond belief by the polite, affable Virginian.[38]

Belvoir, a majestic home, handsomely furnished, had meant a great deal to Washington. He remembered wonderful times with people he respected and admired. Those who subscribe to views similar to Page Smith's find support in a letter Washington wrote Sally near the end of his life, and some years after the death of George William Fairfax. Washington's lengthy missive, dated May 16, 1798, dealt with various subjects of mutual interest. (In all probability, Washington would not have written except that Sally's in-law Bryan Fairfax, preparing for a trip to England, agreed to deliver personally mail to his relatives there.) He recalled "those happy moments—the happiest in my life—which I have enjoyed in your company." But the statement is in the context of Washington's describing gay times at Belvoir, brought to mind by a recent visit to the ruins there. He passed the letter on to Martha to read and to add a message of her own. Washington had recorded a similar observation about spending the "happiest moments of my life" at Belvoir to Sally's husband George William thirteen years earlier.[39] Few letters were exchanged between the Washington and Fairfax families during the war and afterward. Both George and Martha's 1798 letters to Sally suggest that there had been no direct communication between them for over twenty-five years, although Washington and George William had corresponded infrequently until the latter's death in 1787. The Washingtons, at least, had retained their warmth and affection for the other couple. Evidently Sally never replied to her old Mount Vernon neighbors.

Washington's love affair was with the entire Fairfax family—Thomas, Lord Fairfax, who gave Washington his first employment as a surveyor; Colonel William Fairfax, whom Washington described as the key to his advancement in public life; George William and Sally, and the former's siblings, including Washington's sister-in-law Ann and Bryan Fairfax, a man who sat out the Revolution without losing Washington's warm friendship.

Because there is so much more evidence about Washington's relationship with his wife Martha than with the other two women studied in this essay, only a few observations about their forty-year marriage seem in order.

The traditional treatment of Martha Washington is of a rather pudgy, plain-looking woman of modest intellect, but certainly kind and pleasant, as well as loyal and dutiful, an ideal wife of a domestic type. Historians usually have set descriptions of her: "simple," "stolid," "practical," "bustling," "a good housekeeper." In hindsight, "good Martha's plump hand was the more suitable" than that of "pretty Sally" "for the office of helping" Washington "to fame during life and to immortality after death."[40]

Assuredly her virtues extended far beyond some of these, most of which fall into the "Plain Jane" category. First, John Custis IV, father of Daniel Parke Custis, Martha's first husband, considered her to be "beautifull & sweet temper'd," possessed of the highest "Character." A hard man to please when it came to a bride for his son, he kept Daniel Parke a bachelor until age thirty-seven, when his son married the best "Lady in Virginia."[41] Her portrait, painted by John Wollaston about a year before her engagement to Washington, reveals a remarkably pretty face and an appearance consistent with the eighteen-century ideal of femininity: "buxom, yet small and delicate," with "sensuality coy and indirect."[42] According to the British architect Benjamin H. Latrobe, Martha, nearly forty years later, "retains strong remains of physical beauty."[43]

Second, she displayed an independence of mind that has not been appreciated. Her years as a young widow and without Washington at Mount Vernon during the Revolutionary War led her to see the benefits of self-reliance. She advised her niece Fanny Bassett Washington, recently widowed, to learn to manage her own affairs. Fanny should be "as independent as your circumstances will admit." "Dependance is I think a wrached state and you will have enough if you mannage it right."[44]

Third, the Washingtons' few surviving letters show a tenderness and closeness consistent with outside observations about their deep affection for each other.[45] It should not be forgotten that she traveled great distances under primitive conditions to be with her husband in the Continental army's winter encampments for eight consecutive years during the Revolutionary War. As she said, she was truly a "perambulator" of the Revolution.[46] Washington, age forty-three when he first beseeched her to come and stay as many months as possible, had reached a stage in life that finds countless men growing restless and feeling a void in their intimate spousal relations; the French call it *le dèmon du midi,* the devil at high noon. Not so Washington, whose marriage never suffered even a hint of scandal, then or later, from any reputable source, although one encounters occasional reckless stories by British and loyalist propagandists in the Revolutionary War and by Jeffersonian Republican hacks during his presidency, all of which John C. Fitzpatrick refuted in *The George Washington Scandals.*[47]

All this, of course, does not tell us exactly what Washington thought of his bride-to-be in 1758. No doubt good marriages deepen with the years. If the couple were not passionately in love at the time, that fact tells us little. Because of Washington's military commitments, they had had precious few opportunities for togetherness that year. "It was an age that did not necessarily expect people to marry for love, but trusted that love would come and grow after marriage."[48] Washington, in after years, liked to say that the union of man and woman was the most important step one ever took.[49]

Finally, Washington found Martha to be an asset to his public life. She lent her name and support to the Ladies Association, initiated in 1780 by thirty-three-year-old Esther DeBerdt Reed of Philadelphia, wife of Joseph Reed, who presided over the Pennsylvania state government. The first female war measure in the Revolution, it sought to organize chapters in each of the thirteen states to raise money for enlisted men in Washington's army. All sums collected were to go to Mrs. Washington prior to distribution. Linda Kerber speculates that Martha Washington played a substantial role in trying to make the undertaking a national enterprise. Certainly she sent a copy of the Philadelphia plan directly to Martha Wayles Jefferson, the wife of Virginia's governor. She, like other females involved in Philadelphia, hoped that each chief executive's spouse would head the fund-raising drive in her state. Martha Washington also recommended to Mrs. Jefferson that she enlist the cooperation of an influential woman in Williamsburg, Sarah Tate Madison, wife of the president of the College of William and Mary. No doubt Mrs. Washington's name lent visibility and significance to the effort. Even so, the Ladies Association achieved only partial success, partly owing to a shortage of currency in the country. Virginia, perhaps because of its link to the Washington name, stood out as one of the few states to raise substantial sums for the soldiers.[50]

Washington, appreciative of his wife's tact and social skills, likely employed her talents in various ways. On one occasion at Valley Forge, he turned to Martha for assistance in dealing with a group of Quaker women from Philadelphia, distraught over the exile of their husbands from home for refusing to sign a loyalty oath to the Pennsylvania Revolutionary government. He asked Martha to entertain them before he met with them, and then, after he expressed sympathy for their concerns (he could do little in a matter for state authorities), he had Martha assuage their feelings as best she could in her private living quarters. Mrs. Elizabeth Drinker, who described Martha as "a sociable pretty kind of woman," and the rest of her party traveled on to Lancaster, carrying a pass from the general, to plead their case to the Supreme Executive Council.[51]

Martha Washington's significant public role as the president's wife has rarely been fully recognized. To critics of the Washington administration's style and legislative endeavors, who depicted them as British and monarchical in tone and content, Martha Washington's "republican court" served as an antidote. On Friday evenings her drawing room filled with congressmen and other officials of the federal government and their spouses from throughout the nation. Martha, dressing modestly, offered her guests lemonade and tea, not wine, hardly reminiscent of London or Paris high society. Sharing the president's passion to expand the ties between the various regions of America, partly through these gatherings, she brokered sixteen marriages.

Though hardly one of the most intellectual women of her time, she nonetheless seems to have been conversant on the issues of the day. Often expressing an interest in education, she once read a book, still in manuscript, on the proper schooling for females and gave the author permission to cite her name as an advocate of better education for women.[52] She had the respect and friendship of such bright and well-versed women as Mercy Otis Warren, Elizabeth Willing Powel, Hannah Stockton Boudinot, Elizabeth Schuyler Hamilton, and Abigail Adams. If, to some people at least, the president seemed stiff and formal, his wife must have softened or moderated this side of her husband. Mrs. Adams, wife of the vice president, described her "great ease" and "modest and unassuming" behavior, "not a tincture of ha'ture about her."[53]

Why was Washington a sound man to lead a revolution? To be sure, some of the reasons involve his previous military and political experience. Besides these traditional answers to that question, I would stress that his relationship with three women, which certainly has needed clarification, indicates he was emotionally and psychologically stable. Never a part of a dysfunctional family, he gained social skills and other forms of sophistication from the Fairfax family at Belvoir. He had an addiction to the whole Fairfax family—and not just to Sally Fairfax, from whom he probably learned how to be comfortable in the presence of charming young women. He prized marriage and family life. He hardly fits the characterization of a modern revolutionary ascetic, of a man alienated from such things as society and family and often displaying unhealthy attitudes about women and sexuality.[54]

Notes

1. Winthrop D. Jordan, *White over Black: American Attitudes toward the Negro, 1550–1812* (Chapel Hill, N.C., 1968), 461–68; Jack McLaughlin, *Jefferson and Monticello: The Biography of a Builder* (New York, 1988); Kenneth Lockridge, *On the Sources of Patriarchal Rage* (New York, 1992), chap. 3; Joseph J. Ellis, *American Sphinx: The Character of Thomas Jefferson* (New York,, 1996), esp. 90–97; David S. Shields, *Civil Tongues and Polite Letters in British America* (Chapel Hill, N.C., 1997), 322–24, 326–28, and "George Washington: Publicity, Probity, and Power," ibid., 143–54.

2. A full examination of Washington and the distaff side would have to include, among other subjects, his relationship with his nieces, with his step-granddaughter Nelly Custis, and with his friend and correspondent Mrs. Eliza Powell of Philadelphia.

3. Some feminist writers who were influential in attacking stereotypical gender roles include Simone de Beauvoir, *The Second Sex,* Eng. trans. (New York, 1953); Betty

Friedan, *The Feminine Mystique* (New York, 1963); Kate Millett, *Sexual Politics* (New York, 1970); and Germane Greer, *The Female Eunuch* (New York, 1971).

4. For Weems's approach to Washington and for Washington mythology in general, see Mason L. Weems, *The Life of Washington,* ed. Marcus Cunliffe (Cambridge, Mass., 1962), esp. Cunliffe's introduction (ix–lxii); and Bernard Mayo, *Myths and Men* (Athens, Ga., 1959), chap. 3.

5. Douglas S. Freeman et al., *George Washington: A Biography,* 7 vols. (New York, 1948–57), 1:xix–xx, 193, 195, 198, 202, 2:17–18, 49, 107, 199, 246. Freeman, of course, was not the first historian to describe Mary Ball in unflattering terms. The 1920s, a decade of debunking great men, then and earlier, saw the beginning of such a trend, but it did not become the dominant view of Washington's mother before Freeman's work. See, for examples, William E. Woodward, *George Washington: The Image and the Man* (New York, 1926), 15, 85, 434–35; Rupert Hughes, *George Washington: The Savior of the States, 1777–1781* (New York, 1930), 44–45; Bernard Fay, *George Washington: Republican Aristocrat* (New York, 1931), 29; Michael De La Bedeyere, *George Washington* (Philadelphia, 1935), 40.

6. James Thomas Flexner, *George Washington,* 4 vols. (New York, 1965–72), 1:18–25.

7. Frederick Bernays Wiener, "Washington and His Mother," *American History Illustrated,* July/August 1991, 44, 47, 68–72; Howard C. Rice and Anne S. K. Brown, trans. and eds., *The American Campaigns of Rochambeau's Army, 1780, 1781, 1782, 1783,* 2 vols. (Princeton, N.J., 1972), 1:73; *Mount Vernon: Yesterday, Today, Tomorrow* 12 (Summer 1998): 18. A new, generally well-received novel, William Martin's *Citizen Washington* (New York, 1999), also limns an unflattering image of Mary Ball Washington. Young George's slave companion calls her "Ball-and-Chain."

8. *PGW: Col. Ser.* 1:268–69, 304–5, 336–38, 359–60, 4:430; *PGW: Conf. Ser.* 5:33–37. Washington's diaries show that he usually visited his mother when in the vicinity of Fredericksburg. *PGW: Diaries.*

9. Benjamin Harrison to Washington, Feb. 25, 1781, Washington to Benjamin Harrison, March 21, 1781, Washington to John Augustine Washington, Jan. 16, 1783, *GW: Writings* 21:341–42, 26:42–44. Although Washington said that his mother thus far had never complained directly to him of severe economic distress, she had written to his overseer, Lund Washington, with requests a number of times. John A. Ferling, *The First of Men: A Life of George Washington* (Knoxville, Tenn., 1988), 343–44. But several years later he did have trouble containing his exasperation with her over what seemed to be incessant requests for more financial assistance. Washington to Mary Ball Washington, Feb. 15, 1787, *PGW: Conf. Ser.* 5:33–37.

10. Mary Ball Washington to Lund Washington, Dec. 19, 1778, quoted in Flexner, *Washington* 2:337; Mary Ball Washington to Washington, March 13, 1782, Henry E. Huntington Library (transcription courtesy of Philander D. Chase and Beverly Kirsch of *The Papers of George Washington*); Washington to Charles Thomson, Jan. 22, 1784, Washington to the Citizens of Fredericksburg, Feb. 14, 1784, *PGW: Conf. Ser.* 1:71, 122–23.

11. *PGW: Conf. Ser.* 5:157, 158–59; *PGW: Diaries* 5:144. He had only recently "bid an

eternal farewell to a much loved Brother [John Augustine] who was the intimate companion of my youth and the most affectionate friend of my ripened age." *PGW: Conf. Ser.* 5:157.

12. *PGW: Conf. Ser.* 6:332–33, 334n; *PGW: Pres. Ser.* 1:368 and n, 404 and n.

13. Patricia Brady, ed., *George Washington's Beautiful Nelly: The Letters of Eleanor Parke Custis Lewis to Elizabeth Bordley Gibson, 1794–1851* (Columbia, S.C., 1991), 2.

14. William Fairfax to Lawrence Washington, Sept. 9–10, 1746, Robert Jackson to Lawrence Washington, Sept. 16, 1746, in Moncure Daniel Conway, *Barons of the Potomack and Rappahannock* (New York, 1892), 236–40.

15. Joseph Ball to Mary Ball Washington, May 19, 1747, quoted in Freeman, *Washington* 1:198–99.

16. Ibid., 42–45, 530–34.

17. Lucy Brown Beale, "Colonel George Eskridge," *Northern Neck Historical Magazine* 3 (1953): 233–36; *Genealogies of Virginia Families,* 2 vols. (Baltimore, 1981), 2:732–34.

18. The continued use of certain traditional given names within a family seems to be a clue to family closeness and cohesion, whereas family tensions could lead to dropping such names in subsequent generations. Martin H. Quitt, "Immigrant Origins of the Virginia Gentry: A Study of Cultural Transmission and Innovation," *William and Mary Quarterly,* 3d ser., 45 (1988): 629–55.

19. Washington to Mary Ball Washington, Feb. 15, 1787, *PGW: Conf. Ser.* 5:33–36; *PGW: Pres. Ser.* 1:368, 368. A recent, highly publicized contribution to the nature versus nurture literature, which places genetics and environmental influences outside the family above child-rearing techniques in importance, is Judith Rich Harris, *The Nurture Assumption: Why Children Turn Out the Way They Do: Parents Matter Less Than You Think and Peers Matter More* (New York, 1998).

20. Will of Mary Ball Washington, May 20, 1788, in Worthington Chauncey Ford, ed., *The Writings of George Washington,* 14 vols. (New York, 1889–93), 14:416–18; Washington to Betty Lewis, Sept. 13, 1789, *PGW: Pres. Ser.* 4:32–35. President Washington, residing in New York, the temporary capital, ordered that his household wear "mourning Cockades & Ribbon." City officials advised that men wear "black crape or ribbon on the arm or hat" and that women display "a black ribbon and necklace."

21. Wilson Miles Cary, *A Long Hidden Romance of Washington's Life* (New York, 1916); Kenton Kilmer and Donald Sweig, *The Fairfax Family in Fairfax County: A Brief History* (Fairfax, Va., 1975).

22. If twentieth-century historians have found Washington's marriage one of mutual convenience, his early biographers all but ignored it, sometimes giving the subject a few lines at best. John Marshall, *Life of George Washington,* 5 vols. (Philadelphia, 1804–7), 2:71; Jared Sparks, *The Writings of George Washington . . . with a Life of the Author,* 12 vols. (Boston, 1834–37), 1:105; Weems, *Life of Washington,* 53–54.

23. Freeman, as he did in regard to Washington's relationship with his mother, had a substantial impact on subsequent accounts of Washington's interest in Sally Fair-

fax. Freeman, *Washington* 2:335–39. Though the story was hardly original with Freeman, his reputation undoubtedly explains why his treatment became the standard one. The first serious account to document the story seems to have been in 1916. Cary, *A Long Hidden Romance*. Cary seems uncertain or ambivalent about Sally's reaction to Washington's feelings for her.

24. Thomas A. Lewis, *For King and Country: The Maturing of George Washington, 1748–1760* (New York, 1993), 25. The Washington and Sally romance is unquestioned in numerous sophisticated publications. See, for example, Wayne Barrett, "George and Betsy and Polly and Patsy and Sally . . . and Sally . . . and Sally," *Smithsonian* 4 (1973): 90–99; John F. Stegeman, "The Lady of Belvoir: This Matter of Sally Fairfax," *Virginia Cavalcade* 34 (1984): 4–11.

25. The term was coined by Nathaniel W. Stephenson, "The Romantics and George Washington," *American Historical Review* 38 (1933): 274–83. Three careful Washington scholars doubted the reputed love affair, although they tended to dismiss it without seriously endeavoring to disprove it. See John C. Fitzpatrick, *George Washington Himself: A Common Sense Biography* . . . (Indianapolis, 1933), 75–80, 110–14; Nathaniel W. Stephenson and Waldo H. Dunn, *George Washington*, 2 vols. (New York, 1940), 1:441–42. The editors of *The Papers of George Washington* also exercise caution in dealing with the relationship. *PGW: Col. Ser.* 6:13.

26. For an analysis of the documents dealing with the presale inventory and accounts of the sales from Belvoir, see William M. S. Rasmussen and Robert S. Tilton, *George Washington: The Man behind the Myths* (Charlottesville, Va., 1999), 25–28. King Laughlin, a member of the staff of the Mount Vernon Ladies' Association, informed me of the location of the two chests of drawers. One cannot be certain that these pieces always remained juxtaposed as described. An early nineteenth-century painting of the room showed the furniture as described here.

27. Washington to Sarah Cary Fairfax, Sept. 12, 25, 1758, *PGW: Col. Ser.* 6:10–13, 41.

28. Peter Gay, *Voltaire's Politics: The Poet as Realist* (Princeton, N.J., 1959), 148.

29. Claude-Anne Lopez and Eugenia W. Herbert, *The Private Franklin: The Man and His Family* (New York, 1975), 274–75, quotation on p. 274; Claude-Ann Lopez, *Mon Cher Papa: Franklin and the Ladies of Paris* (New Haven, 1966).

30. William Howard Adams, *The Paris Years of Thomas Jefferson* (New Haven, 1997), chap. 7.

31. Richard K. Showman et al., eds., *The Papers of Nathanael Greene*, 11 vols. to date (Chapel Hill, N.C., 1976–), 1:14–65.

32. George William Fairfax makes mention of the first letter he received from Washington, the one of September 12, 1758, in a reply of September 15, 1758. Washington's letter to George William of September 25, 1758, survives. See *PGW: Col. Ser.* 6:12, 19–20, 38–41. Sometimes overlooked is the fact that George William also knew of the letter that his wife wrote to Washington on September 1, 1758. In fact, George William asked his wife to write it. George William Fairfax to Washington, Sept. 1, 1758, ibid., 5:436. That is the now-missing Sally Fairfax letter that prompted Washington's fascinating missive of September 12, which has stirred so much historical controversy. George William Fairfax to Washington, Sept. 1, 1758, ibid., 436–37.

33. Washington to Sarah Cary Fairfax, April 23, 1756, ibid., 3:418–19.

34. Washington to Sarah Cary Fairfax, Nov. 15, 1757, Feb. 13, 1758, [March 4], 1758, ibid., 5:56–57, 93–94, 100.

35. Peter R. Henriques, "Major Lawrence Washington versus the Reverend Charles Green: A Case Study of the Squire and the Parson," *Virginia Magazine of History and Biography* 100 (1992): 233–64.

36. Page Smith, *A New Age Now Begins: A People's History of the American Revolution,* 2 vols. (New York, 1976), 1:549–51, quotation on p. 551.

37. Wilson, *Honor's Voice,* 114–27, quotation on p. 126.

38. L. H. Butterfield et al., eds., *The Book of Abigail and John: Selected Letters of the Adams Family, 1762–1784* (Cambridge, Mass., 1975), 100. Another woman whom Washington captivated and became her genuine friend, quite open with her on a variety of subjects, was Lady Henrietta Liston, wife of the British minister Robert Liston. The Listons were guests at Mount Vernon several times after Washington retired from the presidency. James C. Nicholls, "Lady Henrietta Liston's Journal of Washington's 'Resignation,' Retirement, and Death," *Pennsylvania Magazine of History and Biography* 95 (1971): 511–20.

39. *PGW: Ret. Ser.* 2:272–75; *PGW: Conf. Ser.* 2:387–88.

40. The final sentence is from Bedeyere, *Washington,* 57.

41. Jo Zuppan, ed., "Father to Son: Letters from John Custis IV to Daniel Parke Custis," *Virginia Magazine of History and Biography* 98 (1990): 86. These quotations are in letters to Daniel Parke Custis from two friends, who declared they were repeating his father's words about Martha Dandridge. Ibid. Flexner, *Washington* 1:230, departs from numerous other Washington biographers in calling Martha "an extremely pretty woman." This conclusion was shared by Freeman, *Washington* 2:285–86.

42. Lois W. Banner, *American Beauty* (New York, 1983), 46.

43. Edward C. Carter II, ed., *The Virginia Journals of Benjamin Henry Latrobe, 1795–1798,* 3 vols. (New Haven, 1977–80), 1:168.

44. Martha Washington to Fanny Bassett Washington, Sept. 15, 1794, in Joseph E. Fields, ed., *"Worthy Partner": The Papers of Martha Washington* (Westport, Conn., 1994), 274–75.

45. Both of Martha's messages to her husband are notes written on the bottom or back of letters written by other family members to Washington. His letters to her escaped her detection since they were stuffed in a small desk drawer apart from other family papers. No doubt for these reasons they escaped destruction when she destroyed her correspondence with her husband before her death in 1802. The two Washington letters to Martha begin with "My Dearest" and so does one of hers to him. Her second letter begins with "my Love." *PGW: Col. Ser.* 7:495; *PGW: Rev. War Ser.* 1:3, 27, 11:674.

46. Fields, *"Worthy Partner,"* 193, 314.

47. John C. Fitzpatrick, *The George Washington Scandals* (Alexandria, Va., 1929). Another president, the product of a revolution, had a less successful marriage than Washington, and there were rumors about his fidelity to his nuptial vows. Carol K.

Bleser, "The Marriage of Varina Howell and Jefferson Davis: 'I gave the best and all my life to a girdled tree,'" *Journal of Southern History* 66 (1999): 3–40.

48. Lopez and Herbert, *The Private Franklin,* 40.

49. "Do not . . . look for perfect felicity before you consent to wed," he advised Elizabeth ("Betsy") Custis, Martha's oldest granddaughter. "Love is a mighty pretty thing; but like all other delicious things, it is cloying; and when the first transports of the passion begins to subside . . . and yield, oftentimes too late, to more sober reflections, it serves to evince, that love is too dainty a food to live upon *alone,* and ought not be considered farther than as a necessary ingredient for that matrimonial happiness which results from a combination of causes." Washington to Elizabeth Parke Custis, Sept. 14, 1794, *GW: Writings 33:* 500–501. Washington informed a French friend that his views on marriage were quite different from those held by many Europeans on "matrimony & domestic felicity." Washington to Charles Armand-Tuffin, Aug. 10, 1786, *PGW: Conf. Ser.* 4:203–4. Christine S. Patrick has edited a collection of Washington letters on love and marriage on *The Papers of George Washington* project Web site www.virginia.edu/gwpapers.

50. Mary Beth Norton, *Liberty's Daughters: The Revolutionary Experience of American Women, 1750–1800* (Boston, 1980), 177–87; Linda K. Kerber, *Women of the Republic: Intellect and Ideology in Revolutionary America* (New York, 1980), 99–105. Martha Washington was in Virginia at the time most of the money arrived. For discussions between General Washington and the women leaders about how to reward the troops, see accounts in Norton and Kerber.

51. Kerber, *Women of the Republic,* 95–98; Elizabeth Forman Crane et al., eds., *The Diary of Elizabeth Drinker,* 3 vols. (Boston, 1991), 1:297. The Quaker men were released a short time later, although it is unclear what role the Philadelphia women played in that development.

52. Shields, *Civil Tongues and Polite Letters,* 322–24, 326–28, and "George Washington: Publicity, Probity, and Power," in *George Washington's South,* ed. Tamara Harvey and Greg O'Brien (Gainesville, Fla., 2004), chap. 6.

53. Stewart Mitchell, ed., *New Letters of Abigail Adams, 1788–1801* (Boston, 1947), 13.

54. Bruce Mazlish, *The Revolutionary Ascetic: Evolution of a Political Type* (New York, 1976). See also, among other relevant literature, Erik H. Erikson, *Dimensions of a New Identity* (New York, 1974).

War and National
Institutions

4 *War and State Formation in Revolutionary America*

I HAD THE PLEASURE of an invitation to participate in a symposium in honor of Professor Jack P. Greene for his many years of graduate teaching at Johns Hopkins University and for his significant contributions to scholarship as the author of almost countless books and articles that range over seventeenth- and eighteenth-century American history. I doubt if any historian in this field has directed the work of as many doctoral students as Greene. At the time of the symposium in Baltimore, October 21–23, 2000, Greene had supervised sixty-seven completed dissertations and had nineteen current doctoral advisees. I ranked among the few presenters who did not study under Greene, but I am certain that I have known him longer than any of the other people in attendance that weekend. Beginning in 1954, we went through graduate school together, first at the University of Nebraska and then at Duke University, where we completed our Ph.D.'s.

I welcomed the opportunity to speak on this occasion about "War and State Formation in America" because it is an important subject that had been passed over. It seemed that historians who wrote on social and political change during the Revolution ignored how the war itself contributed to and sometimes profoundly influenced the subjects they dealt with. My desire to address this relationship stems from the academic year 1998–99, when as a visiting professor I taught the first half of the general military history course at the United States Military Academy at West Point. I had to deal with the impact of early modern wars on the development of the national state in Europe. In doing so, I had fruitful conversations with my colleague Professor Clifford J. Rogers, who had recently edited a provocative book of essays on *The Military Revolution Debate*, which reveals the different ways that historians have viewed the significant changes in weaponry and warfare at the time that states such as England, France, Prussia, and Sweden were taking shape.

I contend that the process of forming the American nation is most properly studied as part of the larger early modern historical experience. I am glad to see several other historians making the same connection. For the slow growth of national feeling, even in the latter stages of the War of Independence, see Peter and Nicholas Onuf's *Federal Union, Modern World: The Law of Nations in an Age of Revolutions* and David Hendrickson's *Peace Pact: The Lost World of the American Founding.* Both books argue persuasively that nationalism did not exist before independence and in fact most Revolutionary leaders thought of America in the European definition of the word *federal:* thus, the relationship between the thirteen states should be examined as examples of a kind of internationalism or multilateralism. True enough, the war brought together a band of committed nationalists, but they did not prevail until 1787. In a stimulating new book, *A Revolution in Favor of Government: Origins of the U.S. Constitution and the Making of the American State,* Max M. Edling sees the framers as ambitious men but actually with limited goals. First and foremost, they sought the creation of a fiscal-military state for the United States, one not unlike those of early modern Europe, with authority to tax, borrow, and spend for national security. This essay first appeared in Peter S. Onuf and Eliga H. Gould, eds., *Empire and Nation* (Baltimore: Johns Hopkins University Press, 2004) and is reprinted with the publisher's permission.

WITHOUT THE War of Independence there would have been no American national state in the eighteenth century. This would have been true even if Britain had agreed to grant the American colonies their independence in 1775 or 1776. Without the burden of fighting for their independence from the world's dominant superpower, the American republics might have formed a loose league or confederacy—weaker than the Articles of Confederation—or several regional confederacies. They might instead have gone at each others' throats like the Greek city-states of antiquity. Or some or all of them might have been wooed back into the imperial fold.

As critical as the War of Independence was to the creation of the American nation-state, it led only slowly to the constitutional settlement of 1787 in Philadelphia. And yet historians have all but totally neglected the connection between war and state formation in the creation of the United States. We can best examine war and state formation in America in a comparative context. The origins of the national state have received considerable attention from scholars who have studied the subject elsewhere, particularly in early modern Europe. Most scholars agree that nations are "constructed" or "invented" in response to war or some other crisis or catastrophe in order to impose a sturdy institutional framework over people who may be quite diverse in language, religion, and ethnicity. To be sure, some measure of social homogeneity may speed the political process, but it is not always critical or paramount. Once the political framework is in place, a "people" may overcome—or ignore—some of their cultural differences and create new symbols of their nationhood. The nation as a political fact comes first, reflecting the aspirations of "nationalists" and promoting the emergence of a widely shared national identity.[1]

The "Military Revolution" in early modern Europe provided the crucial impetus for state formation. Recent work by Michael Roberts on Sweden and Geoffrey Parker on Spain shows that the kingdoms or states that antedated this revolution became "modern" to the extent that war increased enormously centralizing tendencies. Numerous wars stemming from dynastic, geographic, and religious factors produced heavy taxes, large armies, technological advances in weapons, and bureaucratic agencies to manage military undertakings. The forms of centralization and bureaucratization remained with the advent of peace.[2] Charles Tilly has employed the findings of the new military history in his studies of state formation, emphasizing the dramatic expansion of these war powers in governments' long-term fiscal and administrative activities.[3] Parker summarizes the dominant historiographical view: "Military activity and state formation have always been inextricably linked, and periods of rapid military change have usually coincided with major political innovations."[4]

Are states that emerge in wars—or that are radically transformed by conflicts—necessarily inhospitable to representative institutions and the rule of law, turning instead to military-bureaucratic absolutism? The histories of England and its American colonies suggest that different outcomes are possible. Other factors may be crucial as well, including demands on internal resources, the ability to secure financial support abroad, and success in establishing military alliances. Britain's liberal institutions survived more than a century of wars with more populous France because it possessed vast commercial wealth and was able to exploit valuable Continental alliances. After 1660 Britain never faced the threat of a vast standing army because the navy provided a first line of defense. In contrast, France and Brandenburg-Prussia responded to enormous wartime pressures by harnessing the domestic sector and then leaving in place afterward strongly centralized governments.[5]

State formation in America began well before independence. The thirteen colonial polities became more vigorous and self-reliant during a period of institution building and increasing internal unity in metropolitan society. As Linda Colley demonstrates, the years following the 1707 Act of Union with Scotland saw the expansion of British national feeling among the peoples of England, Wales, and Scotland. At the same time, the island kingdom ended its lengthy period of comparative international isolation during which England had been a minor military power. Its post-1688 imperial wars were fueled by a dynamic and flexible economy that could support the financial and political structures of a fiscal-military state that challenged and eventually dominated European rivals.[6]

Fortunately for the political liberties of Britons on the imperial peripheries, metropolitan authorities were always reluctant to pay for military and civil establishments across the Atlantic. As a result, provincial governments enjoyed an extraordinary degree of internal autonomy. The colonial legislatures were thus able to sink intractable roots. It would have been imprudent to challenge colonial institutional development as long as Britain had its hands full with France and its allies and needed the wartime assistance of its distant overseas dependencies.

Although the lower houses increased their powers dramatically during the imperial wars, those were not the only occasions when the provincial bodies ignored the governors' constituted military authority, to say nothing of their other jurisdiction. The lower houses found chief executives particularly vulnerable because of pressures from England to raise men and money promptly for frontier defense and for expeditions against the French. Provincial lawmakers became imperial policymakers by indicating how monies were to be spent, the number of soldiers to be raised, the period of months they would serve, and where they would be deployed. Sometimes provincial legislators even insisted on their right to appoint commanders of expeditionary forces and to select oversight committees from their own membership. Consequently, colonial legislatures seized greater authority over military affairs than the House of Commons ever acquired in Britain.[7]

An institutional transformation had taken place in provincial political life. Massachusetts brought what William Pencak describes as a structural expansion not unlike the state-building process in Europe.[8] The assemblies, writes Jack P. Greene, emerged from the pre-1763 era "with an increased awareness of their own importance and a growing consciousness of the implication of their activities."[9]

This state formation, within an imperial framework, was not replicated elsewhere in the eighteenth century. Some peripheral lands and territories had endeavored to preserve ancient privileges by negotiations, even with the monarchs of France and Spain. Yet these units, however much they might retain from a Louis XIV or Phillip II, faced pressure from consolidating ministers like Richelieu in France and Olivares in Spain. Britain's American polities had not so much bargained to retain old rights, long practiced as part of their English heritage, as they had hammered out new ones, based on behaviors and precedents following 1688.[10]

When imperial reform efforts threatened "traditional" rights and more recently won liberties after 1763, provincial legislators exercised their authority by still other creative methods. They had rarely needed appeals to public opinion, but now they encouraged petitions, memorials, pamphlets, broadsides, patriotic meetings, and associations such as "Sons of Liberty."[11] Beginning with the Stamp Act crisis, royal governors retaliated by dissolving legislatures or by failing to call them into session. They could also attach suspending clauses to colonial laws, employing the crown's relatively infrequently used right of legislative review. But these executives could not do without the assembles indefinitely—and they paid a steep price when they did so.[12]

Gradually, from the Stamp Act crisis onward, the assemblies and a stream of American essayists moved from denying Parliament any authority to interfere in the internal affairs of the provinces to the position that any laws emanating from the metropolis were acceptable only if they benefited the whole empire. Radicals staked out an even more advanced position, insisting that trade legislation and other external statutes required the explicit consent of individual assemblies or of an intercolonial congress. Even before the outbreak of hostilities in 1775, influential writers such as Thomas Jefferson, James Iredell, and James Wilson called for a commonwealth conception of the empire—a "cordial union of many distant people . . . warm in their affection and zealous in their attachment to each other, under the influence of one common sovereign," as Iredell phrased it.[13] It was a concept Britain would finally accept in the twentieth century.[14]

Independence could have come only when it did because so many assemblies had separated themselves from imperial officials. Meeting independently, lower houses announced new elections and renamed themselves provincial congresses or conventions. Militia officers resigned their royal commissions in order to free themselves from interference from the governor (as the assemblies themselves had done) and reconstituted local forces under authority of provincial congresses and conventions. Only highly sophisticated political bodies could have effected this extraordinary transformation.[15] The legislators were aided, declares John Phillip Reid, by the primacy of custom and local law, based on community support, in governing behavior and protecting individual rights. In the 1760s imperial law grew weaker. Provincial law at legislative and judicial levels maintained its popularity and vigor. British authority proved ineffectual in suppressing the resistance. Governors could not declare martial law without the approval of their councils, and magistrates had to issue written approval for redcoats to be sent against civilians. Virtually every colony functioned as an independent state, in control of its political and military establishment, months before July 1776.[16]

The subsequent story of war and state formation for the American nation-state was complicated by the distribution of authority in an evolving federal system. The post-1763 imperial crisis began with the colonies in possession of political and military structures that could be employed creatively. The situation of the colony-states resembled that of the kingdoms of Europe before the onset of wars initiated the process of state formation. But there was also a highly significant difference: the absence of any kind of intercolonial structure or institution to build on; there was nothing like the Holy Roman Empire, nor even a diet or an ancient council of notables to give Americans focus or direction. British generals and governors, foreign visitors, and prominent colonials all commented on jealousies and rivalries between the provinces. The assemblies lacked a precedent for pulling together on common issues, a serious liability during the imperial wars. Furthermore, the success of the assemblies in gaining the upper hand within their own borders made them less than enthusiastic about sharing their newly won supremacy with an American congress or confederacy.

Only the threats to the assemblies themselves and to the liberty of Anglo-Americans in general can explain their bold steps beginning in 1774. It took the Coercive Acts to bring about the First Continental Congress. It took Britain's military action against Massachusetts to transform the Second Continental Congress into a quasi-central government that eventually would declare American independence. No organic growth of an American nation lay behind these actions, nor can American nationalism provide the explanation.[17] Concerns for self-preservation can propel people vast distances.

The initial thrust for an intercolonial congress at Philadelphia was, to most of its principal proponents, somewhat conservative: they hoped to head off radicals agitating for instant retaliatory measures, particularly a suspension of trade with Britain. Although its delegates had been given considerable latitude by their respective colonies, the Continental Congress that met in 1774 was never looked upon as a permanent body.[18] Even so, this First Congress displayed a great deal of unanimity and a toughening stance as the crisis escalated. Delegates denounced Parliament; embraced Massachusetts's Suffolk Resolves, with their threat of military action against Britain; and adopted the Continental Association, thus committing their colonies to an ambitious scheme of economic coercion that would be enforced at the grassroots level. The association was a first, limited step toward American nationhood, for it came to be interpreted as an oath of allegiance to Congress and to extralegal, revolutionary authorities in the colonies.[19]

Congress still hoped for accommodation with Britain, but it continued to have no interest in a constitutional reorganization of the empire that might make it a permanent institution. Its first objective remained gaining repeal of the Coercive Acts and securing redress for other misguided British initiatives since 1763, as set forth in its Declaration of Rights and Grievances.[20] Although delegates called for another congress the following year if Britain failed to address their concerns, they had no plans for future action.

Political moderates such as John Dickinson of Pennsylvania did not see the elections for the Second Continental Congress as dangerously provocative. As the moderate New York City leadership explained, the Second Congress, like its predecessor, sought to keep the lid on anti-British zealots—to focus on negotiating with the mother country and on forestalling violence, not on creating organizations or institutions that could bring about some future union within or without the empire.[21] Virtually all members opposed separation and still sought an imperial settlement.

That mind-set failed to last. When Congress met in May 1775, fighting had erupted at Lexington and Concord, followed in June by the Battle of Bunker Hill. At the urging of Massachusetts, Congress adopted the New England army besieging Boston and selected one of its own members as its commander, the highly visible Virginian George Washington, whose appointment would help pull the southern provinces into the war effort. At the same time, Congress dispatched its Olive Branch Petition to London, still hoping for reconciliation. The delegates displayed "a Strange Oscilation between Love and Hatred, between War and Peace."[22] Dickinson angrily accused John Adams of opposing a negotiated settlement within the English-speaking family. As late as January 1776, James Wilson sought a formal statement from Congress against independence. Yet these reluctant revolutionaries supported Congress's military responses, and they in turn received the support of their more radical colleagues in opposing Samuel Adams and Benjamin Franklin's proposal for some kind of confederation. The appearance of *Common Sense* that January, London's rejection of continued American appeals, and new British hostilities, such as the Prohibitory Act, naval raids on the American coast, employment of mercenaries, and reports of a massive invasionary force soon to be bound for America, turned the tide in favor of independence. A radical step, with implications for a future American union, the break nonetheless came reluctantly, only after congressional head counters anticipated a unanimous vote.[23]

The prestige of the Second Continental Congress crested in 1776, only to erode over the next several years. Before severing ties with Britain, Congress had conducted a war for fifteen months and encouraged the colony-states to write new constitutions. The Declaration of Independence came at a critical juncture. Congress needed a legal base for seeking alliances abroad and running a war effort, especially for controlling an army, for standing armies always posed a threat to liberty.

Despite compelling incentives, the Revolutionary War did not lead to the immediate formation of an American nation-state. Why was it such a vexed undertaking, when the southern revolutionaries of 1860–61 constructed a Confederate nation-state quickly and with a minimum of controversy? Southerners, with a little fine-tuning, kept the predominant features of the federal Constitution. Their concern had not been with that instrument but rather with how it had been interpreted and with what President Abraham Lincoln's Republican Party would do with it. Southerners also had been able to draft their charter before the outbreak of the Civil War at Fort Sumter.[24] The American Congress, on the other hand, had to write and obtain ratification of a constitution in the midst of war. As Richard Henry Lee noted, "the immensity of [that] business" often deflected attention away from their political engineering for weeks on end.[25] Like the Confederates, the revolutionaries of 1776 claimed that they had revered the old institutional framework—in their case, the British constitution. But Congress could not fall back on the British model, for it embraced monarchy and a legislative apparatus based on hereditary social distinctions.

Just as Congress had proceeded at a relatively moderate pace between 1774 and 1776, conscious of the need for consensus, congressmen continued to move cautiously when they confronted the challenge of establishing a constitutional union.[26] Because of the ministry's general policy of "salutary neglect," the British Empire before Parliament's disastrous endeavors to transform it after 1763 had been loosely structured and lightly governed. It is therefore hardly surprising that Congress should form a loosely structured confederacy that had more in common with the pre-1763 empire than with the version of federalism that triumphed with ratification of the federal Constitution. Even so, the Articles of Confederation served as a bridge between the old and the new federalism; the

Union they constituted bore little resemblance to past and present versions of confederated systems in Europe—the Greek city-states, the Swiss Confederation, or the United Provinces of Holland.[27]

At first glance, it seems amazing that Congress, now eager for a confederation with constitutional underpinnings, would take nearly sixteen months to complete its task. (Ten years later the Constitutional Convention forged an unprecedented and much more muscular federalism in seventeen weeks.) The process of state ratification then dragged out from the fall of 1777 to the spring of 1781. In the meantime, Congress—though still an extralegal body—managed the war and concluded the French alliance. In the short run, a patriotic outpouring, a *rage militaire,* muffled provincial jealousies. Patriotic fervor combined with pressing military concerns—particularly the well-founded report in the spring of 1776 of a major British offensive against New York City and the middle colonies—to enable congressmen to obtain "powers in an ad hoc fashion" as they "responded to contingencies."[28]

History showed that military despotism loomed as the foremost danger to liberty during revolutions and the formation of new states. But so long as Washington remained alive and served as commander in chief of the Continental army, that possibility remained remote. Already, after only a year in his post, Washington's relations with Congress had set precedents for deference and respect for civil control that would be hard for any successor to overturn. He also had increased Congress's standing and prestige with the states by clarifying the chain of authority. All calls for assistance from him must be routed through Congress.[29]

The Confederation that Congress drafted in 1776–77 invested the government of the Union with specific responsibilities that would reappear in the federal Constitution: making war and peace, raising an army and navy, concluding treaties, appointing ministers, conducting Indian relations, organizing a postal service, issuing currency, and borrowing money. All of these powers were related more or less directly to defense, security, and the international order, the preeminent concerns of early modern national states everywhere.

The jealousies and rivalries of the Seven Years' War that had led to the failure of Franklin's Plan of Union alerted delegates to the obstacles ahead. Sensitive subjects struck closest to home: how to raise monies without giving Congress the taxing power, how to determine representation in Congress, and how to control the western lands. In their deliberations delegates deferred to their state legislatures; during the ratification process the legislatures raised objections and demanded changes. Legislative "egotisms" thus blocked progress. If Parliament in the 1760s and 1770s was reluctant to share powers with colonial assemblies that it had won from the crown in the seventeenth century, the American state legislatures after 1776 were similarly loath to concede much of their jurisdiction to Congress. They had existed too long as corporate entities to contemplate absorption in a wholly new continental state during the Revolution.[30] State-level politicians were willing enough to go along with ad hoc acts of Congress—for instance, when it bestowed temporary dictatorial authority on Washington at several critical junctures—so long as these emergency measures were understood not to entail any formal recognition of Congress's expanded powers. Throughout the war the absence of historical or theoretical debate about America's first national constitution is striking, especially compared to the lively exchange of ideas about government that characterized both the controversy with Britain prior to independence and the subsequent movement to draft and ratify a new federal Constitution. The possibility of establishing an "extended republic," a crucial theme of political debate in the late 1780s, was also conspicuously missing during the war years.[31]

The question of sovereignty failed to receive careful attention in debates over the Articles, despite its centrality in the imperial crisis and in later controversy over the distribution of authority in the federal republic. Congressman Thomas Burke of North Carolina proposed what became the second of the Articles of Confederation, that "each state retains its sovereignty, freedom, and independence," in all areas except those "expressly delegated to the United States, in Congress assembled." But Burke's measure elicited little debate and received a nearly unanimous vote.[32] Historians who maintain that sovereignty was truly divisible in the first national constitution would have had trouble convincing George Washington and other leaders who thought in increasingly continental terms as the war wore on. Sovereignty can only be divided if each political component can effectively perform its assigned functions. This was possible in the old empire before 1763 because the metropolitan government had the means to manage the external affairs of the empire: war and peace, foreign affairs, and trade and commerce. Samuel Johnston, North Carolina's most powerful political figure of the era, reminded his states' rights friend Burke that Americans should face the fact that until they won the war and enjoyed opportunity for deeper reflection, all "Leagues, Confederations, and Constitutions are . . . temporary expedients."[33] Gouverneur Morris, a New York delegate, complained that Congress was "inadequate to the Purposes of Execution" for performing the functions assigned it under the Articles.[34]

Morris hit the nail on the head. Because Congress possessed no mechanism for enforcing treaty terms on the states, the effectiveness of agreements with foreign powers always remained doubtful. Because Congress lacked the taxing power and the states contributed such a small percentage of their annual requisition monies, congressional indebtedness soared, the principal victims being officers and men of the Continental army.

Because the states insisted that their Continental soldiers be formed into state regiments and demanded some form of equitable representation among the general officers, Congress's authority to raise an army suffered. Congress also floundered concerning the militia. Although the Articles stipulated that the states "shall always keep up a well regulated and disciplined militia" "and constantly have ready for use" all necessary "arms, ammunition, and camp equipage," Congress had no way of enforcing these provisions or of calling out the state militias. In numerous other instances the states subverted congressional jurisdiction as prescribed in the Articles of Confederation: creating state navies, sending agents abroad, and failing at times to provide Congress with a quorum so that it could conduct business.

Tensions between the states and federal authorities persisted throughout the Revolutionary conflict. They recalled friction between the colonists and British officials in the Seven Years' War over such issues as raising money, contributing men for the regular army, and employing militia to cooperate with professional troops. British generals had complained of royal governors who were intimidated by their assemblies. Revolutionary generals fumed about state legislatures that prevented their own state governors from moving decisively. Governor Thomas Jefferson chafed at executive impotence in Virginia. So did James Madison, member of Virginia's Council of State, which had a veto over major gubernatorial decisions.[35] Generals Robert Howe and Benjamin Lincoln, each at one time head of the Southern Department, faced deliberate obstructions from civilian leaders in Georgia and South Carolina.[36] The Confederation seemed to hit rock bottom in the final year of the conflict. Thanks to Washington, the Newburgh Conspiracy aborted when the commander in chief put his reputation on the line with disgruntled officers over back pay and other emoluments. Later in the year angry Continental enlisted men surrounded Congress in the Pennsylvania State House. Pennsylvania officials refused to turn out their militia to protect the federal legislators, a painful reminder that the Confederation government had no jurisdiction over the capital of the United States, a point not forgotten later when the framers provided for a national capital on soil belonging to the nation, not a state. Adding insult to injury, the unhappy Continentals then expressed more confidence in Pennsylvania than in the United States when they asked the state to settle their accounts. Even the treaty of peace, which should have brought rejoicing in Congress, prompted near panic because the lawmakers lacked a quorum to ratify it. The British, as tired of war as the Americans, ignored the technicality. The two sides exchanged ratifications in Paris early in 1784.[37]

Rarely have victors in a major war been so troubled and unclear about their future as were the American Revolutionaries. John Dickinson feared that Americans might become the victims of their own success. What would replace the old British imperial structure, which, for all its inadequacies, had held the colonies together? Like Gouverneur Morris, many congressmen had been pessimistic about the viability of the Articles of Confederation well before that document finally received unanimous state approval. Charles Thomson, who knew Congress better than anybody, serving as its secretary throughout its fifteen-year existence, doubted that the Union would long survive the war's end. Between 1780 and 1783 Washington, Colonel Alexander Hamilton, and General Henry Knox all advocated the calling of a convention to examine ways to make Congress more effective and to tighten the Union. Washington was recognized as the most persistent and eloquent critic of the American political system, and he never let up until the federal Constitution achieved implementation nearly a decade later.[38] Such sentiments became more evident in Congress during the last three years of the war, though to speak of a "nationalist ascendancy" overstates the numbers and cohesiveness of reform-minded critics. Hamilton, who switched from the army to a seat in the legislative councils, was one of the most vocal nationalists, whose ranks also included James Madison, Robert Morris and James Wilson of Pennsylvania, ex-general John Sullivan of New Hampshire, Samuel Johnston of North Carolina, and John Mathews of South Carolina.[39] At the state level too, some legislators advocated more vigorous support of the national war effort and were willing to interpret congressional power under the Articles more broadly in the postwar years than many of their fellow representatives. Jackson Turner Main shows that these "cosmopolitan" activists generally lived close to coastal areas or on other waterways impacted by commerce. By contrast, "localists" who were preoccupied with their state's internal concerns and suspicious of federal encroachments were concentrated in the interior and backcountry of their states and were more likely to have been in the militia than in the Continental army.[40]

As advocates of greater continental cohesion pondered the future, they could acknowledge some achievements beyond independence itself over the past eight and a half years. If their national institutions were disappointingly weak, they had not seen the lengthy struggle tear apart the fabric of society, or strain American resources to the breaking point, or lead to extreme forms of centralization. The War of Independence did not bring a European-style absolutist state. Substantial amounts of foreign aid in terms of military stores, cash contributions, and loans (from Holland as well as France) and the French military alliance helped keep either extreme possibility, absolutism or anarchy, from occurring.

Postwar America looked to be moving in the opposite direction from even the modest form of centralization authorized by the Articles of Confederation. The several executive departments established by the Confederation Congress seemed to be eroding. The office of secretary at war, filled by General Benjamin Lincoln during 1781–83, had no occupant from 1783 to 1785. After appointment as superintendent of finance in 1781, the energetic and enterprising Robert Morris devised schemes to pay some of the nation's bills, but he resigned in frustration in 1784 over his failure to secure permanent federal revenues; Congress thereafter resumed control of the Confederation's business affairs. The Department of Marine never became operative because Congress failed to form a postwar navy. Although the final administrative unit voted by Congress, the Department of Foreign Affairs, kept its doors open, its successive secretaries, Robert R. Livingston and John Jay, were thwarted by Congress's impotence in their efforts to negotiate with foreign powers. America had only two permanent ministers in foreign posts, London and Paris, by 1784. In short, the dangerous signs of disintegration in 1783 became even more conspicuous. By that year the negative results were in on Congress's impost of 1781, when the states failed to provide the unanimous vote for ratification needed to give the Confederation an independent source of revenue from duties on incoming foreign products. The impost of 1783, a second attempt, also foundered, even though its time limit of twenty-five years and its provision that duties be collected by state appointees should have made it more palatable to states' rights advocates. Such an income would have made at least a dent in the foreign and domestic debt of the Revolution and would have indirectly provided some resources for a modest peacetime military establishment, which never reached as many as a thousand men after 1783, although the minuscule army had responsibility for controlling the vast American West. Crippled finances also explain why Secretary of Foreign Affairs Jay refused to support the recommendation of Jefferson, then minister to France, that America join an alliance of European nations to protect their Mediterranean trade from the Barbary pirates. To do so, Jay said bluntly, would have required a navy.[41]

Of the variety of other frustrations that plagued the Confederation in the immediate postwar years, two are particularly relevant here, namely, the government's inability to provide either for national security or for internal order. No polity can survive without resolving these fundamental security dilemmas. Wherever sovereignty is supposed to reside, whether with the king-in-Parliament or with the people collectively, who may in turn delegate different functions to governments at the center and the peripheries of the federal republic, it is a meaningless fiction if unwanted foreign troops occupy a nation's soil. America confronted that painful reality when, after the treaty of peace in 1783, Britain retained its military posts at Detroit, Niagara, Michilimackinac, and elsewhere in the Northwest. The British justified their continued presence as retaliation for Congress's failure to implement peace treaty provisions concerning the loyalists, although the desire to retain control over the Indians and the fur trade in the region was clearly an important consideration. American diplomats in Paris, mindful of Congress's absence of muscle over the states, had felt constrained to promise in the peace treaty merely to "earnestly recommend" to the states that the provisions for restitution of loyalist property be followed. Loyalist issues were, with the exception of debates over paper money and other debtor matters, the most hot-button items in domestic politics between 1783 and 1787.[42]

Internal discord also exposed the Confederation's grave inadequacies. When Shays's Rebellion erupted in Massachusetts in 1786, Congress feared that similar debtor-creditor tensions, which existed in every state, might bring further disorder and violence. Congress enacted modest steps to enlarge its tiny army, but even if they had been promptly carried out, most delegates doubted that the federal lawmakers had the authority to use force to restore internal order in the states. When some congressmen argued that the nearness of the federal arsenal at Springfield to the center of rebel strength justified intervention, Secretary at War Knox refused to act in a matter he considered one for "the internal government" of Massachusetts.[43]

The Confederation appeared to be unraveling within even as it faced danger abroad. Southern spokesmen denounced Don Diego de Gardoqui and Secretary for Foreign Affairs Jay because of their tentative agreement in 1786—never approved by Congress—on the terms of a Spanish-American trade treaty, which would have included relinquishing America's claim to the free navigation of the Mississippi River to the Gulf of Mexico. Some southerners and westerners talked of secession, but disunionist impulses lessened north of the Ohio River with Congress's adoption of the Northwest Ordinance in 1787, providing automatic statehood for transmontane territories once an area's population reached 60,000. Secessionist grumbling abounded in the Maine District of Massachusetts. Similar breakaway sounds came from Nantucket. Islanders spoke of cutting their own deal with Britain, which imposed a heavy duty on their whale oil and bone.[44]

Given this decline in the vitality of the Union, how do we account for the fact that four years after the Revolutionary War, Americans produced the federal Constitution? If the war had been the glue that brought the colony-states together, however belatedly, into a union that finally became legitimized in 1781, with the ratification of the Articles, what was the cement in 1787? We have no single answer to a conundrum that has long divided and perplexed historians. In 1787 constitutional reformers could call on more than a decade of experience at the state and federal levels; in 1776, by contrast, Revolutionaries had no such frame of reference—no point of departure. For all their defects, state and federal charters served as springboards for discussion and analysis. Willi P. Adams argues that the constitutions adopted in Massachusetts in 1780 and New Hampshire in 1784 provided particularly valuable models for the framers of 1787. Peter Onuf shows that the states, although failing to agree on amendments to the Articles, still needed the Union, for Congress remained a forum for airing their grievances against one another and a potential locus for resolving boundary and other interstate controversies. To Washington and other centralists, the states were culprits. Yet individually in the post-1783 years various states, including Virginia, North Carolina, and New Jersey, came up with schemes for strengthening the "federal head."[45] But leadership to coordinate and implement reform proposals always seemed lacking.

What made the Constitutional Convention possible was a sense that the federal system required a shot of adrenaline. Future Antifederalists who were knowledgeable about the affairs of the Union conceded that point. But they would have denied a crisis existed—not a crisis, at any rate, that was the equivalent of war, the phenomenon that drove nation-state formation from the sixteenth century onward in Europe.[46]

But the crisis analogy to European state formation applies to those public figures who spearheaded the campaign to revise the federal structure in 1786 and 1787. These centralizers occupied major positions in the Revolution outside their own states. They were profoundly distressed by conditions in the country and by the failure in the late summer of 1786 of the Annapolis Convention, with a meager agenda confined to commercial affairs. Events that year aroused them

to call for a more broadly conceived convention to meet at Philadelphia the following May. These activists, by virtue of service as army officers, congressman,
diplomats, and Confederation officials, had learned to view America continen-
tally. They included not only such well-known figures as Washington, Madison,
Hamilton, Jay, Knox, Wilson, Robert Morris, Gouverneur Morris, and James
Duane but almost every general in the Continental army and the great majority
of former members of the Continental Congress. (By more than a three-to-one
ratio, the signers of the Declaration of Independence and the Articles of Confederation backed the new political system.)[47] To that category must be added
Jackson Turner Main's "cosmopolitan" state legislators: 92 percent of their
leaders supported the adoption of the federal Constitution.[48]

Reform was in the air. But Washington cautioned that did not mean that the
reformers would coalesce on a proper revision of the government or that the
public would agree to a fresh approach to federal government.[49] Though constitutional reform was the work of many hands, Washington emerged as the crucial
figure. He had consistently criticized the Confederation as inadequate, and almost everyone who shared those views corresponded with him. Washington
had expressed a vision of America, strong and united, possessed of a national
character, in his Circular to the States before resigning his commission as commander in chief of the Continental army. Disseminated in newspapers at the
time, it now reappeared in gazettes everywhere.[50]

If by deeds and words and by being the most meaningful symbol of unity and
nationhood, Washington had laid the groundwork for reform, James Madison
became its principal strategist, both in generating momentum in the fall of 1786
and in the spring of 1787 for the convention and later in defense of the Virginia
Plan on the floor of the State House in Philadelphia. The "Washington-
Madison collaboration" leaves small doubt that without their respective contributions a constitutional reformation would never have taken place in Philadelphia. One can even question whether the convention ever would have been
held. Madison and his Virginia allies, who quickly selected their state delegation, made it known that Washington would attend the Philadelphia gathering
as head of the Virginia representatives (before he had agreed to do so!), which
prompted the other states to send their own distinguished men to this "assembly of demigods," as Jefferson described it. Madison and his colleagues
elected Washington president of the convention, and they had no difficulty getting him to allow the Federalists to use his name during the ratification contest.
In fact, Washington took a more active part than he had intended. Antifederalists, reflecting on their eventual defeat, often said he was a major difference,

especially in key battleground states such as Virginia, where Antifederalist Monroe said that without Washington the Constitution's opponents would have prevailed.[51]

Although Washington's influence as a general, constitutionalist, and president will always remain somewhat elusive to us, his performance would have seemed explicable to the architects of national states in the two centuries before 1776. Their belief in a great-man theory of history remained alive in the eighteenth century. Voltaire, Rousseau, and Hume attributed state formation largely to the accomplishments of remarkable men. Voltaire agreed with Rousseau's contention in the *Social Contract* that the statesman "is the engineer who invents the machine." Peter Gay observes that despite the philosophes' cynicism about much in their day, the Enlightenment itself hardly rejected great-man history. Such figures as Peter the Great or Frederick the Great received praise "as the founder of states, the preceptor of his country, and the father of his people."[52] For Revolutionary Americans, Washington personified the great-man theory at its best. He had proved that he could be trusted with the power that he had willingly relinquished at the end of the Revolution. Moreover, in 1787 it was well known that he had preached the gospel of American unity to the Congress, the states, and the people since 1775. If we described Washington in European terms, we would call him Washington the Unifier, a role he continued to assume during the ratification contest and during his presidency.[53]

The American nation-state that emerged between 1763 and 1787–88 revealed both similarities and dissimilarities with the national polities that appeared in early modern Europe. Those European entities, with the notable exception of Britain, were unitary national states. Britain still adhered to long-held concepts of individual liberties anchored in the common law and the Bill of Rights of 1688–89. And its transatlantic settler societies had a significant degree of de facto internal autonomy. With the adoption of the Constitution of 1787, the American nation-state continued to be federal in nature, as the colonies had been in their relationship with the mother country before the Revolution and as the United States had been under the Articles of Confederation.

But the United States, when the government began to function under President Washington in 1789, displayed an energetic and consolidated form of federalism previously unknown in America. The Constitution mixed national and federal features to create the new federalism.[54] Not only did the Constitution provide, as had the Articles, that the central government could make war and peace, raise an army and navy, conclude treaties, coin money, create a postal service and so on, but it now possessed the crucial power to enforce its authority. The lack of legal ways to compel compliance had been the most signal weakness of the Articles. The term employed by students of state formation for such superintendency is *coercion*. The Constitution provided multiple means of enforcing obedience. Under certain circumstances the army could be employed to enforce the laws and to maintain order; and so could the state militias, which could be taken into national service. The Constitution stipulates that the Constitution and "the Laws of the United States . . . shall be the supreme Law of the Land." State officials are also compelled to take an oath to uphold the Constitution. Failure to do so means that federal courts can take action against state-level officeholders. Even Elbridge Gerry, who refused to sign the Constitution, admitted the value of linking "officers of the two Governments" into "the General System."[55]

Because the framers addressed so fully the Articles' deficiencies by providing for both internal and external security and order, Walter Millis calls the Constitution a military and a political document. As Governor Edmund Randolph of Virginia explained, government's first responsibility was to be "a shield against foreign hostility, and a firm resort against domestic commotion." The Constitution proved so successful in these areas that Americans have not added a single amendment concerning war making and security.[56] For many years the American centralized state appeared weak by European standards, but by 1800, writes Richard H. Kohn, America had established the military institutions that would remain largely unchanged until the twentieth century. For the people of the West, says Andrew Cayton, "the use of an army" during the Washington administration "became crucial to proving the value of the national government. Nothing else it did was more important in attaching people to the United States." Because of America's "free security" from Europe for nearly a century following the War of 1812, America did not need a sizable military apparatus to counter threats from outside the hemisphere, but the constitutional basis existed in the Constitution should the need arise, which came about only after 1900.[57]

Throughout the course of state formation, America had become a nation without a well-developed sense of nationalism, although leaders with a continental vision such as Washington, Hamilton, and Madison—nationalists by any definition—had created an institutional structure in which nationalism evolved in the nineteenth century. After 1815 the process seems to have quickened. Scholars are not of one mind about this process or all of its ingredients; but some are indisputable: Washington, the Revolution, and the Constitution. Cultural common ground probably came more slowly for Americans, a pattern noted previously for European nation-states. It increased following the War of 1812, when Americans jettisoned the foolish notion that the Federalist and Republican Parties were respectively ideological clones of monarchical Britain and revolutionary France. Had the Articles of Confederation continued to operate into the 1790s, confronting internal and external threats stemming from the French Revolution, it is doubtful that the United States would have survived under one flag. The third and final phase of federalism and state formation came just in the nick of time.[58]

Notes

1. By the early eighteenth century, virtually every major European state seems to have been "invented": France, Spain, the Netherlands, Austria, Prussia, Russia, and Britain. An applicable term for them is *composite* states. For national identity and the nationalization of culture, I have been especially influenced by Ernest Gellner, *National and Nationalism* (Oxford, Eng., 1983); Bruce D. Porter, *War and the Rise of the State* (New York, 1994); Benedict Anderson, *Imagined Communities: Reflections on the Origins and Spread of Nationalism,* rev. ed. (London, 1991); Lawrence Stone, ed., *An Imperial State at War: Britain from 1689 to 1815* (London and New York, 1994).

2. The best introduction to this literature and the controversies surrounding the subject is Clifford J. Rogers, ed., *The Military Revolution Debate* (Boulder, Colo., 1995).

3. Charles Tilly, ed., *The Formation of National States in Western Europe* (New York, 1975), and *Coercion, Capital, and the European States, AD 990–1990* (Oxford, Eng., 1990).

4. Geoffrey Parker, "In Defense of the Military Revolution," *Military Revolution Debate,* 341. John A. Lynn, however, warns against oversimplifications about the connection between centralization, bureaucratization, and armies in the early modern era. For France, as an example, see his *Giant of the Grand Siècle: The French Army, 1610–1715* (New York, 1997), "Epilogue: Insights on State Formation."

5. Brian M. Downing, *The Military Revolution and Political Change in Early Modern Europe* (Princeton, N.J., 1992), examines the relationship between major wars and the political character of European states. See also Stone, *An Imperial State at War,* chaps. 1–3, 8.

6. Linda Colley, *Britons: Forging the Nation, 1707–1837* (New Haven, 1992); John Brewer, *The Sinews of Power: War, Money, and the English State, 1688–1783* (New York, 1989); Stone, *An Imperial State at War,* chaps. 3, 5.

7. Leonard W. Labaree, *Royal Government in America: A Study of the British Colonial System before 1783* (New Haven, 1930), esp. chaps. 3, 10; Jack P. Greene, *The Quest for Power: The Lower Houses of Assembly in the Southern Royal Colonies, 1689–1776* (Chapel Hill, N.C., 1963), 297–309.

8. William Pencak, *War, Politics, and Revolution* (Boston, 1981), xi, xii, 5, 6.

9. Jack P. Greene, *Negotiated Authorities: Essays in Colonial and Constitutional History* (Charlottesville, Va., 1994), 178, 179.

10. Ibid., chap. 1; Mark Greengrass, *Conquest and Coalescence: The Shaping of the State in Early Modern Europe* (London, 1991).

11. The best treatment of American Whigs' methods and tactics is Pauline Maier, *From Resistance to Revolution: Colonial Radicals and the Development of American Opposition to Britain, 1765–1776* (New York, 1972).

12. Detailed narratives of the dozen years before independence include ibid.; Lawrence Henry Gipson, *The Coming of the Revolution, 1763–1775* (New York, 1954); Bernard Knollenberg, *Origin of the American Revolution, 1759–1766* (New York, 1960), and *The Growth of the American Revolution, 1766–1775* (New York, 1975); Merrill Jensen, *The Founding of a Nation: A History of the American Revolution, 1763–1776* (New York 1968).

13. Don Higginbotham, ed., *The Papers of James Iredell, 1767–1783,* 2 vols. (Raleigh, N.C., 1976), 2:19.

14. The rich literature on the evolution of American constitutional thinking includes Charles H. McIlwain, *The American Revolution: A Constitutional Interpretation* (New York, 1923); Andrew C. McLaughlin, *The Foundations of American Constitutionalism* (New York, 1932); Jack P. Greene, *Peripheries and Center: Constitutional Development in the Extended Polities of the British Empire and the United States, 1607–1788* (Athens, Ga., 1986); Bernard Bailyn, *The Ideological Origins of the American Revolution,* enlarged ed. (Cambridge, Mass., 1992). The most prolific author in the last generation on constitutional issues is John Phillip Reid. A preliminary evaluation of his work is Jack P. Greene, "From the Context of Law: Context and Legitimacy in the Origins of the American Revolution: A Review Essay," *South Atlantic Quarterly* 85 (1986): 56–77.

15. Don Higginbotham, "The American Militia: A Traditional Institution with Revolutionary Responsibilities," in *Reconsiderations on the Revolutionary War,* ed. Higginbotham (Westport, Conn., 1778), 87–89, 92, 93, 95–96; William H. Nelson, *The American Tory* (New York, 1961), 17–20, 31–32; Jensen, *Founding of a Nation,* chaps. 18–24; Benjamin Woods Labaree, *The Boston Tea Party* (New York, 1964), chaps. 11–13; David Ammerman, *In the Common Cause: American Response to the Coercive Acts of 1774* (Charlottesville, Va., 1974), chap. 8.

16. John Phillip Reid, *In a Defiant Stance: The Conditions of Law in Massachusetts Bay, the Irish Comparison, and the Coming of the American Revolution* (University Park, Pa., 1977), and *In a Rebellious Spirit: The Argument of Facts, the Liberty Riot, and the Coming of the American Revolution* (University Park, Pa., 1979).

17. Studies that offer a cautionary note as to claims for cultural and evolutionary national feeling in eighteenth-century America are S. N. Eisenstadt, *Revolution and the Transformation of Societies: A Comparative Study of Civilizations* (New York, 1978); Yehoshua Arieli, *Individualism and Nationalism in American Ideology* (Cambridge, Mass., 1964).

18. Congress refused even to consider Joseph Galloway of Pennsylvania's proposed

Plan of Union, which advocated intercolonial defense and control of Indian affairs, as well as a legislative union with Britain. The plan is analyzed in Julian P. Boyd, *Anglo-American Union: Joseph Galloway's Plans to Preserve the British Empire* (Philadelphia, 1941). A recent reexamination of Congress's negative reaction to Galloway's proposal is in Paul H. Smith, ed., *Letters of Delegates to Congress, 1774–1789*, 26 vols. (Washington, D.C., 1976–99), 1:112–13, 116–17.

19. Rakove, *Beginnings of National Politics* (New York, 1979), chaps. 1–3; Ammerman, *In the Common Cause,* chaps. 1–3; Greene, *Peripheries and Center,* chap. 7; Jerrilyn Greene Marston, *King and Congress: The Transfer of Political Legitimacy, 1774–1776* (Princeton, N.J., 1987), chaps. 1–4.

20. The delegates resorted to both "assertiveness and deference" in their desperate effort "to combine empire and liberty." Neil L. York, "The First Continental Congress and the Problem of American Rights," *Pennsylvania Magazine of History and Biography* 122 (1998): 354–83, quotations on 376, demonstrates the difficulties that congressmen felt about asserting their principles without implying a threat to secede from the empire.

21. One scholar even calls the Second Continental Congress "a more conservative body than the first." Nelson, *American Tory,* 116–17.

22. John Adams to James Warren, July 6, 1775, in Smith, *Letters of Delegates* 1:589.

23. Rakove, *Beginnings of National Politics,* chaps. 5–6; John Ferling, *John Adams: A Life* (Knoxville, Tenn., 1992), 123; Smith, *Letters of Delegates* 3:63–68, for Dickinson's proposed resolutions for negotiating with the king.

24. Emory M. Thomas, *The Confederate Nation, 1861–65* (New York, 1979), 58–66; Richard E. Beringer, Herman Hattaway, Archer Jones, and William N. Still Jr., *Why the South Lost the Civil War* (Athens, Ga., 1986), 75–81; William C. Davis, *"A Government of Our Own": The Making of the Confederacy* (New York, 1994).

25. Richard Henry Lee to Thomas Jefferson, Aug. 25, 1777, in Smith, *Letters of Delegates* 7:551.

26. Divisions in Congress were never as ideological as the Progressive school of historians maintained. For a review of Progressive historiography, see Richard B. Morris, "The Confederation Period and the American Historians," *William and Mary Quarterly,* 3d ser., 13 (1956): 139–56. See especially the work of Merrill Jensen and a number of his students. For example, Jensen, *The Articles of Confederation: An Interpretation of the Social-Constitutional History of the American Revolution, 1774–1781* (Madison, Wis., 1940); Joseph L. Davis, *Sectionalism in American Politics, 1774–1787* (Madison, Wis., 1977).

27. McLaughlin, *The Foundations of American Constitutionalism,* chap. 6., and *A Constitutional History of the United States* (New York, 1935), chaps. 1–3, remain the most thoughtful accounts of American federalism from before 1763 to 1787.

28. Charles Royster, *A Revolutionary People at War: The Continental Army and American Character, 1775–1783* (Chapel Hill, N.C., 1979), chap. 1, describes the *rage militaire.* For quotation, see Peter S. Onuf, *The Origins of the Federal Republic: Jurisdictional Controversies in the United States, 1775–1783* (Philadelphia, 1983), 7.

29. H. Trevor Colbourn, *The Lamp of Experience: Whig History and the Intellectual*

Origins of the American Revolution (Chapel Hill, N.C., 1965); Lois G. Schwoerer, *"No Standing Armies": The Antiarmy Ideology in Seventeenth-Century England* (Baltimore, 1974); Don Higginbotham, *George Washington and the American Military Tradition* (Athens, Ga., 1985), chap. 2.

30. Richard R. Johnson, "'Parliamentary Egotisms': The Clash of Legislatures in the Making of the American Revolution," *Journal of American History* 74 (1987): 338–62; Onuf, *Origins of the Federal Republic,* 21–22; Greene, *Peripheries and Center,* 164–65.

31. The last two paragraphs draw heavily on Rakove, *Beginnings of National Politics,* 133–215; Morris, *The Forging of the Union,* chap. 4; Greene, *Peripheries and Center,* chap. 8.

32. David C. Hendrickson argues convincingly that Burke's amendment, contrary to the view of most historians, "was supremely unimportant" and merely repeated the conventional understanding of Congress's limited authority. See his *Peace Pact: The Lost World of the American Founding* (Lawrence, Kans., 2003), 134.

33. Samuel Johnston to Thomas Burke, April 19, 1777, Early University Papers, University of North Carolina at Chapel Hill.

34. "Gouverneur Morris' Proposals on Fiscal and Administrative Reform," [June–July? 1778], Smith, *Letters of Delegates* 10:202–16, quotation on p. 208. Throughout the history of the Continental Congress and the Confederation, Morris offered penetrating commentaries on the federal government and the Union. See also Mary-Jo Kline, *Gouverneur Morris and the New Nation, 1775–1778* (New York, 1978), 109–26.

35. Jefferson criticized the constitutional division of powers that enfeebled Virginia's chief executive in his *Notes on the State of Virginia,* ed. William Peden (Chapel Hill, N.C., 1954), Query XIII, "The Constitution of the State."

36. Charles E. Bennett and Donald R. Lennon, *A Quest for Glory: Major General Robert Howe and the American Revolution* (Chapel Hill, N.C., 1991), chap. 7; John S. Pancake, *This Destructive War: The British Campaign in the Carolinas, 1780–1782* (University, Ala., 1985), 63–67.

37. Richard H. Kohn, *Eagle and Sword: The Federalists and the Creation of the Military Establishment in America, 1783–1802* (New York, 1975), chap. 2; Kenneth Bowling, "New Light on the Philadelphia Meeting of 1783: Federal-State Confrontation at the Close of the War for Independence," *Pennsylvania Magazine of History and Biography* 101 (1977): 419–50; Richard B. Morris, *The Peacemakers: The Great Powers and American Independence* (New York, 1965), 440–48.

38. Don Higginbotham, "George Washington's Contributions to American Constitutionalism," in Don Higginbotham, *War and Society in Revolutionary America: The Wider Dimensions of Conflict* (Columbia, S.C., 1988), 193–213.

39. Merrill Jensen, *The New Nation: A History of the United States during the Confederation, 1781–1789* (New York, 1950), 54–84; E. Wayne Carp, "The Origins of the Nationalist Movement of 1780–1783: Congressional Administration and the Continental Army," *Pennsylvania Magazine of History and Biography* 107 (1983): 363–92. For the argument that there was no cohesive centralist movement in Congress in the

early 1780s, see Rakove, *Beginnings of National Politics,* 307–24; Lance Banning, "James Madison and the Nationalists, 1780–1783," *William and Mary Quarterly,* 3d ser., 40 (1983): 227–55.

40. Jackson Turner Main, *Political Parties before the Constitution* (Chapel Hill, N.C., 1973), esp. chaps. 12–13.

41. Rakove, *Beginnings of National Politics,* chaps. 12–14; Morris, *Forging of the Union,* 95–97; Michael McShane Burns, "John Jay as Secretary for Foreign Affairs" (Ph.D. diss., Univ. of North Carolina at Chapel Hill, 1974), chap. 6, esp. 284–87; Julian P. Boyd, "Two Diplomats between Revolutions: John Jay and Thomas Jefferson," *Virginia Magazine of History and Biography* 67 (1959): 131–46.

42. Morris, *The Forging of the Union,* 194–204; Charles R. Ritcheson, *Aftermath of the Revolution: British Policy toward the United States, 1783–95* (Dallas, 1969), chaps. 4–5; Burns, "John Jay," chap. 4; Rakove, *Beginnings of National Politics,* chap. 14; Roberta Jacobs, "The Treaty and the Tories: The Ideological Reaction to the Return of the Loyalists" (Ph.D. diss., Cornell Univ., 1974).

43. For the military fortunes of the Confederation, see Don Higginbotham, *The War of American Independence: Military Attitudes, Policy, and Practice, 1763–1789* (New York, 1971), 438–52; Harry M. Ward, *The Department of War, 1781–1795* (Pittsburgh, 1962), chaps. 7–9, Knox quotation on p. 80.

44. Burns, "John Jay," chap. 5; Morris, *Forging of the Union,* chap. 9; Onuf, *Origins of the Federal Republic,* chap. 7; Peter S. Onuf, "Anarchy and the Crisis of the Union," *To Form a More Perfect Union: The Critical Ideas of the Constitution,* ed. Herman Belz, Ronald Hoffman, and Peter J. Albert (Charlottesville, Va., 1992), 272–302.

45. Willi Paul Adams, *The First American Constitutions: Republican Ideology and the Making of the State Constitutions in the Revolutionary Era* (Chapel Hill, N.C., 1980), 86–93, 268–69, 273, 290; Onuf, *Origins of the Federal Republic.* "All states— landed or landless, large or small, old or new—looked to the states collectively in Congress to recognize and uphold their claims." Conflicts between states "provided an important impetus toward enlarging the scope of federal authority." Ibid., xv.

46. The secondary literature of Antifederalism has reached substantial proportions. Still quite valuable for an overview is Jackson Turner Main, *The Antifederalists: Critics of the Constitution, 1781–1788* (Chapel Hill, N.C., 1961). A recent monograph that stresses Antifederalist thought and its place in the American political tradition is Saul Cornell, *The Other Founders: Antifederalism and the Dissenting Tradition in America, 1788–1827* (Chapel Hill, N.C., 1999).

47. Stanley Elkins and Eric McKittrick, *The Founding Fathers: Young Men of the Revolution* (Washington, D.C., 1961), an American Historical Association pamphlet; Main, *The Antifederalists,* 260.

48. Main, *Political Parties,* 455.

49. Higginbotham, "George Washington's Contributions to American Constitutionalism," 208–209; Stuart Leibiger, *Founding Friendship: George Washington, James Madison, and the Creation of the American Republic* (Charlottesville, Va., 1999), 60, 64, 67–68; Glen A. Phelps, *George Washington and American Constitutionalism*

(Lawrence, Kans., 1993), 92–95. No single letter better captures Washington's apprehension than his missive to Henry Lee, April 4, 1786, *PGW: Conf. Ser.* 4:4.

50. Circular to the States, June 1783, *GW: Writings* 23:483–96; Merrill Jensen, John P. Kaminski, Gaspare J. Saladino, et al., eds., *The Documentary History of the Ratification of the Constitution,* 18 vols. to date, not numbered consecutively (Madison, Wis., 1976–), 13:60–61.

51. The recent study of the Washington-Madison alliance and Madison's overall role is Leibiger, *Founding Friendship,* chap. 3. A more detailed account of Madison's part in the writing and ratification of the Constitution is Lance Banning, *The Sacred Fire of Liberty: James Madison and the Founding of the Federal Republic* (Ithaca, N.Y., 1995), chaps. 4–8. Monroe's interpretation of the outcome in Virginia is in Julian P. Boyd et al., eds., *The Papers of Thomas Jefferson,* 30 vols. to date (Princeton, N.J., 1950–), 13:351–52. For Jefferson's letter to Adams, Aug. 30, 1787, see Max Farrand, ed., *Records of the Federal Convention of 1787,* rev. ed., 4 vols. (New Haven, 1937), 3:76.

52. Peter Gay, *Voltaire's Politics: The Poet as Realist,* 2d ed. (New Haven, 1988), quotations on pp. 180, 181.

53. These remarks on Washington are drawn from my *George Washington: Uniting a Nation* (Lanham, Md., 2002), which examines his public life and imagery in the context of leadership in Europe and America in the early modern era. See also, for views of Washington in his own time, Gary Willis, *Cincinnatus: George Washington and the Enlightenment* (New York, 1984); Barry Schwartz, *George Washington: The Making of an American Symbol* (New York, 1987); Paul K. Longmore, *The Invention of George Washington* (Berkeley, Calif., 1988).

54. Jacob E. Cooke, ed., *The Federalist* (Wesleyan, Conn., 1961), 250–57, for Madison's analysis.

55. Madison's Notes, in Farrand, *Records of the Federal Convention* 2:88.

56. Walter Millis, *Arms and Men* (New York, 1956), 41. See also Richard H. Kohn, "The Constitution and National Security: The Intent of the Framers," in *The United States Military under the Constitution of the United States, 1789–1989,* ed. Kohn (New York, 1991), 61–94. For Federalist thinking on how a nation's economic power strengthened its hand in both domestic and foreign affairs, see Cathy D. Mason and Peter S. Onuf, *A Union of Interests: Political and Economic Thought in Revolutionary America* (Lawrence, Kans., 1990). Another insightful volume showing how ideas on the European balance of power and state system influenced the framers' conception of a new American federalism is Peter S. Onuf and Nicholas G. Onuf, *Federal Union, Modern World: The Law of Nations in an Age of Revolutions, 1776–1814* (Madison, Wis., 1993). Randolph's statement is in Jensen, *Documentary History of Ratification* 15:123.

57. Kohn, *Eagle and Sword,* esp. chap. 14; Andrew R. L. Cayton, "'Separate Interests' and the Nation-State: The Washington Administration and the Origins of Regionalism in the Trans-Appalachian West," *Journal of American History* 79 (1992): 39–67, quotation on p. 47. C. Vann Woodward described the military significance of America's noninvolvement in European wars after 1815 in "The Age of Reinterpre-

tation," *American Historical Review* 66 (1960–61): 1–20. John A. Lynn argues that students of European state formation stress the state's coercive power over its citizens and ignore the possibility of a more positive image (as noted by Cayton for western settlers and the American army in the 1790s). By protecting citizens, European armies could also symbolize beneficent government and attract converts to a strong monarchy. Lynn, *Giant of the Grand Siècle.*

58. John Murrin maintains that Revolutionary America lacked a sense of nationalism that was deeply embedded in American culture and that nationalism grew slowly in the nineteenth century. See his three essays: "A Roof without Walls: The Dilemma of American National Identity," in *Beyond Confederation: Origins of the Constitution and American National Identity,* ed. Richard Beeman et al. (Chapel Hill, N.C., 1987), 333–48; "Nationalism," in *The Oxford Companion to American Military History,* ed. John Whitclay Chambers (New York, 1999), 465–68; and "War, Revolution, and Nation-Making: The American Revolution versus the Civil War," MS cited with the author's permission. The complexities of the subject are further illuminated in Andrew R. L. Cayton, "We Are All Nationalists, We Are All Localists," *Journal of the Early Republic* 18 (1998): 521–28. For a recent study that contends the 1790s "represent a critical era in American history equivalent to that of the Civil War," see James Roger Sharp, *American Politics in the Early Republic: The New Nation in Crisis* (New Haven, 1993), quotation on p. 1.

5 ┊ *The Federalized Militia Debate*

I HAVE HAD THE GOOD FORTUNE to receive several invitations to speak in the Canadian maritime provinces, always in the spring or fall (thank goodness!), lovely times of the year for visitors to Prince Edward Island, New Brunswick, and Nova Scotia. This article grew out of a presentation at a conference on "Military Aid to the Civil Authority: The Anglo-Saxon Tradition" held at Acadia University in Wolfville, Nova Scotia, April 4–5, 1991. The sponsors were Acadia University and the Centre for Foreign Policy Studies at Dalhousie University. Understandably, most speakers addressed this tradition as it related to Britain, Canada, and Northern Ireland. I participated in a panel on European and American Analogues. I came away from Wolfville with an awareness that the British and American traditions were alike only in superficial ways. Despite the existence of the centuries-old British militia, it does not appear to have been a first line of defense against riots, rebellions, and other forms of uprisings. Shakespeare poked fun at its moribund condition. In the early modern period, wardens of the Northern Marches called out untrained bands of locals or other civilian groups known for their ferocity such as the Scottish Highlanders. By the eighteenth century, whether confronting disturbances in Britain or Canada, the crown turned to its professional army. In later years Canadians often employed their own militias in these undertakings.

In United States history it was the militia that served as a domestic police force in the colonial and Revolutionary eras. That was also true after the adoption of the Constitution in 1788. Contrary to the fearful predictions of the Antifederalists, the national government has taken state militias into federal service for use at home on relatively few occasions—two of the most notable occurrences were when Washington led a militia force to subdue the Whiskey Rebellion in western Pennsylvania in 1794 and when Jefferson called out militia to assist the army in enforcing the Embargo of 1807. Although the states on many occasions have turned to their militias for a variety of domestic reasons, the federal government did not do so a single time between 1867 and 1957. In examining the militia debate during the ratification of the Constitution, I concluded that the controversy was over a problem in federalism, over whether the states should share their traditional control of the militia with the national authority. I found extremely little evidence for the contention of those legal scholars and historians who assert that the subject is relevant to current debates on gun control. If, as some of these writers believe, the Antifederalists and the authors of the Second Amendment maintained that Americans wished to protect the individual right of citizens to hold guns for hunting, recreation, and self-defense, in addition to seeing gun ownership as a collective right as members of the militia, my own research runs in the opposite direction: it does not lend support to the individual right interpretation. Indeed, a simple either-or approach to the meaning of the Second Amendment does not help us comprehend the eighteenth-century world. An enlarged version of the address appeared in the *William and Mary Quarterly*, 3d ser., 55 (January 1998): 39–58, and is reprinted with the editor's permission.

THE PAST TWENTY YEARS or so have brought heated debate on one aspect of the Second Amendment. Does its gun ownership language provide both a personal right to keep firearms—for protection and other private purposes such as hunting and recreation—and a collective right to defend society as a member of the militia? Historians such as Robert E. Shalhope, Lawrence Delbert Cress, and Joyce Lee Malcolm have addressed these issues.[1] They have been joined in increasing numbers by members of the legal academy. The lawyers have concentrated on the individual rights question, which the great majority of them answer affirmatively.[2]

Virtually absent from these gun ownership and gun rights arguments, in both the legal and the historical literature, is what Americans had to say about control of the state militias before, during, and after the writing of the Constitution. The subject is important because it shows how radical was the shift from the states' total control of their militias to the sharing of that authority under the Constitution, how disturbing this development was to the Antifederalists, how James Madison dealt with Antifederalist concerns in the Second Amendment, and, finally, how the issue was gradually resolved in the first half of the nineteenth century. In all the discussions and debates, from the Revolution to the eve of the Civil War, there is precious little evidence that advocates of local control of the militia showed an equal or even a secondary concern for gun ownership as a personal right.

The language of the Constitution provides the base for the militia control controversy in the late 1780s. Article I, Section 8 declares that "the Congress shall have power . . . To provide for calling forth the militia to execute the laws of the Union, suppress insurrections and repel invasions." Although the states retain the authority to train the militia and to appoint its officers, Congress has the power "to provide for organizing, arming, and disciplining the militia, and for governing such part of them as may be employed in the service of the United States." The Antifederalists gave initial definition and drive to the controversy over the meaning and application of these terms, but none of their proposals for limitations or prohibitions on the federalized militia appears in the Second Amendment, which, writes Leonard W. Levy, is "as vague as it is ambiguous."[3] It therefore became the responsibility of Congress, with some assistance from the Supreme Court, to implement the Constitution's militia clauses.

After showing that colonial and Revolutionary Americans were virtually of one mind in espousing a well-regulated militia under local authority, this essay reviews the breakdown of that consensus brought about by the militia's performance in the War of Independence and during Shays's Rebellion. After looking into the militia provisions of the Constitution, it examines the Antifederalists' negative reaction to those provisions and their failure to accomplish their agenda in the Second Amendment. It then shows how Congress and the Supreme Court resolved the constitutional questions concerning the federalization of the militia for domestic purposes. That resolution, together with the limited extent to which the national government actually called out the militia in peacetime—the subject of the final part of this article—explains why, for all practical purposes, a long and hotly disputed ideological issue disappeared. That the states were rarely called on to send their militias into national service, however, proved no guarantee that the institution itself was, in the classic phrase, the great palladium of liberty that Antifederalists and other states' rights advocates claimed it to be.

In their newspaper and pamphlet responses to Britain's new imperial policy after the Seven Years' War, the colonists decried, among other ominous developments, the decline of the metropolitan militia and the increasing use of redcoats to preserve law and order in both the parent kingdom and its transatlantic dominions.[4] Americans asserted that if their civil officials encountered domestic commotions, they should appeal only to their local militias for support, a contention that reflected both their reading of the dangers of standing armies in English history and their own colonial experience. It became a tenet of faith that colonial authorities should retain jurisdiction over their provinces' militias and other forces. That view brought displeasure to royal governors during the imperial wars, for the provincial assemblies claimed and exercised such power over the militia to set salaries, to authorize the stores and equipment to be raised, to determine the number of men called for service, to prescribe organization and training, and to forbid or limit duty outside their provinces. Consequently, American lawmakers hamstrung royal administrators and British officers who sought to establish control over colonial fighting men.[5] The colonists predictably reacted vigorously when royal governors in 1775 attempted to seize militia arsenals at Williamsburg and Concord. The latter episode ignited the War of Independence.

The pattern of home control of local military organizations continued in the Revolution. Both conviction and precedent explain why the language of the thirteenth article of the Virginia Declaration of Rights in 1776 resounded through similar state charters. The Virginia document declared "that a well-regulated militia, composed of the body of the people trained to arms, is the proper, natural and safe defense of a free state . . . and that in all cases, the military should be under strict subordination to, and governed by, the civil power." The new state constitutions gave the legislatures the power to mobilize the militia, and mustering them for campaigns usually required the approval of the state executive council, which the legislatures themselves elected in most states. For Congress or the army to attempt to take over the militias or to send them against their will outside their own states would constitute "a Subvertion of all Liberty," asserted Abraham Clark of New Jersey, who lectured the speaker of his state's assembly on the need to "Oppose Tyranny in all its Strides."[6] Noting that few if any structures symbolized state sovereignty more than the militia, Cress calls the institution "central to the political stability and constitutional balance that sustained a republican constitution."[7]

George Washington, critical of a system that at best provided poorly trained men for limited service in his Continental army, addressed the sensitive issue of militia control near the war's end in 1783. His "Sentiments on a Peace Establishment," a document that anticipates crucial elements of military policy debate for the next two centuries, proposed that America retain its Revolutionary practice of regular and state forces but with fundamental alterations in the militia system. Congress should create two classes of militia within each state, each more effectively organized than the present militias. The first and larger class would, as in the past, include all men from ages sixteen to fifty. It would represent an improvement over the old system in that its establishment, exercise, and weapons would be uniform in all the states. Even so, the class could hardly be trusted to meet the nation's most critical needs. For "amongst such a Multitude of

People . . . there must be a great number, who from domestic Circumstances, bodily defects, natural awkwardness or disinclination, can never acquire the habits of Soldiers." The second class, drawn from the first, would be composed solely of young, able-bodied volunteers or draftees. While on active duty, this class would be under direct federal jurisdiction. Its primary task would be to resist "any sudden impression which might be attempted by a foreign Enemy," affording time for Congress to begin full-scale mobilization.[8]

Militia reform, like other schemes for empowering Congress under the Articles of Confederation, found a chilly reception. Washington's "Sentiments," though approved in revised form by a congressional committee, elicited scant support in the full legislative body. In 1786 Henry Knox, secretary at war for the Confederation, advanced a militia plan that resembled Washington's blueprint in some respects and also responded to parochialists' fears that a nationalized militia might be corrupted and cease to embody republican virtue. Knox proposed that militiamen in federal training would hear lectures on the glories of republican institutions and would engage only in recreation and amusements that were morally and physically uplifting. Moreover, militia units called outside their states to deal with threats and emergencies would be returned in no more than a year, a provision Knox believed would dampen apprehensions of misusing the militia or turning the state troops into a standing army. Even so, Knox's recommendations suffered the fate of Washington's "Sentiments."[9]

The articles referred to every state's maintaining "a well regulated and disciplined militia," yet they contained no authorization for the central government under any circumstances to assemble for training or any other reason even some small part of the state militias. Only the broadest interpretation of congressional authority could read into the Articles a power to dictate militia regulations or responsibilities to the states. Short of amendments—and they required unanimous approval from the thirteen states—Congress could not reform the militias, even had it a mind to do so.[10]

Although the Confederation's main line of defense in the post-1783 years consisted of a single regiment under the control of Congress, the states proved unwilling to upgrade the militias on their own initiative. David Ramsay, a former South Carolina congressman, complained that "our governments are too relaxed to bear any [militia] system . . . attended with . . . time & expense."[11] Part of the problem stemmed from opposition of local elites. In Virginia, for example, the legislature, responding to Washington's recommendation that the states replace their militia officers with former officers of the Continental army "so far as can be done without creating uneasiness and jealousy," authorized Governor

Patrick Henry to make wholesale replacements.[12] Henry made a number of appointments but ran into strong resistance, for loss of office also meant diminution of the senior officers' local standing and influence. As one appointee who declined to accept his commission explained, he did not hail from one of the foremost Augusta County families and did not wish to be "an object of . . . utmost resentment." The following year the legislature, beating a retreat, returned the displaced militia officers to their commands.[13]

The nationalists, persistent advocates of a more consolidated political union, saw the uneven performance of the Massachusetts militia in Shays's Rebellion as a further indication of the need for improving militia by the central government. In 1786 several thousand men took up arms, closed the courts in western counties, and threatened the Confederation's arsenal at Springfield. Some militia units in the insurgent counties supported the rebels. A battle between state troops and dissidents at Springfield produced defections to the rebel ranks. In time the government forces prevailed, but not before the Confederation was gravely shaken.[14] Other states likewise suffered from postwar economic dislocation; would they be spared similar tumults? A less publicized confrontation had occurred almost simultaneously in New Hampshire. There angry debtors led by militia officers surrounded the building in Exeter where the legislature was in session and announced that none could leave until the besiegers obtained an acceptable response to their petitions for relief. The following day militia from the state's eastern towns dispersed the insurgents.[15] Everywhere, newspaper essays and letters echoed Washington's exclamation that "combustibles in every State" menaced the tranquillity of the states and the stability of the Union itself.[16]

The authors of the federal Constitution saw a critical need to impose controls over the internal affairs of the states in general and over the state militias specifically, to counter domestic turmoils. They added a new component to the idea of a federalized militia as detailed by Washington, Knox, and several other generals of the Continental army. It now appeared insufficient to provide better training and a measure of congressional oversight. Consequently, the Philadelphia Constitutional Convention gave Congress authority to employ the militia against the states or any of their citizens in certain cases involving internal disturbances and breaches of federal law.

Owing to a preoccupation with such major concerns as the structure of the central government and representation issues, the subject of militia control was not formally addressed by the full convention until August 6, when the committee of detail reported the first draft of a constitution. Surprisingly, in light of earlier negative views on militia reform and the presence in the convention of men who held such views, the delegates agreed with little debate to accept the committee's all-embracing language empowering the national legislature "to call forth the aid of the militia" not only to "repel invasions" but also "to execute the laws of the Union" and to "suppress insurrections." Some of the more state-minded delegates, however, favored a limit on the portion of any state's militia that might be subject to federally imposed rules for training and that might be called up for national service at one time. But these were mainly differences of degree; the idea of some measure of federal oversight and control in these two areas was questioned on the floor by only two delegates: Elbridge Gerry of Massachusetts and Luther Martin of Maryland. The task of dealing with the delegates' differences over this part of the militia wording fell on August 18 to a committee of eleven. Three days later the committee reported militia language almost identical to that in the final document: Congress was "to make laws for organizing, arming, and disciplining the militia, and for governing such part of them as may be employed in the service of the United States, reserving to the States respectively, the appointment of the Officers, and the authority of training the militia according to the discipline prescribed by the United States." The convention then agreed to accept the committee report in two votes: 9–2 and 7–4, the four negatives in the second vote coming from states that wished to reduce the federal role in training the militia.[17]

The militia provisions of the Constitution flew in the face of much American thinking and experience and so became subject to Antifederalist attack. On December 12, 1787, at the Pennsylvania ratifying convention, the first to be held, Robert Whitehill introduced one of the most detailed Antifederalist resolutions on the militia to appear during the ratification contest. It stated "that the power of organizing, arming, and disciplining the militia (the manner of disciplining the militia to be prescribed by Congress) remain with the individual states, and that Congress shall not have authority to call or march any of the militia out of their own state, without the consent of such state and for such length of time only as such state shall agree."[18] Whitehill's resolutions set the stage for the militia debate that would be repeated in subsequent conventions and the press.

The absence of stated limits to congressional control, asserted the Antifederalists, would generate repeated military interventions in the domains of the states and the lives of the people, especially because, as Patrick Henry warned, the Constitution did not define the meaning of executing the laws or suppressing insurrections.[19] Critics of the Constitution feared that only military coercion could hold together a consolidated republic in a sprawling country like the United States, with its diverse regions and heterogeneous population, but such use of force, declared the "Federal Farmer," would "very soon destroy all elective governments in the country, produce anarchy, or establish despotism."[20] Antifederalists warned that the people's resistance to unjust and discriminatory taxation would prompt the federal government to resort to arms. "Is it not well known," asked Virginia's George Mason, "that what would be a proper tax in one State would be grievous in another?"[21]

An oft-repeated Antifederalist scenario explained how the sword would be employed. The national government would quite possibly be too shrewd to send a standing army to enforce the laws and intimidate the people, a step that would raise specters of Caesar, Cromwell, and George III. Rather, it would resort to the federalized militia: it would confuse the people by using the body of the people against the people. Mason had endeavored to address this fear at the Constitutional Convention. He wanted to preface the section on federalizing the militia by stating that to do so would have made it transparent that the purpose of the militia in national service was to protect freedom, not to threaten it. But Gouverneur Morris of Pennsylvania—supported by Charles Pinckney of South Carolina and Gunning Bedford of Delaware—called the Mason addition a slap in the face of American professional soldiers, "the military class of Citizens," and it met defeat.[22]

As Antifederalists saw it, the militia under federal control would possess all the evils associated with a standing army. Congress's power to impose harsh discipline would brutalize the militia into submission by fines, corporal punishment, and fear of death by court-martial. Having been thus transmogrified into myrmidons, citizen-soldiers would become the mirror image of European professionals. These "meer machines as Prussian soldiers" would lose their devotion to freedom and to the dignity of the individual as they became walled off from the body politic. Of course, some yeomanry might be too sensitive and independent-minded to be deceived or to knuckle under. It would be terribly distasteful, for instance, for Pennsylvania militiamen, many of them doubtless Quakers opposed to military obligations in principle and antislavery in sentiment, to be sent to Georgia to suppress slaves revolting for "*sacred liberty.*" To avert such defection or disobedience, the national administration would concentrate its energies on militiamen from "the young and ardent part of the community, possessed of but little or no property."[23]

Although the means might vary, the result would be the same: the militia would become, in effect, a standing army maintained by the states but controlled by the central government.[24] Militias might be dispatched from one end of America to the other to quell insurrections sparked by the most terrible oppressions, leaving their home states defenseless, particularly from Indians on the frontier. This military arm, the erstwhile palladium of liberty, would become an instrument of tyranny. As one Maryland "Farmer and Planter" put it, if you "think you are imposed upon by Congress[,] . . . your great Lords and Masters, and refuse or delay to pay your taxes, or do any thing that they shall think proper to order you to do, they can . . . send the militia of Pennsylvania, Boston, or any other state or place, to cut your throats, ravage and destroy your plantations, drive away your cattle and horses, abuse your wives, kill your infants, and ravish your daughters, and live in free quarters, until you get into a good humour, and pay all that they may think proper to ask of you, and you become good and faithful servants and slaves."[25] In sum, moaned John Smilie in the Pennsylvania convention, the militia, "the last resource of a free people[,] is taken away" and put in the hands of Congress. "It ought to be considered as the last *coup de grace* to the *State governments,*" lamented Luther Martin.[26]

Antifederalists objected in general to the Constitution's bestowal of concurrent powers on the federal government and the states, and nowhere did this shared authority appear more starkly than in the militia provisions. Antifederalists maintained that either the central government or the states would ultimately control the militia. This concern found vociferous expression in the Virginia convention. The new government would be consolidated in character, complained Henry, pointing to the militia language; Congress did not have to receive the approval of the states to call out the militia. The concept of shared jurisdiction was a myth: "To admit this mutual concurrence of powers will carry you into endless absurdity:—That Congress has nothing exclusive on the one hand, nor the States on the other!" All such absurdities would resolve to the advantage of the central power. If, for example, a state needed its militia at the same time as the federal government, "Which call is to be obeyed, the Congressional call, or the call of the State Legislature? The call of Congress must be obeyed."[27]

Antifederalists sought means for redress—for tilting the balance toward the states' retaining greater control of their armed forces—either by changing the text of the Constitution or by adding a national bill of rights. At the Pennsylvania convention they tried—and failed—to delay approval of the Constitution until adoption of amendments that would have included stipulations for lessening federal authority over the militias. Beginning with the Massachusetts convention, Federalists faced stiffer opposition and increasingly agreed to propose recommendatory amendments in a variety of areas. Massachusetts and four other states offered such recommendations.[28] When the First Federal Congress took up the issue of constitutional change in 1789, it had approximately one hundred separate proposals on a broad range of topics available for consideration.[29]

Because Madison, who introduced amendments in the House of Representatives after pledging to do so at the Virginia convention, supported almost exclusively stipulations guaranteeing individual and collective rights, he avoided all recommendatory amendments that would have created structural changes in the Constitution, including weakening the power of Congress over the militia.[30] Recommendations for limiting the militia's numbers in federal employment, restricting its time under national control, regulating its out-of-state service, subjecting its rank and file to martial law, and providing for its training all failed to find their way into what became the Second Amendment. One measure advocated by some Antifederalists, freeing conscientious objectors from military participation, passed in the House but lost in the Senate. Still another proposal popular with some Antifederalists—that the militia would remain under state control except when in the employment of the United States—was introduced in the House but received little support, perhaps because it failed to go beyond the language already in the Constitution. In any case, Congress, composed largely of Federalists, showed no inclination whatsoever to mollify Antifederalists on the subject of the militia.[31] The members, with few exceptions, shared Madison's belief that a bill of rights should be a statement of general principles rather than a document that included particulars and policies that, in their view, were more properly determined by statute law.

Federalists, in refusing proposals for change, responded as they had done during ratification. They dismissed Antifederalist apprehensions as totally unrealistic. In *The Federalist,* Hamilton branded them as "far fetched and . . . extravagant," and Madison dismissed them as "misguided exaggerations."[32] Denying that Congress would enact legislation that would be harsh or discriminatory toward states or large numbers of people, Federalists further contended that civilian officials, including judges, would almost always have the means to uphold federal law and maintain the peace without resorting to the nationalized militia or the army. William Samuel Johnson of Connecticut argued that the Constitution goes to great lengths to avoid military responses to internal difficulties: rather than "armed force . . . the power which is to enforce these laws is to be a legal power vested in proper magistrates."[33] Consequently, as Virginia Federalists repeatedly pointed out, militias, with very rare exceptions, would remain under direct control of the states, which would be free to increase their arms and their training as they saw fit. Edmund Randolph reminded Virginia's convention that militia officers, appointed by and subject to removal by the states, would hardly give up their state loyalties if and when they entered federal service. Randolph, reflecting other supporters' sentiments, ridiculed the opposition's lack of "common sense" in "interpreting this Constitution."[34]

The rhetoric of Antifederalists and Federalists will never enable us to understand fully what the members of the First Congress intended by the language of the Second Amendment: "A well-regulated militia, being necessary to the security of a free State, the right of the people to keep and bear arms shall not be infringed." The problem is that, with exceedingly few exceptions, we do not know how individuals in either camp understood the amendment as it moved through the Congress to the state legislatures. Neither side displayed unanimity of views about the strengths and weaknesses of the Constitution. Much has been said over the years about the difficulty of determining the original intent of the authors of the Constitution; the same holds true of those who voted—warmly or halfheartedly—for rights amendments or for the Bill of Rights itself, a subject that gained the serious attention of Congress only as a result of Madison's prodding in 1789.[35]

We can only speculate about Madison's motives in introducing the Second Amendment. He may well have done so partly for psychological or symbolic reasons and partly to satisfy—in some measure, at least—the Virginia convention, which wanted not only alterations in the body of the Constitution that would have weakened jurisdiction over the militia but also a bill of rights containing militia language fairly close to Madison's own Second Amendment wording. By conceding something heavy in emotional content but thin in substance, something that could be interpreted as each reader chose to do, Madison and his supporters in Congress probably hoped to calm Antifederalist fears. Without dealing with specifics, the amendment seems to imply that the concurrent power of the state and federal governments over the militia will not threaten the states or obstruct their use of the militia when not in federal service. That would include the states' arming and equipping their respective militias if Congress failed to do so. It can surely be seen as a confirmation of their views by that small number of Antifederalists who are known publicly to have favored citizens' right to keep arms for private purposes as well as for collectively defending society as members of the militia.[36] If most Antifederalist writers feared that the central authority would make the militias so muscular that they might serve as a standing army, others saw another disturbing possibility: that the national government would keep the militias too weak to resist the power of a future standing army.[37]

It is clear, in any case, that Congress was less than enthusiastic about a bill of rights and that some Antifederalists were disappointed with the Bill of Rights, including Virginians Richard Henry Lee and William Grayson, the former judging the amendments "much mutilated and enfeebled," the latter calling them "good for nothing."[38] Also opposed was Gerry of Massachusetts, like the two Virginians an Antifederalist member of the First Congress. Gerry singled out the militia amendment as his most serious objection to the Bill of Rights. He saw in it the continuation of a dangerous precedent that had begun with the militia provisions of the Constitution: the sacrificing of the states' total control of the militia to a central government that also had the authority to create a standing army. It reminded him of Britain's efforts during the earlier imperial crisis to keep the Massachusetts militia weak at the same time that royal troops were sent to coerce the Bay Colony.[39]

The new national charter remained in 1789 a skeleton to be fleshed out by laws and judicial interpretation. President Washington's administration encountered difficulty in getting Congress to implement the Constitution's provisions for bringing the state militias under federal jurisdiction for training. The reasons are complex and not always ideological. The large Federalist majority in the First Congress had refused to weaken Congress's control of the militia in the Second Amendment but was not of one mind about creating a centralized militia establishment.

Congressional divisions on that subject became apparent immediately after Secretary of War Knox, borrowing liberally from militia plans that he and Washington had advanced in the Confederation years, presented an implementation package to the national lawmakers in January 1790.[40] Stressing the need for quick legislative action because of Indian uprisings on the frontier, Knox once again called for a system of classing the militia by age and providing summer encampments and standardized weapons and equipment for the younger militiamen, who would constitute the elite class. Knox, like Washington and other former generals of the Continental army, knew that not all militiamen were well armed and familiar with their weapons.[41] Equally bold, and certainly unprecedented, was Knox's recommendation that young men should be denied the full benefits of citizenship until they completed their terms of service in the elite class.

Knox's proposals produced heated opposition in and out of Congress. Critics asserted that classing and summer camps for younger men would be unworkable and exceedingly expensive. The cost, estimated at over $400,000 a year for the "advanced corps," prompted Benjamin Goodhue of Massachusetts, a Federalist member of the House of Representatives, to exclaim, "I believe Knox to be" nearly "the most extravagant man . . . living." Others called for exemptions for numerous occupations and for conscientious objectors, and they denounced Knox for stipulating that citizenship rights should be linked to compulsory military service.[42] According to a satirical piece in Benjamin Bache's Philadelphia *General Advertiser,* one Charlotte informed her friends Sophia and Thalestris that because Quakers, tradesmen, students, and farmers sought exemptions from militia duty, "I suppose that we young women must learn militia duty, and turn out with both musquet and bayonet." Two authorities state that "nothing [the First Federal Congress] considered raised as much organized public opposition as Knox's militia plan."[43]

Congress backed off, taking the customary route of legislative bodies that seek to escape the heat: a committee drafted a bill, encouraged further public commentary, and put the controversial measure aside for months while lawmakers dealt with other divisive issues such as Hamilton's financial program and the location of the national capital.[44] The Knox legislation eventually limped through a succession of ad hoc committees in 1790 and 1791, each one further weakening its original contents. The first and only full debate on the much-revised militia bill terminated with the end of the First Congress in early 1791. The national legislators, hopelessly divided on the subject, went home without voting on it.[45]

When the Second Congress finally passed the Uniform Militia Act of 1792, it eliminated almost all the parts Washington and Knox considered crucial. The act lumped together all men between the ages of eighteen and forty-five in a huge, undifferentiated militia force, with every man responsible for securing his own weapon, regardless of its condition, unless the states elected to furnish arms. The law provided only loose guidelines for training and organizing the militia under state, not federal, supervision. It provided no penalties if the states proved unwilling to enforce these guidelines.[46] The statute continued to be the basic structural legislation for the militia until the twentieth century, despite reform-minded efforts of various presidents. None made more persistent attempts than Thomas Jefferson, who addressed the matter in seven of his annual messages to Congress. Like Washington and Knox before him, Jefferson embraced the idea of Congress's classing the militia and supplying the best-trained component with standardized weapons. But when he persuaded lawmakers to consider the matter seriously in 1805–6, he met a resounding defeat.[47]

Congress in 1792 also enacted the Calling Forth Act to define procedures for federalizing state militias. Some Federalists wanted to leave the decision to the president, but a majority of the lawmakers insisted on safeguards against hasty action by the administration. In the event of an insurrection against a state government, the act made it "lawful for the President . . . on the application of the legislature of such state, or the Executive (when the legislature cannot be convened)" to call out militia from other states. The new law also passed on some of Congress's power relative to executing national law to the chief executive, mostly pertaining to when it was not in session. To act, however, the president needed notification from a federal judge that civil authority was inadequate to bring order. Furthermore, before ordering out militia, he had to issue a cease-and-desist proclamation.[48]

The first and greatest test case, practically and constitutionally, for the employment of the federalized militia came soon after Congress enacted the 1792 militia laws. In 1794 Washington called out 13,000 militiamen from four states to suppress the Whiskey Rebellion in western Pennsylvania, where angry farmers blocked the collection of a federal tax on distillers of spirituous liquors. Though Washington received criticism from within the emerging Republican Party, the protesters could hardly argue that the president had failed to remain inside the letter of the law; their concerns focused on the need to resort to force and the number of men taken into national service. Most congressmen, however, approved Washington's performance: he had delayed forceful means until after conciliation had apparently failed, he released most of the militiamen after a short time in arms, and he pardoned the two rebels convicted of treason.[49]

Congress subsequently reinforced and strengthened the "calling forth" authority of the federal government in general and of the president in particular. Revising the Calling Forth Act in 1795, it made the law permanent and deleted the stipulations that the president, before implementing part of it, had to obtain a judicial certificate and secure congressional approval if the lawmakers were in session.[50] In 1799 President John Adams, displaying less hesitancy than Washington did in 1794, dispatched federalized militia to put down the Fries Rebellion in Pennsylvania where, again, an unpopular federal tax generated agrarian resistance. Even Jefferson, who had faulted both Washington and Adams for federalizing militia for use against Pennsylvania farmers, when president followed their lead during the Burr Conspiracy and again during the disorders stemming from his controversial Embargo in 1807.[51] Once the leaders of both political parties had turned to federalized militia, the question of employing that military force to maintain or restore domestic tranquillity could hardly arouse as much dispute as a party issue as it had in the 1790s.

Remaining constitutional issues were resolved by the Supreme Court under Chief Justice John Marshall in the 1820s. From time to time militia had been reluctant or unwilling to serve the federal government. President Jefferson had a greater problem in this respect than his predecessors, owing to the extreme un-popularity of the Embargo in New England, and Federalists saw danger in Con-gress's enabling Jefferson to deploy both the army and the militia to enforce the Embargo. The Massachusetts legislature condemned Jefferson's assembling militia at the ports as "irregular, illegal, and inconsistent with the principles of the constitution . . . subversive of the militia system, and highly dangerous to the liberties of the people."[52] In *Houston v. Moore* (1820), the Supreme Court ruled that a militiaman who refused to respond to a federal call-up violated na-tional law. Justice William Johnson, in a concurring opinion, found the central government empowered to stipulate "both the officer and private who shall serve, and to call him forth or punish him for not coming."[53] Even more sweep-ing was the court's unanimous decision in *Martin v. Mott* (1827) that, in the words of Justice Joseph Story, upheld the constitutionality of all portions of the Calling Forth Act of 1795. Addressing concerns about presidential tyranny, Story declared that it must be assumed that chief executives would demonstrate "public virtue and honest devotion to the public interests." He added that con-gressional oversight and frequent elections would ever "guard against usurpa-tion or wanton tyranny."[54]

The settlement of constitutional questions about militia control hardly guaran-teed that Americans would live comfortably with the outcome. Rather, a combi-nation of laws and judicial opinions and the infrequency of federal militia call-ups explain why the militia control issue in peacetime became moot. Since the time of Jefferson's Embargo, the central government has seldom assembled state units under its direction, and in every instance they have acted in conjunction with troops of the United States Army.[55] For ninety years following the Civil War, from 1867 to 1957, although often activated by a state to maintain order, the militia saw no federal service in internal disturbances. Beginning in the latter year and continuing into the next decade, the militia, by then known as the Na-tional Guard, performed short-term duty in enforcing racial integration in the South and restoring order in several northern cities racked by racial violence. Since the 1960s the guard's responsibilities have been carried out under state ju-risdiction, with only a single two-day exception in Arkansas in 1980.[56]

The Antifederalists lost the battle but, in a sense, won the war. They largely prevailed in that the federal government showed little interest in federalizing the militia for domestic reasons or in subjecting it to intensive training overseen by the national military establishment. Presidential administrations have not dis-patched militiamen from one end of America to the other or, typically, kept them on duty for more than a few days to a few months. With the major exception of the Civil War, federal law could normally be upheld and enforced by civil authorities and by the judiciary. Strong sentiments of localism and states' rights also are factors that worked against federalizing the militia and subjecting it to demanding training. So too is the fact that America hardly had an activist government in Washington, D.C., before the twentieth century.

Ironically, state control, a reality during by far the greater part of American history, failed to produce the positive results that its admirers predicted. Although Antifederalists feared that national authorities either would fail to train the militia or would remove it from the states, the truth is, as the Federalists maintained at the time, the states could train their militias above and beyond whatever regulation the central government imposed. The states have displayed scant initiative in providing substantial appropriations and rigorous training for their units—to the point that, by 1861, save for volunteer units (usually elitist in character), the state militias had virtually ceased to exist, especially in the South, and they revived but slowly after the Civil War.[57] The deterioration of the militias provides the explanation why, after the War of 1812, the federal government took into active service in time of national conflict very few militia units as such prior to the twentieth century, preferring instead to fight its wars with the regular army and federal volunteers.

Nor has state control ensured that the militia would be the bulwark of liberty its proponents had claimed it to be from the time of seventeenth-century English opponents of the Stuarts through the colonial period and the Revolution to the Antifederalists and beyond. When called out by state authorities, the militia and the National Guard often have been accused of heavy-handed behavior against various minorities, including Catholics in antebellum cities, labor unionists, Native Americans, Asian Americans, African Americans, and Vietnam War protesters.[58]

The militia and National Guard never served as splendid repositories of freedom and equality. They were highly politicized instruments that reflected majoritarian views in the states, except during Reconstruction. Because governors or legislatures appointed general and staff officers, political affiliation became a critical factor in the selection process; this can be seen as early as 1802 in Tennessee when Andrew Jackson won the post of commanding general over John Sevier. The opportunity to be a member of the guard has always been influenced by political factors. Just as some antebellum northern states limited participation to non-Irish whites, so blacks by 1900 had all but disappeared from the guard in the southern states. Conversely, the National Guard became a haven for countless young men seeking to avoid the draft during the Vietnam War, their ability to join often depending on their having political or social connections.[59]

Since the adoption of the Constitution in 1788, control of the militia has never been an either-or matter. It rarely received a call-up for peacetime domestic duty. Patrick Henry, who doubted that concurrent powers could work, was wrong, but for reasons he could not have foreseen, which have been enumerated in this essay. Rather than becoming agents of oppression in the name of the national government, as Antifederalists feared, the militia and National Guard have more often been agents of state-level discrimination against minorities, in acting against such elements, excluding them from joining the state forces, or both.[60]

James Madison, at the Constitutional Convention and in *The Federalist* No. 10, declared that personal rights were more likely to be endangered by the state governments than by the national government. That is why he included in his initial draft of the Bill of Rights in the House an amendment stating: "No state shall violate the equal rights of conscience, or the freedom of the press, or the trial by jury in criminal cases." (Though this prohibition failed to gain the Senate's approval, Madison considered it "the most valuable amendment on the whole list.")[61] Hence, in still another way the Antifederalists were mistaken in believing, as they did, that freedom was more secure in small, homogeneous republics. History vindicates Madison's new and daring counterargument of 1787: namely, that rights are more secure in large and diverse republics in which majorities are slow to form and thus have difficulty discriminating against minorities. The history of the militia and the National Guard, viewed from a comparison of their federal and state services, points in that direction.

Notes

1. Robert E. Shalhope, "The Ideological Origins of the Second Amendment," *Journal of American History* 69 (1982): 599–614; Lawrence Delbert Cress, "An Armed Community: The Origins and Meaning of the Right to Bear Arms," ibid., 71 (1984): 22–42; Shalhope and Cress, "The Second Amendment and the Right to Bear Arms: An Exchange," ibid., 587–93; Joyce Lee Malcolm, *To Keep and Bear Arms: The Origins of an Anglo-American Right* (Cambridge, Mass., 1994). Cress, rejecting any Second Amendment guarantee of gun ownership as a basic right, sees the amendment solely as reflective of Americans' belief in the citizen's collective obligation to defend society as a member of the militia. Shalhope and Malcolm view the amendment as recognizing both the individual's personal right and the collective rights to possess arms. Unlike Cress and Shalhope, Malcolm, in her very recent

book, pushes the argument back beyond the ratification struggle over the Constitution and the Revolution itself to the English Bill of Rights and subsequent British laws and judicial writings. She contends that the ownership of guns, apart from any responsibility for the common defense, became a well-recognized right in England long before the American Revolution. In time, according to Malcolm, this attitude about gun rights became conventional wisdom in British America, as did certain other dimensions of English common law. It evolved and became generally understood and accepted, regardless of how often or in what form it received articulation. According to Malcolm, this "English influence on the Second Amendment is the missing ingredient that has hampered efforts to interpret its intent correctly." Ibid., xii.

2. Scott Heller, "The Right to Bear Arms: Some Prominent Scholars Are Taking a New Look at the Second Amendment," *Chronicle of Higher Education* 41 (July 21, 1995): A8, A12. See also "An Open Letter on the Second Amendment," a full-page ad from "Academics for the Second Amendment," ibid., Aug. 11, 1995, A23. Thirty-one of the 51 signers are members of the legal academy. For a scathing attack on the individual rights view of the Second Amendment, see Garry Wills, "To Keep and Bear Arms," *New York Review of Books* 42 (Sept. 21, 1995): 62–73.

3. Leonard W. Levy, *Original Intent and the Framers' Constitution* (New York, 1988), 341.

4. T. A. Critchley, *The Conquest of Violence: Order and Liberty in Britain* (London, 1970); Tony Hayter, *The Army and the Crowd in Mid-Georgian England* (London, 1978); Pauline Maier, *From Resistance to Revolution: Colonial Radicals and the Development of American Opposition to Britain, 1765–1776* (New York, 1972); Hiller B. Zobel, *The Boston Massacre* (New York, 1970); John Shy, *Toward Lexington: The Role of the British Army in the Coming of the American Revolution* (Princeton, N.J., 1965).

5. The substantial literature on friction concerning control of provincial forces in wartime includes Jack P. Greene, *The Quest for Power: The Lower Houses of Assembly in the Southern Royal Colonies, 1689–1776* (Chapel Hill, N.C., 1963), 297–309; Don Higginbotham, *The War of American Independence: Military Attitudes, Policies, and Practice, 1753–1789* (New York, 1971), chap. 1; Alan Rogers, *Empire and Liberty: American Resistance to British Authority, 1755–1763* (Berkeley, Calif., 1974); Fred Anderson, *A People's Army: Massachusetts Soldiers and Society in the Seven Years' War* (Chapel Hill, N.C., 1984); Douglas Edward Leach, *Roots of Conflict: British Armed Forces and Colonial Americans, 1677–1763* (Chapel Hill, N.C., 1986).

6. "Virginia Bill of Rights," in S. E. Morison, *Sources and Documents Illustrating the American Revolution,* 2d ed. (Oxford, Eng., 1929), 151; Ruth Bogin, *Abraham Clark and the Quest for Equality in the Revolutionary Era, 1774–1794* (Rutherford, N.J., 1982), 22, 25.

7. Lawrence Delbert Cress, *Citizens in Arms: The Army and the Militia in American Society to the War of 1812* (Chapel Hill, N.C., 1982), 73.

8. George Washington, "Sentiments on a Peace Establishment," *GW: Writings*

26:374–98, quotations on pp. 389–90. An overall assessment of the Revolutionary militia's performance appears in Don Higginbotham, *War and Society in Revolutionary America: The Wider Dimensions of Conflict* (Columbia, S.C., 1988), 106–31.

9. Henry Knox, *A Plan for the General Arrangement of the Militia of the United States* (Philadelphia, 1786). The best treatment of militia reform efforts, including congressional attitudes on the subject, is Cress, *Citizens in Arms,* chap. 5.

10. Articles of Confederation, Article VI.

11. David Ramsay to Knox, March 12, 1786, in Robert L. Brunhouse, ed., *David Ramsay, 1749–1815: Selections from His Writings,* American Philosophical Society, *Transactions,* new ser., 55, pt. 4 (Philadelphia, 1965), 98–99.

12. Washington, "Sentiments on a Peace Establishment," 394.

13. Robert Porterfield, quoted in Harrison E. Ethridge, "Governor Patrick Henry and the Reorganization of the Virginia Militia, 1784–1786," *Virginia Magazine of History and Biography* 85 (1977): 456. Madison, in describing the opposition to the new law as limited to a minority of counties, may have underestimated the number of critics. Madison to Thomas Jefferson, Jan. 22, 1786, in William T. Hutchinson et al., eds., *The Papers of James Madison,* Congressional Series, 17 vols. (Chicago and Charlottesville, Va., 1962–91), 8:478.

14. Robert J. Taylor, *Western Massachusetts in the Revolution* (Providence, 1954), chap. 7; David P. Szatmary, *Shays' Rebellion: The Making of an Agrarian Insurrection* (Amherst, Mass., 1980), chaps. 6–7; Cress, *Citizens in Arms,* 95–97. For recent interpretations of Shays's Rebellion, see Richard D. Brown, "Shays's Rebellion and the Ratification of the Federal Constitution in Massachusetts," in *Beyond Confederation: Origins of the Constitution and American Identity,* ed. Richard Beeman, Stephen Botein, and Edward C. Carter II (Chapel Hill, N.C., 1987), 113–27, and Robert A. Gross, ed., *In Debt to Shays: The Bicentennial of an Agrarian Rebellion* (Charlottesville Va., 1993).

15. Jeremy Belknap, *History of New Hampshire . . . ,* 3 vols. (Boston, 1813), 2:350–54; Alan Taylor, "Regulators and White Indians: The Agrarian Resistance in Post-Revolutionary New England," in Gross, *In Debt to Shays,* 145–50. Debtor violence on a lesser scale also took place in the backcountry from New Jersey to South Carolina. See Richard B. Morris, *The Forging of the Union, 1781–89* (New York, 1987), 264–65.

16. John K. Alexander, *The Selling of the Constitutional Convention: A History of News Coverage* (Madison, Wis., 1990), 20–21, 34, 54–55, 99–101, 142–43, 169–70; Washington to Knox, Dec. 26, 1786, *PGW: Conf. Ser.* 4:482.

17. Max Farrand, ed., *Records of the Federal Convention of 1787,* rev. ed., 4 vols. (New Haven, 1937), 2:182, 323, 326, 330–33, 352, 355–56, 380–81, 382, 384–88, 390.

18. Whitehill, resolution II, in *The Documentary History of the Ratification of the Constitution,* ed. Merrill Jensen, John P. Kaminski, Gaspare J. Saladino, et al., 17 vols. to date (Madison, Wis., 1976–), 2:598. For similar views expressed by Pennsylvania Antifederalist delegate John Smilie, see ibid., 508–09.

19. Henry's speeches, ibid., 10:1277, 1300.

20. "Federal Farmer," ibid., 14:29.

21. George Mason's speech, ibid., 9:937; "Centinel I" and "Dissent of the Minority of the Convention," ibid., 2:162, 635–39; Henry's speech, ibid., 10:1300; Jackson Turner Main, *The Antifederalists: Critics of the Constitution, 1781–88* (Chapel Hill, N.C., 1961), 143–45.

22. Mason's proposed preface to the militia language in Article I, Section 8 of the Constitution declared: "And that the liberties of the people may be better secured against the danger of standing armies in time of peace." Farrand, *Records of the Federal Convention of 1787* 2:616–17.

23. Quotations from "Centinel III," "Philadelphiensis II," and "Federal Farmer," in Jensen, *Documentary History Ratification* 14:60, 253–54, 37–39; "Aristocrotis," "The Government of Nature Delineated," in *The Complete Anti-Federalist,* ed. Herbert J. Storing, 7 vols. (Chicago, 1981), 3:16.9; Jonathan Elliot, comp., *The Debates in the Several State Conventions on the Adoption of the Federal Constitution, as Recommended by the General Convention at Philadelphia in 1787,* 5 vols., 2d ed. (Philadelphia, 1861–63), 2:552; Mason's speech, in Jensen, *Documentary History Ratification* 10:1269–72. A broadside published in Maryland, signed J. T. Chase and J. F. Mercer, endeavored to generate public opposition to the Constitution without a bill of rights, which should include "no whipping militia, nor marching them out of the state, without consent of the general assembly." *Documentary History of the Constitution of the United States of America,* 5 vols. (Washington, D.C., 1894–1905), 4:641–42. Daniel Carroll informed Madison that the broadside had "alarm'd" many people with its "positive assertions." Carroll to Madison, May 28, 1788, in Hutchinson, *Madison Papers* 11:63.

24. Connecticut Antifederalists voiced some of the earliest fears that the federalized militia would become a standing army. Jensen, *Documentary History Ratification* 3:378, 427, 428–29.

25. "Essay by A. Farmer and Planter," in Storing, *Complete Anti-Federalist* 5:2.3. For examples of other predictions of federalized militia outrages, see Jensen, *Documentary History Ratification* 2:509, 13:540. I find no evidence of Antifederalists' quoting an intellectual ally, Sir William Blackstone, who wrote that English militiamen "are not compellable to march out of their countries, unless in case of invasion or actual rebellion, nor in any case compellable to march out of the kingdom" *Commentaries on the Laws of England* 4 vols. (Oxford, 1765–69), 1:399.

26. Jensen, *Documentary History Ratification* 2:508–9, 15:411.

27. For examples of attacks on the concurrent powers idea, see Henry's speeches, ibid., 9:957–58, 10:1276 (quotation), 1309–11, 1419; Mason's speech, ibid., 9:936–37; William Grayson's speech, ibid., 10:1306.

28. For a state-by-state analysis of the tactics and strategies of the Federalists and Antifederalists in the ratifying conventions, see Michael Allen Gillespie and Michael Lienesch, eds., *Ratifying the Constitution* (Lawrence, Kans., 1989).

29. Helen E. Veit, Kenneth R. Bowling, and Charlene Bangs Bickford, eds., *Creating the Bill of Rights: The Documentary Record from the First Federal Congress* (Baltimore, 1991), xi, 14–28; Edward Dumbauld, *The Bill of Rights and What It Means Today* (Norman, Okla., 1957), 173–205. The number can be placed as high as 210 if

one counts duplicate proposals, many of which did not relate to rights but instead focused on structural changes in the central government. In fact, structural "alterations formed a clear majority of both the 210 and the 100." Kenneth R. Bowling, "'A Tub to the Whale': The Founding Fathers and Adoption of the Federal Bill of Rights," *Journal of the Early Republic* 8 (1988): 228.

30. Stuart Leibiger, "James Madison and Amendments to the Constitution, 1787–1789: 'Parchment Barriers,'" *Journal of Southern History* 59 (1993): 441–68.

31. Veit, Bowling, and Bickford, *Creating the Bill of Rights,* 12, 30, 38–39, 182–85, 267. Charles A. Lofgren argues that the conscientious objector issue came up mainly in discussions of the militia rather than in regard to federal armies and navies because both Federalists and Antifederalists considered the Constitution as limiting the citizen's military obligation to compulsory service in the militia. "Compulsory Military Service under the Constitution: The Original Understanding," *William and Mary Quarterly,* 3d ser., 33 (1976): 61–88.

32. Nos. 29, 46, *The Federalist,* ed. Jacob E. Cooke (Middletown, Conn., 1961), 185, 321.

33. Jensen, *Documentary History Ratification* 3:546. For the same point, see Hamilton, *Federalist* No. 27, in Cooke, *Federalist,* 171–75. In *Federalist* No. 28, ibid., 176–80, Hamilton conceded that there might be rare exceptions when force would be needed. Although he was unclear whether the federalized militia or regular troops would be employed in such circumstances, he stated that the decision would be made by the representatives of the people. He went on to say, in *Federalist* No. 29, ibid., 181–87, that the well-trained, properly disciplined federalized militia is preferable because standing armies are more likely threats to liberty.

34. Jensen, *Documentary History Ratification* 9:1014, 1074, 1102, 10:1288 (quotation), 1289, 1293–94, 1296, 1311–12, 1324–25, 1486, 1531. Hamilton and Madison also stressed officers' loyalty to the states that appointed them as a safeguard against federal misuse of the militia, in *Federalist* Nos. 29, 46, in Cooke, *Federalist,* 185, 321–22.

35. Because the Senate did not initially hold open sessions, little is known about the details of its members' response to Madison's amendments. John Randolph, in New York City at the time the future Second Amendment reached the Senate, informed his stepfather, St. George Tucker, that "a Majority of the Senate were for not allowing the militia arms & if two thirds had agreed it would have been an amendment to the Constitution. They [the senators] are afraid that the Citizens will stop their full Career to Tyranny & Oppression." The House held open sessions, which enabled several men from the press to record its debates, though none did so in a full and systematic way. Much of what later appeared in print on the Bill of Rights debates in the House is technical and procedural rather than substantive. See Veit, Bowling, and Bickford, *Creating the Bill of Rights,* 55–213, quotation on p. 293.

36. Ibid., 19, 20. Although Jefferson, from Paris, plied Madison with suggestions for changes in the Constitution, particularly for adopting a national bill of rights, he expressed no reservations about the militia clauses of the document. See especially Jefferson to Madison, Dec. 20, 1787, July 31, 1788, Aug. 28, 1789, in Hutchinson, *Madison Papers* 10:336, 11:212–13, 12:364.

37. "Essays of John DeWitt," in Storing, *Complete Anti-Federalist* 4:3.27–28; Martin's speech, in Jensen, *Documentary History Ratification* 14:290–91; Henry's speech, ibid., 9:957–58; Mason's speech, ibid., 10:1270, 1271; Grayson's speech, ibid., 1306; Henry's speech, ibid., 1535. A Federalist writer correctly noted that the Antifederalists tried to have it both ways: they spoke of the dangers of the federal government's both arming and its failing to arm the state militias. "The Landowner No. X," ibid., 16:267.

38. Richard Henry Lee to [Francis Lightfoot Lee], Sept. 13, 1789, in James Curtis Ballagh, ed., *The Letters of Richard Henry Lee*, 2 vols. (New York, 1911–14), 2:500; Grayson to Henry, Sept. 29, 1789, in William Wirt Henry, ed., *Patrick Henry: Life, Correspondence, and Speeches*, 3 vols. (New York, 1891), 3:406. There is a disappointing lack of information about the public's reactions to Congress's proposed amendments that became the Bill of Rights, probably because there seems to have been strong public support for most of them. The subject is not even mentioned in Donald H. Stewart, *The Opposition Press of the Federalist Period* (Albany, N.Y., 1969), x, based on "nearly all" of the approximately 550 newspapers published between 1789 and 1801. The existing sources are mainly skeletal outlines of legislative measures. The ratification literature is listed and evaluated by Saladino, "The Bill of Rights: A Bibliographic Essay," in *The Bill of Rights and the States: The Colonial and Revolutionary Origins of American Liberties*, ed. Patrick T. Conley and John P. Kaminski (Madison, Wis., 1992), 484–85. The continued strength of Antifederalism in post-1788 Virginia is discussed in Richard Beeman, *The Old Dominion and New Nation, 1788–1801* (Lexington, Ky., 1972), 61–66, and J. Gordon Hylton, "Virginia and the Ratification of the Bill of Rights, 1789–1791," *University of Richmond Law Review* 25 (1991): 433–74. These accounts suggest that Virginia Antifederalists were less interested in the congressionally proposed individual rights amendments than in the absence of amendments that would have specifically restricted the powers of the federal government in its dealings with the states. Richard Henry Lee and William Grayson to the Speaker of the Virginia House of Representatives, Sept. 28, 1789, cited in Beeman, *Old Dominion*, 61. By contrast, Georgia, whose convention unanimously ratified the Constitution, appears to have taken the view, as reflected in the action of its legislature in rejecting the Bill of Rights, that amendments were premature until the people had a chance to observe the actual workings of the new government after the Constitution went into effect. Julia M. Bland, comp., *Georgia and the Federal Constitution: Proceedings of the State Constitutional Convention, and Proceedings of the State Legislature with Respect to the Amendment Proposed by the Untied States Congress on September 25, 1789* (Washington, D.C., 1937), 9–15.

39. George Athan Billias, *Elbridge Gerry: Founding Father and Republican Statesman* (New York, 1976), 232–35; Veit, Bowling, and Bickford, *Creating the Bill of Rights*, 182–84.

40. Henry Knox, "A Plan for the General Arrangements of Militia of the United States," in *Documentary History of the First Federal Congress*, ed. Charlene Bangs Bickford, Kenneth R. Bowling, Linda Grant DePauw, and Helen E. Veit, 14 vols. to date (Baltimore, 1972–), 5:1435–57.

41. In 1794 Secretary of War Knox stated that of 450,000 men in the militias, probably 100,000 at most owned guns or had been supplied them by their states. *American State Papers: Documents, Legislative and Executive, of the Congress of the United States,* class V, *Military Affairs,* 7 vols. (Washington, D.C., 1832–61), 1:70.

42. As early as April 16, 1790, about seven months before Congress formally debated the measure, Senator William Maclay of Pennsylvania predicted that it had no chance of adoption. Kenneth R. Bowling and Helen E. Veit, eds., *The Diary of William Maclay and Other Notes on Senate Debates, March 4, 1789–March 3, 1791* (Baltimore, 1988), 246–47. An excellent summary of the early reaction to Knox's plan is in Richard H. Kohn, *Eagle and Sword: The Federalists and the Creation of the Military Establishment in America, 1783–1802* (New York, 1975), 128–33, Goodhue quotation on p. 131.

43. Charlene Bangs Bickford and Kenneth R. Bowling, *Birth of the Nation: The First Federal Congress, 1789–1791* (Madison, Wis., 1989), 82–83. For the satire on militia legislation see "C. to Mr. Bache," Philadelphia *General Advertiser,* Jan. 20, 1791, copy provided through the courtesy of Kenneth R. Bowling.

44. *Documentary History First Congress* 3:256–69, 379, 484, 631–48.

45. First Congress militia debates, ibid., 14:48–189.

46. *Annals of Congress,* 2d Cong., 1st sess., 103, 418–24, 436, 1392–95; 1 *Statutes at Large* 271.

47. James D. Richardson, ed., *A Compilation of the Messages and Papers of the Presidents, 1789–1897,* 10 vols. (Washington, D.C., 1896–99), 1:329, 345, 372, 385, 410, 428–29, 455; Paul Leicester Ford, ed., *The Writings of Thomas Jefferson,* 10 vols. (New York, 1892–99), 8:409–12; *Annals of Congress,* 9th Cong., 1st sess., 69–70, 141, 327–30.

48. *Annals of Congress,* 2d Cong., 1st sess., 554–55, 574–80; 1 *Statutes at Large* 264. See also for the 1792 militia legislation Robert W. Coakley, *The Role of Federal Military Forces in Domestic Disorders, 1789–1878* (Washington, D.C., 1988), 19–23, and John K. Mahon, *History of the Militia and the National Guard* (New York, 1983), 51–54.

49. There is a sizable literature on the Whiskey Rebellion. Accounts of the martial dimensions are in Kohn, *Eagle and the Sword,* 157–73; Coakley, *Role of Federal Military Forces,* chaps. 3–4; Bennett Milton Rich, *The Presidents and Civil Disorder* (Washington, D.C., 1941), chap. 1. The subject is treated more broadly in Leland D. Baldwin, *Whiskey Rebels: The Story of a Frontier Uprising* (Pittsburgh, 1939); Thomas P. Slaughter, *The Whiskey Rebellion: Frontier Epilogue to the American Revolution* (New York, 1986).

50. 1 *Statutes at Large* 422.

51. W. W. H. Davis, *The Fries Rebellion, 1798–99* (Doylestown, Pa., 1899); Coakley, *Role of Federal Military Forces,* 69–77.

52. 2 *Statutes at Large* 506. Massachusetts General Court, quoted in Coakley, *Role of Federal Military Forces,* 89. Jefferson's military enforcement of the Embargo is criticized in Leonard W. Levy, *Jefferson and Civil Liberties: The Darker Side* (Cambridge, Mass., 1963), chaps. 5–6, and viewed somewhat sympathetically in Dumas

Malone, *Jefferson the President: Second Term, 1805–1809* (Boston, 1974), chaps. 28, 32–35.

53. 5 Wheat. 1, 12–32, 37 (U.S., 1820).

54. 12 Wheat. 19, 29–39 (U.S., 1827).

55. Coakley, *Role of Federal Military Forces,* is a detailed account covering the years through Reconstruction, the first of a projected three-volume work on military interventions.

56. Robin Higham, ed., *Bayonets in the Streets: The Use of Troops in Civil Disturbances,* 2d ed. (Manhattan, Kans., 1989), although comprehensive, focuses on post–Civil War activity. See also Jerry M. Cooper, "Federal Military Intervention in Domestic Disorders," in *The United States Military under the Constitution of the United States, 1789–89,* ed. Richard H. Kohn (New York, 1991), 120–50.

57. Mahon, *History of the Militia and the National Guard,* chaps. 6, 8; Don Higginbotham, "The Martial Spirit in the Antebellum South: Some Further Speculations in a National Context," *Journal of Southern History* 58 (1992): 3–26; Kenneth Otis McCreedy, "Palladium of Liberty: The American Militia System, 1815–1861" (Ph.D. diss., Univ. of California at Berkeley, 1991).

58. Robert Reinders, "Militia and Public Order in Nineteenth-Century America," *Journal of American Studies* 11 (1977): 81–101; Mahon, *History of the Militia and National Guard,* chaps. 6, 8, 16; Stephen E. Ambrose, "The Armed Forces and Civil Disorder," in *The Military and American Society: Essays and Readings,* ed. Ambrose and James A. Barber Jr. (New York, 1972), 241–48. Few state guards displayed more partisan behavior than that of Colorado. See Alvin R. Sunseri, "The Ludlow Massacre: A Study in the Mis-employment of the National Guard," *American Chronicle: A Magazine of History* 1 (1972): 21–28; Clarence C. Clendenen, "Super Police: The National Guard as a Law-Enforcement Agency in the Twentieth Century," in Higham, *Bayonets in the Streets,* 90–91; George G. Suggs Jr., *Colorado's War on Militant Unionism: James H. Peabody and the Western Federation of Miners* (Detroit, 1972); Alan M. Osur, "The Role of the Colorado National Guard in Civil Disturbances," *Military Affairs* 46 (1982): 19–24. At least three Vietnam-era studies address the guard's performance on the home front: *Report of the National Advisory Committee on Civil Disorders* (New York, 1968), 497–506; American Civil Liberties Union, *The National Guard and the Constitution* (New York, n.d.); Renata Adler, "A Reporter at Large," *New Yorker* 46 (Oct. 3, 1970): 40–64, which in some respects remains the most penetrating analysis of the guard's domestic role at the time.

59. Mahon, *History of the Militia and National Guard,* chap. 8, and 149, 212, 236–37, 243, 246, 264; Willard B. Gatewood Jr., "North Carolina's Negro Regiment in the Spanish-American War," *North Carolina Historical Review* 48 (1971): 370–87. On none of the four major occasions the guard was called out by state governors in the 1950s to deal with racial strife are blacks known to have served. W. Ronald Wachs, "'Off Guard': The National Guard and Race Relations in the 1950s" (Ph.D. diss., Univ. of North Carolina at Chapel Hill, 1977), 416. The political activities of the

militia and National Guard, especially at the federal level, are developed in William H. Riker, *Soldiers of the States: The Role of the National Guard in American Democracy* (Washington, D.C., 1957), and Martha Derthick, *The National Guard in Politics* (Cambridge, Mass., 1965).

60. Perhaps the harshest scholarly judgment is in Ambrose, "Armed Forces and Civil Disorder," 241–48.

61. Veit, Bowling, and Bickford, *Creating the Bill of Rights,* 13, 41, 19, 188.

6 | *Military Education before West Point*

I HAVE HAD A LONG AND REWARDING relationship with the United States Military Academy that began with a lecture that I gave there in 1973. I was a visiting professor at that institution in 1975–76, when I helped plan and organize a symposium on the bicentennial of the American Revolution. Subsequently I edited a volume, based on the papers given there, *Reconsiderations on the Revolutionary War,* published in 1978. I did a second "tour of duty" as a visiting professor in 1998–99. Soon after my return to Chapel Hill, I took part in planning another bicentennial event at West Point, this one to commemorate the founding of the military academy in 1801. One of my former doctoral students, Professor Robert M. S. McDonald of the academy's history department, played the major role as architect of the commemorative undertaking, which took place October 31–November 3, 2001.

My presentation looked at European and American ideas on military education in the century or more before the founding of the military academy. Certainly there is little evidence that Americans had any remarkable new ideas on the education of men for professional service, but I discovered that American officers in the Revolutionary War were much better acquainted with European military thought than I had realized. In fact, I contended that Washington, the most persistent advocate of such an academy from the time of the War of Independence, saw such a school as having twofold benefit: it would inform cadets of the most recent European military thought and practice, and it would foster a sense of nationality, of American oneness, by drawing student-officers together from the different parts of the country. Washington's desire to foster national cohesion also explains his paramount motive for seeking a national university. It is ironic that Washington failed in his efforts to gain the approval of Congress for these two institutions when he was able to do so much as commanding general in the War of Independence and as president of the United States to create a sense of nationhood.

Perhaps the most important papers at this gathering, in terms of Jefferson as founder, dealt with his motives, given his seeming indifference to many matters military in the 1790s and even earlier. A forceful argument has it that Jefferson created the academy, in part at least, because he was out to republicanize the officer corps, which he saw as a bastion of aristocratic Federalism. A school that was open to all and operated largely at government expense would make in the long run an army that was more politically healthy. A second contention brought out at the conference was that Jefferson wished to shape an educational institution with his own ideas about the curriculum, which would include science, mathematics, engineering, and languages. Such graduates of West Point, both in the army and later on their return to civilian life, would make significant contributions to American society. In all likelihood, the president and Congress acted from multiple motives. My essay, along with others from the symposium, is found in Robert M. S. McDonald, ed., *Thomas Jefferson's Military Academy: Founding West Point* (Charlottesville, Va.: University of Virginia Press, 2004) and is reprinted here.

———— ·•· ————

TWO CENTURIES OF discussion and debate about the nature of military education had taken place in the Western world before President Thomas Jefferson established the United States Military Academy at West Point, New York, in 1802. Jefferson, himself never a soldier, had been interested generally in state-supported education as early as his years in the Virginia legislature during the War of Independence. But his focus had been on education for civilian boys and young men. His elaborate scheme (it failed to secure adoption) had called for a pyramid of institutions. Male students, depending on their performance or financial means, would progress from elementary (girls were included at this first level) and then grammar schools to the capstone institution: the College of William and Mary. To Jefferson, a liberally educated citizenry provided the key to successful republican government.[1] When, after 1800, he finally showed an interest in a national military school, his desire to strengthen republican ideals and practices again came into play. In fact, Jefferson's West Point came into being before the more famous military schools of the nineteenth century, which resulted from the profound changes in warfare during the Napoleonic era.

And yet, given the emphasis of military historians and other students of military education, one might think that officers received little or no academic training before the Prussians created their famous War School. Certainly, whatever institutions that existed get short shrift. Undoubtedly influential scholars such as Samuel P. Huntington and other American apostles of Emory Upton have played a role in creating this image. Of course, Prussia exercised a profound influence. In 1807, following its disastrous defeat by Napoleon at Jena and the Treaty of Tilsit, which imposed humiliating terms, Prussia shook up its military establishment. It opened military careers to seventeen-year-olds by competitive examination and revamped military schooling, with its capstone eventually being the War College, associated with Gerhard Johann Scharnhorst, then the best-known military writer in Prussia, and with Carl von Clausewitz, the future father of theoretical and strategic studies. The institution came to prescribe a three-year course in strategy and other advanced subjects. Clausewitz, at one time its director, wrote his study *On War,* which reached print posthumously in 1832. His quest for fundamental strategic principles took the form of comparing the wars of the French Revolution with those of the old regime.

If Clausewitz failed to offer a satisfactory fare, students of conflict had more down-to-earth alternatives, including the Swiss writer and member of Napoleon's staff Antoine-Henri Jomini, whose *Summary of the Art of War* bristled with maxims about maneuver, attack points, and lines of communication. American officers, including those with West Point educations and West Point educators, found little of relevance in the period before the French upheaval. And surprising as it may seem to us, that included the War of Independence and the life of America's one Great Captain, George Washington.[2]

If Jomini and somewhat later Clausewitz and their interpreters dominated American military writing and teaching, what did eighteenth-century Americans know and think about military education at the time of the imperial wars, the War of Independence, and the subsequent years before the creation of the United States Military Academy in 1802? Americans knew about the rise of the nation-state in the early modern period and the wars that it spawned from the sixteenth century to their own era in the late eighteenth century. They were also aware that there occurred simultaneously what historians now call the "Military Revolution." Part of this change can be explained by technological advances that made for more destructive weaponry, but part of it was owing to the need for a more bureaucratic apparatus to harness the engine of the state to collect heavier taxes and to supply armies and navies made larger by the succession of wars involving the nation-states over nearly three centuries.[3] An examination of military education in Europe and America before the French Revolution shows that on both continents governments and their military men were aware, however imprecisely, of choices in military education between a growing emphasis on institutional learning and a tutorial tradition. In America and possibly elsewhere, these tensions remained alive and well at the end of the century—and even, in the United States, after the founding of the military academy at West Point.

Military schools emerged to provide more systematic training for larger armed forces that now fought and maneuvered in ways brought about by technological innovations. In 1616 John of Nassau, from a distinguished Dutch military family, created an academy for officers, one of the earliest and most influential for its time. His students already had available a body of published soldierly literature in their own language, including at least one illustrated drill manual. Emphasizing distinct, numbered steps for loading muskets and volley fire, the Dutch publications on infantry tactics went through various editions in Danish, German, French, and English. Dutch experts traveled to numerous friendly states to impart the new methods. Gustav II Adolph of Sweden borrowed and revised these tactical reforms, demonstrating their great potential. A 1726 German military manual showed the continued influence of the Dutch for loading and shooting a musket. In 1653 Prussia established a cadet corps to train officer elites in military science. France, Austria, and Denmark soon followed, as did Russia in 1731.

Thinkers and teachers about war also lavished time on geometric fortifications as the infantry-dominated battlefield increasingly receded in relative importance. In western Europe at least, what might be termed fortress warfare dominated the landscape. Huge, geometric structures signaled the significance of military architecture and artillery. Officers had to know how to defend or besiege and capture fortresses. Technical awareness became imperative as artillery and engineering, together or separately, became a distinct branch or component of armies by the eighteenth century. In time serious soldiers everywhere talked and read about Sébastien Le Prestre de Vauban, Louis XIV's great military engineer, who besides his influence as a teacher and writer conducted countless sieges and drafted plans for a hundred or more fortresses and other defense works. To Vauban, such citadels served a dual purpose: they guarded against foreign invasion and served as staging points for taking the offensive. His polygonal forts with their protruding bastions dotted the landscape of western Europe, especially in the Low Countries and northern Italy, and could occasionally be found in central and eastern Europe as well.[4]

Sieges and siegecraft characterized the climactic campaigns of the Seven Years' War in Britain's thirteen colonies against such French strongholds as Carillion (later Ticonderoga) and Louisbourg. Colonial and British detachments even erected Vaubanesque forts of their own in the wilderness, such as Fort William Henry in New York and Fort Ligonier in Pennsylvania. Siege warfare also formed a major component of the critical stages of the War of Independence, a conflict that began with the siege of Boston in 1775 and ended, for all practical purposes, with the siege of Yorktown in 1781. In between those events were the sieges of Savannah and Charleston, which, unlike the first-mentioned ones, ended disastrously for Americans. But Nathanael Greene and his militia allies used such tactics in reducing several British posts in the South Carolina backcountry. The longest siege of the war, the French and Spanish investment of Gibraltar, brought 40,000 men and fifty ships to bear on the rocky fortress, but after three and a half years it ended in failure.[5]

Although military schools became more important in the eighteenth century, it is difficult to generalize about them in terms of their objectives and course of study. And educational institutions, then and now, change for better or worse over time. In Russia, Prussia, and Austria, they served as institutions for inculcating or reinforcing the culture of the nobility. In Russia the French language, fencing, music, and other cultural arts found their way into the course of study, and the minimum age for entry in 1766 was lowered from thirteen to five because of the fear that older boys might already have acquired bad habits and materialistic values before admission. But until they reached the age of nine, boys were taught by women because they still needed "maternal sweetness." (The Russian Cadet Corps remained an institution under firm imperial direction until its demise in the Russian Revolution of 1918.)

Similar thinking influenced Prussia's Berlin Cadet Corps, where the age requirement dipped from thirteen to ten. At times academic standards looked quite rigorous, but many boys complained of being ordered by Frederick II to enroll, and the hazing of newcomers seems to have been a common practice, as would be true later at the United States Military Academy. Some of the more talented young scholars received career options, possibly what we might call the civil service, including the diplomatic branch. Maria Theresa of Austria, like her royal contemporaries elsewhere, saw her newly created military school, the Wiener Neustadt Academy, as a training ground for the next generation of nobles. If the institution lived up to the claims for it, the school may well have been one of the best in that day, with its study of drill, fortifications, artillery, mathematics, and foreign languages.[6]

In Britain fewer opportunities existed for formal military education than in these Continental kingdoms. The only military school of note before the American Revolution was the Royal Military Academy at Woolwich, founded in the 1740s, which focused on officers for the artillery and engineers. If technical military education received the greatest emphasis in Russia, Prussia, and elsewhere, it seems to have been all that Woolwich offered, except for languages. Not until about the time of West Point's founding did Britain have a formal institution, Sandhurst, to train infantry and cavalry officers.[7]

It would have been unthinkable for the British elite to have attended Woolwich and entered an inferior branch of the army. High rank and field command did not go to officers with such a background. At best, writes William B. Willcox, "any such quasi-specialist who rose above the junior grades was as likely as not to find himself governing a city or commanding an expedition."[8] One reads of rare exceptions. Major General William Phillips of the artillery came from modest origins, a sound officer who earned the respect of his social superiors, as did another commoner, Major General James Robertson, who served as military governor of New York City between 1780 and 1783.[9] One reads biographies of Britain's ranking generals in the War of American Independence—Gage, Howe, Clinton, Burgoyne, Cornwallis, and Carleton—without learning much if anything of their having formal military schooling in their home country. If an officer really wanted even a smattering of time in the classroom, he might do as Cornwallis did when the young officer traveled to Turin in the Kingdom of Sardinia, where he entered the military academy, reputedly one of the best in Europe. Doubtless he profited from the experience, even though he stayed only a few months and received special treatment because his father was a friend of King George II's son the duke of Cumberland, the general who put down the Scottish Rebellion of '45 in ruthless fashion.[10]

Another junior officer enrolled at Brunswick, and two more studied at Caen, including the son of General Jeffery Amherst, who gained fame in the conquest of Canada. The complexity of our subject is reflected in a comparison between Britain and Prussia. The absence of a stigma upon an officer with a formal military education is seen in Frederick's Prussia, with a third of its generals having been in the Berlin Cadet Corps.[11]

In any case, it is clear that France under the leadership of Choiseul, Saint-Germain, and Gribeauval led the way in military innovation and education in the latter half of the eighteenth century.[12] Low-level academies had existed for years, but by the eve of the French Revolution a variety of advanced specialized schools had appeared. Reformers were sounding off well before 1789, or even 1763, the year of France's humiliating treaty concluding the Seven Years' War. The heated discussions over field artillery and cannon design have been called the "Star Wars" debate of its time. French military reformers, according to Ken Adler, "refashioned the artillery service into a new kind of military machine that, in conjunction with the Revolutionary mass armies, spearheaded the destruction of the old Europe under the command of their disciple, Napoleon Bonaparte." (Americans would later be mindful of these innovations.) More than any other influence, the French inspired armies of the time to increase the use of artillery as opposed to other arms, a greater proportional shift than would be witnessed again until the twentieth century.[13]

A variety of officer-training schools also exposed young officers to new ideas about the use of light infantry, to the mixed order of line and column, and to the separation of armies into large administrative components, which during the wars of the French Revolution would become combat divisions. Napoleon, to be sure, was hardly a typical general. But his early soldierly career shows the possibilities available. He attended the Royal Military School at Brienne, where during those five years he gained some of his most important ideas. Graduating in 1784, he entered the École Militaire in Paris, completing its two-year program in one. Three years later he matriculated at Auxonne, studying at the preeminent artillery school in France.[14]

Even though military education differed in some measure from one country to another, with the French certainly out in front after 1763, some commonalties held true for a majority of them during much of the period in question—ones not yet discussed. Rulers displayed an intense interest in military schools and their officer corps in general. The preference for officers from the nobility reflected the monarch's desire to increase the loyalty of the highest elites to the reigning monarch. The notion stands out with particular clearness in looking at Louis XIV, Frederick II, Maria Theresa, and George II.

In a sense, the crown's behavior retarded the development of creative military leadership. Senior officers often remained in the dark as to national goals and planning, including orders given to other generals in the same campaign, a characteristic of Frederick II's dealings with his uniformed underlings. For an army or naval officer to cross the king, or to be perceived as engaging in a political flirtation with the king's opponents, or to bring humiliating defeat to his arm of the service could result in court-martial or death. Although the American Revolutionaries eschewed monarchy, the early days of independence witnessed concerns about where the loyalty of military men rested. Was their allegiance to Washington, or, later, to the Federalists, or, later still, to President Jefferson and the Republicans? And was there danger that an American military school would be politicized?

Many officers as late as the American Revolution and afterward either had no opportunity for formal military schooling or rejected the concept even if such a possibility existed. Professionalism as the word would be used in the nineteenth century did not exist, even for those who gained valuable know-how from Woolwich, the Wiener Neustadt Academy, or similar schools. At best, officers were highly proficient technicians. A general was born, not made, declared Marshal Saxe, the famous eighteenth-century French commander. "Application rectifies ideas," he pronounced, "but does not furnish a soul, for that is the work of nature." These views he shared with other military writers, including Henry Lloyd and the comte de Guibert.[15]

In an era before Clausewitz and Jomini, generals had no strategic or theoretical doctrine to draw on. They did not know how to analyze a problem from different vantage points and seek the best of several approaches. If they saw themselves as professionals, they looked amateurish to a later age. Sir Henry Clinton, alone among Britain's military commanders in the War of Independence, seemed capable of some measure of analytical thinking.[16] But even he, like his colleagues, had no clear understanding of the difference between strategy and tactics. Indeed, strategy seems to have been a word little used. Stratagem appears, but usually in the context of describing a ruse or a surprise. If a general spoke of grand tactics, as opposed to elementary tactics, which applied to the battlefield, he likely meant the movement of armies over large spaces, outside or beyond the field of action.

General John Burgoyne, who lost an army at Saratoga, illustrates the deficiencies of British military leadership. He plunged into the wilderness of upper New York in 1777 without a sense of the obstacles that lay ahead. He lacked a clear-cut objective for the campaign. And he failed to seek any agreement with General Sir William Howe in New York City as to how their respective forces would cooperate with or complement each other. "Gentleman Johnny" brought with him through the woods and thickets along the Hudson more than a dozen wagons carrying his own personal wardrobe, store of wine, and other personal effects, as well as those of his mistress. And yet Burgoyne predicted an easy triumph over the Americans because, as he put it, the rebels lacked "men of military science."[17]

Burgoyne, Clinton, and the rest of the ranking generals in America had never held major commands, nor had they seen active service for many years. To a degree, Thomas Gage stands out as an exception, for he held the post of commander in chief in North America from 1763 to 1775. But his duties were strictly administrative until he arrived in Boston after the tea party and the Intolerable Acts. Certain generals even found ways during their assignments to put down the American rebellion to obtain leaves of absence to return to England for a time. Whatever their seemingly valid excuses, such as to see a dying wife, the truth is that a desire to lobby for a better command or to attend Parliament usually provides the real explanation. The records of those officers who commanded British naval forces in America hardly excelled those of the generals in terms of hands-on commitment during their careers. Richard Howe, Augustus Keppel, and Charles Hardy had not been before the mast for fifteen years or more prior to the colonial uprising.

In fact, the tutorial or apprenticeship method provided most officers with the tools of their trade, just as it did for young men in fields such as law and medicine. Despite the existence in Europe of some medical schools and institutions for legal training, including the British Inns of Court, direct observation and hands-on training predominated in all fields.[18] Observers noted repeatedly that one learned soldiering from fighting in battles and not from sitting in the classroom. For the young man with military aspirations or for the father who had them for his son, some experts recommended the provision of toy soldiers (metal ones were available by 1600 or so). Instead of childish things like wooden horses, dolls, and toy carts, a boy by the age of ten might be knowledgeable about drawing up companies, posting sentinels, and storming walled cities. Despite Frederick II's heavy investment in the Berlin Cadet Corps and lesser institutions, most Prussian officers considered assignments in the field to be the most valuable experience of all.[19]

George Washington, as the youthful commander of the Virginia Regiment in the Seven Years' War, illustrated how the tutorial system worked at its best. He observed the command techniques of such able British superiors as Colonel Henry Bouquet and General John Forbes, he took notes on useful ideas and information, he read military treatises, and he took fencing lessons. He could not take the so-called grand tour of Europe, an experience available to British and Continental officers. To the extent that other nations permitted it, which depended on the relations between a young man's kingdom and the states he proposed to visit, an officer might take in a military school, an army encampment, a fortress, and a famous battlefield such as Bergen (Clinton went over the terrain for four hours), as well as engaging in a series of conversations with foreign officers—in the course of much socializing—on their soldierly profession.

Washington, denied the chance to travel in Europe, made the most of his opportunities to develop informative relationships with British officers in America, including Colonel Thomas Gage, with whom he subsequently corresponded. Gage became his first military antagonist in the Revolutionary War because Washington commanded the New England forces that besieged Gage's troops in Boston.[20] What he learned from Gage and other crown officers in the 1750s he then imparted to the officers who served under him. No doubt Washington also drew on accounts from his brother Lawrence, who held a royal commission for a time and led Virginia troops that participated in the Cartagena expedition against the Spanish in the early 1740s. In his Mount Vernon office, Washington placed only one painting on the wall: Lawrence in his crimson regimentals, where it still hangs today. In particular, Washington stressed to his Virginia officers military reading, firm discipline, uniform dress, and new drill techniques introduced into the British army by the duke of Cumberland. Since Washington and his Virginia Regiment received high praise from several able royal officers, it is safe to conclude that he had learned a good deal. And his letters show that he enjoyed military life, even to the point of trying hard but unsuccessfully to obtain a British regular commission and to have his Virginia Regiment placed on the regular establishment.[21]

Reading constituted a form of military education that seems to have had fairly wide appeal to officers in Europe and America, whether they attended war schools or pursued the tutorial method of Washington and Sir Henry Clinton and many other British officers. But it is difficult to measure the effect of such literature on the ability of bookish officers to influence their peers or to conduct campaigns in ways that reflected their learning. Ira D. Gruber provides helpful accounts of the British army, based particularly on new information about Sir Henry. Several decades after William B. Willcox published his magisterial biography of Clinton, *Portrait of a General,* significant sources on the general's reading habits became available to historians: eleven "small leather-bound books containing notes and reflection on nearly thirty years" of military reading. Gruber's study of the inventories of sixteen other officers' libraries reveals reading tastes remarkably similar to those of Clinton. After the mid-eighteenth century, these Britons increasingly devoured French writings on war, which had not been the case in the previous fifty years.[22] Clinton hardly stood alone in recording his thinking about his reading, nor did he lack company in digesting, in addition to the standard exercise manuals, an array of literature that included histories, biographies, memoirs. Fluent in French, Clinton agreed with his colleague who proclaimed the French language an essential pedagogical tool because the "best modern books upon our profession are written in that language."[23]

A comparison of Clinton's reading with that of Washington is worthwhile because during the War of Independence, Clinton served as deputy British commander in chief or as the supreme commander from 1776 to 1782, roughly paralleling Washington's slightly longer tenure as commander in chief of the Continental army. Gruber persuasively argues that "Clinton's actions in America do seem to have been remarkably consistent with his ideas about war" recorded in his reading notes.[24] He advocated building support among the civilian population—the loyalists—and he recognized the importance of seapower. He displayed a reluctance to engage in large-scale battle unless he had a numerical advantage and an opportunity to flank the enemy. He admired generals who achieved their ends by maneuver and avoidance of battle.

Clinton, who owned or consumed more than thirty military tomes, had more reading material available than did Washington, and we lack the kind of notes for Washington that Clinton used to preserve his interpretation of his reading. But it is certain that Washington read a good deal, and that in both the Seven Years' War and the Revolutionary conflict he encouraged his subordinates to do so as well. On the whole, Washington was much better read than we have realized, not only on warfare but on other topics as well. He informed Jonathan Boucher, who tutored his stepson, Jackie Custis, that "I conceive a knowledge of books is the basis upon which all other knowledge is to be built." In time, he possessed a library of over 900 volumes.[25]

For Washington what would be an ongoing process for many years of acquiring military literature began as early as age twenty-three when the recently appointed colonel of the Virginia Regiment ordered from London Humphrey Bland's *Treatise of Military Discipline*—"Old Humphrey," as generations of officers referred to that work, which went through nine editions. This British staple for drill and regulations had sat on the shelves of Lawrence Washington's study, where his young brother probably first encountered it. Now he sought his own copy, and only a month later he encouraged his officers of the Virginia Regiment to do the same. Reminding them that there was more to being an officer "than the Title," he said, "Let us read." "Bland's and other treatises . . . will give us the wished for information." For the colonel the message became a refrain. "Leisure hours" should be devoted to the "study of your profession."[26] By the time Washington resigned his commission as the war wound down on the Virginia frontier and as he prepared to marry Martha Custis and bring his bride and her children to Mount Vernon, his "knowledge in the Military Art," as he phrased it, had grown substantially. Since he knew the names of the great captains of history, it is reasonable to assume he had heard a good deal about them, possibly even encountering books covering their careers. He ordered from his business agent in Britain statue busts of Julius Caesar, Oliver Cromwell, Marlborough, Charles XII of Sweden, Prince Eugene of Austria, and Frederick the Great. He found them to be unavailable, but he later acquired biographies of Charles and Frederick.[27]

Washington must have been encouraged by the outburst of military publishing in 1775 as Americans prepared for war. The quality of some of these guides and manuals, usually appearing in pamphlet form, is questionable, but Americans snapped them up because, for the time being at least, such works were scarce. The printers invariably gave Washington complimentary copies, beginning when he was a member of the Continental Congress, some weeks before he received his appointment as commander in chief of the Army of the United Colonies on June 15, 1775. Hugh Henry Ferguson dedicated his edition of a British work, *Military Instructions for Officers Detached in the Field,* to Washington, the Virginian's first honor of that nature. Washington himself began to purchase military tracts. He joined other subscribers to finance the publication of Thomas Hanson's *Prussian Evolutions.* Committing to buy eight copies, which arrived on May 20, 1775, he also opened his purse for several other military tracts while still in Congress, which he failed to name, merely describing them as "5 books—Military." One gets a good sense of what Washington had read—or what he considered the best of his reading—from his response to sought-after advice from Colonel William Woodford of Virginia. As for Washington's recommendations, he replied on November 10, 1775, with a list of five works, all part of his library: Bland's *Treatise of Military Discipline;* the comte de Turpin de Crissé, *An Essay on the Art of War,* an English translation; Roger Stevenson, *Military Instructions for Officers Detached in the Field;* Captain Louis de Jeney, *The Partisan; or, The Art of Making War in Detachment,* another translation; and William Young, *Manoeuvres, or Practical Observations on the Art of War.*[28]

The absence of reading notes limits what we can detect about these books' influence on Washington, but we see his awareness that French specialists were now au courant. We can say that his superiors in the 1758 Fort Duquesne campaign, General Forbes and Colonel Henry Bouquet, a Swiss soldier of fortune, recommended Crissé, who urged his readers to study military writings and to be mindful of adequate procurement and logistics, topics often neglected. The French essayist Jeney underscored the growing European interest in light infantry and skirmishers, who might be deployed behind enemy lines to engage in partisan or guerrilla activity.[29] Marshal Saxe's *Reveries,* another favorite of Forbes and Bouquet, influenced the Forbes campaign against Fort Duquesne, and likely made an impression on their subordinate Washington. These writers maintained that even infantry lines could move effectively through rough, uneven terrain if they had received some light infantry training. Though committed to a traditional war, with an army built largely along European lines, Washington put a premium on logistical considerations and recognized the value of Jeney's message, which doubtless underscored lessons he had learned on the frontier, especially in the Braddock disaster. Certainly he put to good use Daniel Morgan's regiment and other rifle-carrying units from the backcountry, and he temporarily detached Morgan's unit to assist General Horatio Gates in the campaign against Burgoyne. It was the corps, reported Gates, that "the army of General Burgoyne are most afraid of." By 1779 every Continental regiment received some light infantry training. That year a special light force under General Anthony Wayne captured the British post at Stony Point, New York, in a night attack.[30]

If Washington carried his prized books with him throughout the war, even buying "a green baise bookcase" to hold them, so did many other officers bring along the primers of the soldier's profession.[31] Numerous officers had served in the militia in the Seven Years' War, including Benjamin Lincoln, Philip Schuyler, and Benedict Arnold. Several former British officers residing in the colonies received commissions from the Continental Congress, including Generals Charles Lee, Horatio Gates, and Richard Montgomery. Nathanael Greene, Henry Knox, Anthony Wayne, and John Sullivan, too young for service in the 1750s, later served in the militia and took a serious interest in military reading and training. Greene frequented Knox's Boston bookstore in the early 1770s and discussed the latest books then being consumed by British officers. Greene seemed to admire most Marshal Saxe and Frederick II. Knox agreed with Greene that one turned first to Saxe for the principles of war, but, for his growing personal interests, artillery and engineering, he held up the famous Vauban and John Muller, "Professor of Artillery and Fortification" at Woolwich, as the preeminent authorities.[32]

At times Washington's generals turned to military history to answer questions the commander in chief put to them concerning a course of action for the army, a reflection perhaps of his continued emphasis on the importance of "the study of Military authors."[33] For example, after American reversals at Brandywine and Germantown in Pennsylvania in 1777, Washington queried them as to whether the army should strike back, possibly continuing the campaign into the early winter, or whether it should go into quarters until the spring; and if so, should they make their encampment relatively near the enemy in Philadelphia. Their written responses brimmed with references to the maxims and conduct of Pyrrhus, Marius, Maurice, Charles XII, Marlborough, Saxe, the duke of Brunswick, and Montcalm, along with others, including Hannibal.[34] Not surprisingly, Greene, probably better read than any of Washington's other senior American officers with the possible exception of Knox, cited authorities from Hannibal to Frederick II in arguing for suspending campaigning and taking up secure positions relatively close to Howe's army.[35]

Captain Johann Ewald, a Prussian officer, believed that Americans took military reading more seriously than their opponents, "who consider it sinful to read a book or to think of learning anything during the war." He discovered that captured American haversacks contained "the most excellent military books translated in their language" such as "the *Instructions* of the great Frederick to his generals," which "I have found more than one hundred times. Moreover, several among their officers had designed excellent small handbooks and distributed them in the army." German and British officers preferred to fill their portmanteaus with bags of powder, sweet-scented hair dressing, and playing cards.[36]

Ewald went on to make a point about Washington's army that is not now appreciated. At the time of his writing, December 1777, the war had been going on for only two and a half years, and he had witnessed two recent American reversals, at Brandywine and Germantown in southeastern Pennsylvania. Yet he could write that the Americans have "excellent officers."[37] A few weeks later another German, Captain Johann Heinrichs of the Hessian Jaeger Corps, also saw real potential in the American army. He informed his minister of state that it would take only "time and good leadership to make . . . [it] formidable."[38] In some ways, Washington and Congress had wanted an army that resembled its British counterpart and other European establishments. Although America had no congressionally mandated military school, what I have described as the tutorial method seems to have worked reasonably well. Officers' experience with battles and campaigns was already extensive—Boston, Quebec, Long Island, Manhattan, Trenton, Princeton, Brandywine, Germantown, and Saratoga. Americans were reading, as Ewald observed, at just about the point in time when Washington's councils of war were responding with historical allusions to his quest for advice on whether to conclude the campaign of 1777 before the onset of winter.

Washington, like European monarchs, wanted an officer corps composed of elites, or of the better sort at least. He did so at the time when in Prussia and France men outside the nobility were being denied entry into the military and others, who were already officers, were being removed at the conclusion of wars.

The very social character of America meant that it would be impossible for Washington to confine his officer corps even to an American kind of aristocracy, a homegrown one based on wealth, education, and lifestyle, although officers such as the Monroes, Marshalls, Laurens, Hamiltons, Schuylers, Livingstons, and Habershams showed that many men above the rank and file could at least measure up to what Washington called gentlemen. For, like his European counterparts, Washington believed that only gentlemen would likely have dedication, commitment, and respect from those they commanded. Colonel Henry Beekman Livingston, frustrated because he could not recruit enough officers who bore the good marks of family and high character, suggested that he be allowed to enlist adventurers from Canada.[39] Washington sensed the likelihood of political opposition to the idea, especially since he felt inundated by foreign officers sent over from Europe by American diplomats.

Even so, the great influx of foreign officers in the Continental army also gave it added military experience and eighteenth-century-style professionalism. Although some foreign appointments were extremely controversial, because a few Europeans were given preferential rank and station over able American senior officers such as Knox and Greene and also because some were both arrogant and incompetent, it is fair to say that a substantial percentage were sound and gained the respect of Washington and his lieutenants.[40] This admixture of Europeans is an example of how the American officer corps bore some resemblance to the polyglot nature of European armies. In addition to the numerous Frenchmen, there were Germans, Poles, and, among other nationalities, at least one Russian. Some of these men were typical European soldiers of fortune, having served in several different European armies. Charles Lee, for instance, the former British army major, spent time in various capacities with the Polish, Turkish, and Russian armies before settling in Virginia in the early 1770s.[41]

Aside from the marquis de Lafayette, whose influential political connections helped cement the Franco-American alliance of 1778, the greatest foreign contributions came from Friedrich Wilhelm von Steuben, the Prussian, and a cluster of French engineers, especially Antoine-Jean-Louis Le Bègue de Presle Duportail. Steuben's arrival coincided with a growing concern on Washington's part. Although there was now almost a surfeit of military treatises available after two years of war (and varying decidedly in quality), the commander in chief needed a manual to simplify and codify standards and procedures for the Continental army. Indeed, "a regular system of discipline, manoeuvers, evolutions, [and] regulations" was imperative.[42] He turned to Steuben, who had extensive experience as both an infantry and a staff officer under Frederick II. Working closely with Washington and other officers, Steuben mixed practices from the British, French, and Prussian armies, adapting them to the backgrounds and needs of Continental soldiers. He slowly formulated his ideas for such a book, experimenting with various procedures as he drilled the Continentals during the Valley Forge winter and into the following campaigning season. He also drew upon his staff experience in Europe in spelling out the duties and responsibilities of regimental officers and men, from the commanding officer to the lowest level of the rank and file. Once Steuben had completed his manuscript, Washington voiced his general approval, but he requested greater clarity of diction because the translation of Steuben's prose into English left some matters obscure. He also made additions and alterations before recommending to Congress that Steuben's revised draft be adopted, published, and distributed throughout the army.[43] Steuben had simplified the manual of arms, added more bayonet training, increased the pace of march, and instituted greater battlefield flexibility. It won the praise of both American and foreign officers.

The Washington-Steuben collaboration resulted in the most important piece of American military writing to come out of the war, a conflict that generated a remarkable political literature from men like Thomas Jefferson, John Adams, and James Madison. There were no comparable military treatises, no parallel to the volumes of Clausewitz or Jomini that emerged from the Napoleonic era. Even so, Steuben's *Regulations for the Order and Discipline of the Troops of the United States* met a critical need in handsome fashion. The first edition comprised three thousand copies of what became known as the Blue Book, since most of them were bound in blue paper boards, although Steuben insisted that Washington's personal copy be tooled in gold leaf with leather binding.[44] As for Steuben himself, his value to the army continued to grow. Appointed inspector general, he functioned as the army's chief administrator and became, in effect, Washington's chief of staff.

As for the French volunteers, they contributed most significantly to the American corps of engineers. There were fewer needs in the artillery owing to the talents of the self-educated Knox, who headed the American artillery throughout the war. The chevalier de Mauduit Du Plessis, a notable exception, graduated from the prestigious Grenoble artillery school and proved himself to Washington and Knox at Germantown and Fort Mifflin and demonstrated his teaching abilities at Valley Forge.[45] Doubtless Knox and Colonel John Lamb, a fine New York artillery officer, shared the contents of their personal libraries with their fellow officers. Time and again that arm of the service proved its effectiveness—at

Trenton, Monmouth, Yorktown, and elsewhere, earning the praise of the French artillerists, unexcelled in Europe, as the two armies conducted the siege of Yorktown. The chevalier de Chastellux, the second-ranking French officer, exclaimed that his troops marveled at the American artillery's "extraordinary progress." Knox's men had approximately as many heavy weapons as the French army commander, the comte de Rochambeau, who reportedly had already participated in fourteen sieges.[46]

By contrast, the French engineers proved indispensable to Washington, for Americans were without talent or experience in that military branch. The French minister of war, Saint-Germain, ensured that the American engineers would not be plagued with incompetents or fortune seekers by, in effect, assigning four highly qualified officers to Washington's army. Louis Le Bègue de Presle Duportail, their ranking officer, so impressed Congress that he received promotion to brigadier general and command of the engineers, which put him on an equal footing with General Knox of the artillery. Duportail then recruited able engineers from France and received superb assistance from Colonel Tadeusz Kosciuszko, a Pole who received his engineering education in France.[47]

Duportail himself had his own library and used his tomes in providing some classroom instruction at West Point late in the war. By the standards of the day, the corps of engineers may well have been the ablest branch of the Continental army. It constructed bridging trains and temporary and permanent fortifications (some of their constructions at West Point and across the river at Constitution Island can be seen today, especially Fort Putnam, which has been completely rebuilt). Combat engineers, called sappers and miners, built the entrenchments and tunnels that allowed Knox's artillery to move into close range at Yorktown. Civil engineers and others with surveying experience constituted the topographical staff. Washington, a former surveyor and mapmaker, relied heavily on this group of officers. A Scot named Robert Erskine, a civil engineer from New Jersey, coordinated six mapmaking teams.[48] According to a leading authority, "the resulting maps equaled those of the French in accuracy and were vastly superior to anything available to British commanders."[49]

Although the last years of the war saw the Continental army suffer from shortages of supplies and pay, to say nothing of desertions and occasional small-scale mutinies, Robert K. Wright is surely correct when he writes that it "fought well under a variety of conditions. The army's organization achieved sophistication; its leadership down to the company level grew experienced, tough, and competent. The 'Europeanization' of the Continental army reflected the contributions of foreign volunteers and also the wisdom of Washington and other American leaders in selecting only those concepts that would work in America."[50]

What the army lacked in professionalism, as defined by that century, was a military school. Although various people proposed such institutions, their endeavors either failed or met with modest, temporary success. Multiple reasons seem to explain the outcome. It was unclear whether Congress—an extralegal body for several years—could create national structures. It did not even establish the Continental army. Instead, it adopted the New England forces besieging Boston at the request—*urging* is a better word—of Massachusetts authorities. The constitutional question hardly faded away with the implementation of the Articles of Confederation in 1781, nor, for that matter, did it disappear completely with the ratification of the federal Constitution. The innovations in warfare taking place in military systems after midcentury—the employment of light infantry and skirmishers, mobile artillery, and large, self-sufficient divisions—were not dramatic enough to alter thinking about officer education. These were evolutionary developments that failed to bring profound transformations before the wars of the French Revolution and Napoleon.[51]

The attempts to found military schools were haphazard and uncoordinated. James Alcock, announcing the opening of a military school in September 1775 in Annapolis, Maryland, declared that "there appears at this time a great alacrity among all ranks of people to perfect themselves in the Military Art."[52] It is not unreasonable to assume that other such quick fixes were available to would-be soldiers. A month before the colonies declared their independence, Congressman John Adams, who became a voracious reader of books on war, wrote Knox that "the Public" should establish "Academies for the Education of young Gentlemen in every Branch of the military Art." Several months later Adams repeated his desire, for "Time, Study and Experience alone must make a sufficient Number of able officers." "This day," he continued, "I had the Honour of making a Motion for the appointment of a Committee to consider of a Plan for the Establishment of a military Academy." Congress responded by appointing Adams to such a committee, but, for whatever the reason, it presumably never presented a report. In fact, it is possible that three separate proposals for military schools were afloat in Congress. Opinions differed on whether to favor general or specialized educational institutions.[53]

Later, when the Continental army encamped at Pluckemin, New Jersey, Knox opened an informal school and rotated his officers through it for brief periods of time. There they read John Muller of Woolwich's *Treatise on Artillery* and the works of other writers.[54] From 1777 to 1779 some educational training took place at Carlisle, Pennsylvania, for an unknown number of artillerymen, but the main purpose of the facility was to repair and make ordnance. The only other attempt at formal instruction resulted from Congress's creation of the Corps of Invalids, a concept adopted from the British army of using men unfit for combat to perform garrison functions. It was to include a "Military School for Young Gentlemen," who would eventually return to active duty as ensigns. Headed by Colonel Lewis Nicola, author or translator of several military tracts and a former British army engineer, the Invalids' educational mission received scant attention. But the unit engaged in important custodial work for the remainder of the war.[55]

It should come as no surprise that efforts to create one or more military academies had met with failure and that informal institutions presided over by Knox, Nicola, and possibly others had not been noteworthy. The fact is that the record of the Continental army, as Robert K. Wright observed, was remarkably good considering the circumstances, for it steadily improved by means of the tutorial method still prevalent in Europe, a method that had served Washington and doubtless other provincial officers rather admirably in the Seven Years' War. The components of the tutorial approach included battlefield experience, military reading, and conversation and observation involving professional officers. Those opportunities had been available to Washington's officers. Even so, Washington, Adams, Knox, and others were undoubtedly correct in seeing infinite value in military schools. The point is that the need was not critical at the time.

But with the war drawing to a close, a better case might now be made for Congress's creating permanent educational facilities. In a future war there might not be time to get the hands-on training, and there might not be foreign officers available to teach skills that few Americans would know. Whatever the nature of the postwar military system in America, it would surely be small, possibly too small to inculcate the tutorial training of the past. It seemed unthinkable, given the low American opinion of European standing armies, that young men from Virginia, New York, and other states would go to the Old World for a military education or even take the grand tour of the Continent, visiting battlefields and conversing with officers in Prussia, Austria, and elsewhere as young Englishmen such as Clinton and Burgoyne had done before the American war. Washington took a dim view of such excursions. American young men would succumb to principles "unfriendly to republican government" and "the rights of man." So did Jefferson, who, in his 1785 letter to John Banister Jr., condemned European education in general and the corrupting influence of old regime society, which would lead American youths to extravagant and immoral lives, including a passion for whores "destructive" of one's "health" and "fidelity to the marriage bed."[56]

When in the spring of 1783 Congress appointed a committee chaired by Hamilton to assess the postwar military needs of the United States, it gave Washington and, through him, his senior officers an opportunity to voice their opinions.[57] The commander in chief received a multitude of proposals, all of which addressed officer education. Most were reasonably sound if sometimes unrealistic. Quartermaster General Timothy Pickering feared an American military academy might generate a kind of nobility, perhaps an indication that he was thinking of current trends in Prussia and France. He then contradicted himself, saying that American officers who wanted formal instruction might enroll in European war schools. Governor George Clinton of New York, who had a modest military background, responded to Washington's solicitation by opposing a specific institution for officer training. But he as well as one other respondent broached the establishment of a professorship in military science at one college in each of the thirteen states, an interesting idea in view of such developments years later at land grant institutions and even earlier at some antebellum schools. (Jefferson, long a highly visible archenemy of the hereditary Society of the Cincinnati, urged the society in 1817 to endow such a professorial chair at his new University of Virginia, even—and he must have swallowed hard—promising to name it the Cincinnati professorship.)[58]

Some of the more serious ideas included the creation of three regional academies, near military arsenals so that training facilities and weaponry would be available. Another recommendation advocated a three-year curriculum featuring a thorough grounding in mathematics and the sciences with some attention as well to geography, literature, and French. Some proposals favored educating men for all branches of the army, not just a standard course leading to engineering and artillery assignments. Summers would be occupied in field training. Breadth in academic education and in preparation for all the military branches particularly appealed to Knox and Steuben. These proposals had merit, although the creation of three army schools would have been exceedingly expensive and would have involved a thin distribution of other resources. And the suggestion for a naval academy, appearing in an occasional proposal, was ahead of its time.[59]

Washington, whose task was to respond to Congress after analyzing these plans, had little to say about military education in a document that focused on maintaining a small well-trained army and a greatly improved militia under a degree of federal supervision. A total realist, Washington realized the Confederation was contracting at the war's end. Congress's request for advice on the military needs of the nation came almost simultaneously with two events that hardly made the general public look positively on the subject of a sound course for national security: the Newburgh Conspiracy and the founding of the Society of the Cincinnati.[60] Although "an Institution calculated to keep alive and diffuse the knowledge of the Military Art would be highly expedient," Washington doubted Congress's ability to enter "great and expensive Arrangements." What seemed possible for the moment was to offer instruction to young men at artillery and engineering posts. As Washington knew from his recent experience with the Continental army, these were the two branches in which Americans had been deficient and where the greatest need would exist in a time of war. These garrisons, then, would become "a nursery from whence a number of Officers for Artillery and Engineering may be drawn on any great or sudden occasion."[61]

Between Congress's failure to act on Washington's "Sentiments on a Peace Establishment" and the election of Jefferson to the presidency seventeen years later, the subject of an educational institution for the military languished.[62] A dreary succession of schemes for producing well-schooled officers appeared in various places. They lacked the freshness and creativity of the blueprints presented to Washington on the eve of disbanding the army. The army itself hardly acted as a pressure group for new military structures, for its numbers ranged from under one hundred to under a thousand men as the feeble Confederation limped through the middle and late 1780s. The First Congress under the Constitution created an army, tiny though it was, because of Indian threats in the Northwest. It soon suffered two humiliating defeats at the hands of the tribesmen. In November 1793 Secretary of the Treasury Hamilton and Secretary of War Knox spoke out in the cabinet for Washington's returning to the cause of a military academy in his forthcoming fifth annual address to Congress, a measure Secretary of State Jefferson opposed as unconstitutional. Hoping to avoid further division among his already fractious department heads, the president elected to refer the matter to the lawmakers without a precise recommendation. He nonetheless reminded Congress that some "branches of the Military art" could "scarcely ever be attained by practice alone."[63]

If the venerable tutorial approach had achieved results in the Revolution, the explanation lay in large part in the availability of men like Steuben, Duportail, and Kosciuszko. Turning to Europe, at least on a large scale, offered no option.

The country seethed with anger and hostility between Federalists and Republicans over the French Revolution and its impact on Europe and America. Even during the War of Independence, the European option had generated tensions.

Congress responded somewhat positively to Washington's concerns about officer preparation. In 1794 it established within the army the Corps of Artillerists and Engineers, stipulating the appointment of two cadets for each company and the purchase of books and other instructional materials for their use. The new corps, quartered at the existing army installation at West Point, New York, on the Hudson River, showed the continuing French influence in these areas of specialization and revealed, as in the Revolution, the shortage of qualified Americans for high positions. Three of the five most senior posts went to Lieutenant Colonel Stephen Rochefontaine, the ranking appointee, a former officer in the French and American armies; Major Louis Tousard, another veteran of French and American service; and John Jacob Rivardi, a Swiss-born officer in the Russian army before arriving in America, who had already been employed by Knox to supervise several fortifications under construction on the Atlantic coast. Secretary of War Timothy Pickering, who succeeded Knox in that office, admitted American deficiencies in technological experience. "To become skillful in either branch of their profession," artillery or engineering, would demand "long attention, study and practice." Although there might be complaints about the selection of "foreign officers" for "this object," they alone seemed well qualified, and several were available in America.[64]

West Point in the 1790s hardly appears as a school in the making. The junior officers resented being treated as students required to attend classes by the imperious Rochefontaine. What Theodore Crackel calls "this experiment in military education" lasted "just a few months," because of rebellious engineers and artillerists and a mysterious fire that destroyed the old Revolutionary War provost building on the plain, where classes met. Tensions increased when Rochefontaine and a junior officer fought a duel.[65] Formal education, such as it was, ended. Moreover, part of the corps moved to other stations, some companies to the coast and some to the interior. Whatever Rochefontaine's failings, he had endeavored to create a respectable military library at West Point. A surviving inventory lists twenty-seven titles and a total of forty-three volumes, mostly artillery, mathematics and science, and fortification studies. But unfortunately the library fell victim to the fire.[66] Even the XYZ affair followed by the Quasi-War with France scarcely led to the creation of a truly educational facility. Although one intent of the 1794 law creating the Corps of Artillerists and Engineers was to educate cadets (young men not yet holding officers' commissions), as late as

1798 no cadets had been appointed. Hamilton, nominal head of the enlarged army during the French crisis, called for a "permanent academy for naval and military instruction" and secured from General Duportail, the head of army engineers in the Revolution, a "plan for a military school."[67]

The Federalists, never working together, especially from 1798 through the end of Adams's one-term presidency, favored an academy without being of one mind about how to achieve it. Secretary of War James McHenry now opted for a proposal submitted by Major Louis Tousard for a school at Carlisle, Pennsylvania, or Springfield, Massachusetts. Adams agreed to it, but Congress did not. Never to be outdone, Hamilton returned to the fray, proposing an academy made up of five schools, a ridiculous idea including everything from cavalry to naval curricula. Moreover, it was terrible timing because the Federalists by then were feeling a political backlash throughout the country because of, among other things, their efforts to vastly increase the size of the army. Even so, the Adams administration went along with a scaled-down version of Hamilton's grandiose blueprint for military education. But the Federalist internal bickering, the Republican opposition, and the election of 1800 all contributed to the future of a military academy being uncertain at best when Jefferson took office.[68]

The story of the Federalists' last efforts to create a school is, in fact, more complicated than what is outlined here. Adams and his secretary of war even decided they could have a de facto academy, whatever it was called, by vigorously implementing the 1794 law, appointing faculty and cadets for instruction at West Point. But Adams, for one, wearied of appointing Frenchmen to army posts, a practice he seems to have felt had been employed too often since the beginning of the War of Independence. Reacting to a freshet of French names, he exclaimed, "I have an invincible aversion to the appointment of foreigners, if it can be avoided."[69] The new scheme was never fully implemented before Adams left office.[70]

In America, as in Europe, there was always some tension between formal military education and the tutorial approach to learning about warfare. And in the new nation, it would continue into the nineteenth century, fueled in part by the age-old myth that the militia constituted the first line of defense in a free country. Of course, neither of the two approaches really supported the militia myth, but that myth further muddied the waters of rational debate. Some congressmen voiced skepticism of "scientific soldiers." General and later President Andrew Jackson was no friend of Jefferson's military academy. Prior to the American Civil War, only one West Point graduate had risen to the rank of general officer:

Joseph E. Johnston in 1860. Yet the military academy survived. To those who still had an eighteenth-century fear of professional officers and standing armies, one could always respond (whatever the truth of the matter) that West Point was primarily an institution for training engineers. But most Americans probably gave little thought to the school. It was not located in a highly visible metropolitan area, although there had been talk in its early days of moving it to New York City. It continued to be out of sight, nestled in the highlands of the Hudson.

Moreover, although new ideas are always unsettling to some people, West Point hardly became associated with innovation. After all, the War of Independence had failed to produce original ideas about how soldiers learned their craft. Even the advanced thinking that one might encounter in French artillery and engineering schools after 1763 seems to have had modest impact on officers on both sides of the Atlantic before the 1790s. An examination of the Continental army and the new federal army of the 1790s, in terms of education and most other matters as well, reinforces the prevailing view that the Revolution looks militarily conservative. To the extent that Americans advocated formal military education, they were mostly of one mind about where it should start, and that was with artillerists and engineers—a strictly European idea.[71]

The influence of French authors, of great significance to military readers in the War of Independence, continued to be felt in the Corps of Artillerists and Engineers at West Point in the 1790s and later. And the impact of America's former ally hardly diminished over the long run at the military academy. Jonathan Williams, the first superintendent, was recognized first and foremost for translating two French military texts. Jefferson himself recommended French titles for the library. In 1803 forty of the one hundred technical books at the school were in French. Superintendent Sylvanus Thayer, a committed Francophile, saw to the wholesale purchasing of French tomes. Alan Aimone writes that "by 1822 books and manuals about engineering, fortification, military art and tactics . . . included only 67 English titles as compared to 174 French manuals and reference books."[72] Frenchmen graced the faculty, and the most famous professor, Dennis Hart Mahan, was a devoted follower of Jomini. The list could go on.[73]

A few concluding comments about the debate over the military academy's origins seem in order. Jefferson's motives in 1801 remain cloudy. He, of course, had opposed such an institution earlier. There now seems less interest in demonstrating a genuine concern for military education on his part. The third president is pictured as desiring to further science or to create an institution with wide-ranging benefits to society. Or, in the opinion of Crackel, Jefferson was out to republicanize the army with Republicans. After all, that was not much different from the Federalist attempt to stock the officer corps of the enlarged army in 1798 with Federalists.[74]

But if military education was not Jefferson's preeminent motive, it should be stressed that it was not number one with Washington either. Surely he saw much value in a well-educated officer corps, but he had avoided the details of a war school, just as he had advocated major constitutional reform in 1787, content to leave the architecture to Madison and others. Washington wanted a military academy first and foremost for the same reason that he long urged the creation of a national university: that is, to create a more centralized government and to foster more national unity. He often remarked that bringing men from the different states into the army during the Revolutionary War had created "a band of brothers," a sense of oneness that would have taken countless years in the normal course of exchanges between Americans from the far-flung regions. Washington repeated those sentiments to Hamilton in 1796 as the two men worked together on what would become known as his Farewell Address, which first appeared in the press on September 19, 1796. Despite Washington's ardent wish to talk about the national benefits of federally sponsored education in the address, Hamilton urged him to keep his valedictory to the American people general in nature and to avoid specificity, pointing out that the president's eighth annual message to Congress would provide him with such an opportunity before stepping down as chief executive. Washington gave in, but only in part. Hamilton reluctantly inserted two sentences toward the middle of the Farewell Address recommending "Institutions for the general diffusion of knowledge."[75] Two months later, in Washington's final speech to the lawmakers, he called for a bold program of federal activity, including a national university and a national military academy.[76]

Congress has never seen fit to establish a national university, but it did, albeit in faltering fashion, finally cooperate with a subsequent president, Jefferson, in the establishment of the United States Military Academy. In the army, at least, the new school fostered that sense of oneness that Washington had passionately advocated since his appointment as commander in chief of the Continental forces more than twenty years earlier. West Point has always done that. Let us hope it always will.

Notes

1. Jefferson's ideas on education while in the Virginia legislature are nicely summarized in Noble E. Cunningham Jr., *In Pursuit of Reason: The Life of Thomas Jeffer-*

son (Baton Rouge, La., 1987), 58–60. For Jefferson's proposed legislation, see "A Bill for the More General Diffusion of Knowledge," in Julian P. Boyd et al., eds., *The Papers of Thomas Jefferson*, 31 vols. to date (Princeton, N.J., 1950–), 2:526–28.

2. The best introduction to Clausewitz is Peter Paret, *Clausewitz and the State: The Man, His Theories, and His Times*, 2d ed. (Princeton, N.J., 1985). For the origins and development of military thought and practice from the Renaissance through the Napoleonic era, see Peter Paret, ed., *Makers of Modern Strategy: From Machiavelli to the Nuclear Age* (Princeton, N.J., 1986), chaps. 1–7. Russell F. Weigley, *Towards an American Army: Military Thought from Washington to Marshall* (New York, 1962), is still the best study of American writers.

3. Geoffrey Parker, *The Military Revolution: Military Innovation and the Rise of the West, 1500–1800* (Cambridge, Eng., 1988); Clifford J. Rogers, ed., *The Military Revolution Debate* (Boulder, Colo., 1995).

4. Henry Guerlac, "Vauban: The Impact of Science on War," in Paret, *Makers of Modern Strategy*, chap. 3.

5. Lee Kennett, *The French Forces in America, 1780–83* (Westport, Conn., 1977), 143; Piers Mackesy, *The War for America, 1775–83* (Cambridge, Mass., 1964), esp. chaps. 14, 18, 21, 28, 29.

6. Joseph L. Wieczynski, ed., *Modern Encyclopedia of Russian and Soviet History*, 6 vols. (Gulf Breeze, Fla., 1976–2000), 6:86–89; Mary West Case, "Catherine the Great, Ivan Ivanovich Betskoi, and Their Schools for a New Society" (M.A. thesis, Univ. of North Carolina at Chapel Hill, 1976), 94–105; Christopher Duffy, *The Army of Frederick the Great* (New York, 1974); Christopher Duffy, *The Army of Marie Theresa* (New York, 1977).

7. John Smyth, *The History of the Royal Military Academy, Woolwich, the Royal Military Academy, Sandhurst . . .* (London, 1961).

8. William B. Willcox, *Portrait of a General: Sir Henry Clinton in the War of Independence* (New York, 1964), 14. In 1803 President Thomas Jefferson's secretary of war, Henry Dearborn, stressed the distinct place of engineering officers in the command system of armies. Engineering officers, he wrote, were staff specialists, and neither in America nor Europe had they been given authority over line officers. Thomas Elliott Shaughnessy, "Beginnings of National Professional Military Education in America, 1775–1825" (Ed.D. diss., Johns Hopkins Univ., 1956), 134.

9. Robert P. Davis, *Where a Man Can Go: Major General William Phillips, British Royal Artillery, 1731–81* (Westport, Conn., 1999); Milton M. Klein and Ronald W. Howard, eds., *The Twilight of British Rule in Revolutionary America: The New York Letter Book of General James Robertson, 1780–83* (Cooperstown, N.Y, 1983).

10. Franklin and Mary Wickwire, *Cornwallis: The American Adventure* (Boston, 1970), 49–50.

11. Duffy, *Army of Frederick*, 29.

12. The duc de Choiseul, foreign minister; the comte de Saint-Germain, minister of war; and Gribeauval, the most influential reformer, who in 1776 won the new post of inspector general of artillery and held it until his death in 1789, a man who profoundly influenced Napoleon's thinking about heavy weaponry.

13. Ken Adler, *Engineering the Revolution: Arms and Enlightenment in France, 1763–1815* (Princeton, N.J., 1997) chaps. 1–3, quotation on p. 3; R. R. Palmer, "Frederick the Great, Guibert, Bulow: From Dynastic to National War," in Paret, *Makers of Modern Strategy*, 105–13.

14. A good introduction to warfare in Napoleon's day, with appropriate emphasis on Bonaparte himself, is Robert A. Doughty and Ira D. Gruber, eds., *Warfare in the Western World: Military Operations from 1600 to 1871* (Lexington, Mass., 1996), chaps. 6–7. For greater detail, see David G. Chandler, *The Campaigns of Napoleon* (New York, 1966); Owen Connelly, *Blundering to Glory: Napoleon's Military Campaigns* (Wilmington, Del., 1987).

15. Maurice de Saxe, *My Reveries upon the Art of War,* trans. R. R. Phillips (Harrisburg, Pa., 1955), 297.

16. Willcox, *Portrait of a General,* and "Sir Henry Clinton: Paralysis of Command," in *George Washington's Opponents: British Generals and Admirals in the American Revolution,* ed. George Athan Billias (New York, 1969), 73–102.

17. Edward B. de Fonblanque, *Life and Correspondence of John Burgoyne, General, Statesman, Dramatist* (London, 1876), 484. Burgoyne's social life while campaigning was disturbing to the wife of the German Brunswicker general. Marvin L. Brown Jr., ed. and trans., *Journal and Correspondence of a Tour of Duty: Baroness von Riedesel and the American Revolution* (Chapel Hill, N.C., 1965), xxxi, 55–56.

18. For the evolution of professionalism in various fields and disciplines, see Howard M. Vollmer and Donald L. Mills, eds., *Professionalization* (Englewood Cliffs, N.J., 1966).

19. J. R. Hale, *War and Society in Renaissance Europe* (New York, 1985), 144–46; Karl Demeter, *The German Officer Corps in Society and State, 1650–1945* (New York, 1965), 68; Don Higginbotham, "Military Leadership in the American Revolution," in *Leadership in the American Revolution,* Library of Congress Symposia on the American Revolution (Washington, D.C., 1974), 91–95, 98–99.

20. For the Washington-Gage correspondence and other numerous references to Gage during Washington's Virginia military career, see *PGW: Col. Ser.,* esp. the index to vol. 10.

21. Don Higginbotham, *George Washington and the American Military Tradition* (Athens, Ga., 1985), esp. chaps. 1–2.

22. Ira D. Gruber, "The Education of Sir Henry Clinton," *Bulletin of the John Rylands University Library of Manchester* 72 (1990): 131–51. This essay is one of Gruber's pieces in his ongoing study of eighteenth-century British military education. See also his "Classical Influences on British Strategy in the War for American Independence," in *Classical Traditions in Early America,* ed. John W. Eadie (Ann Arbor, Mich., 1976), 175–90; "British Strategy: The Theory and Practice of Eighteenth-Century Warfare," in *Reconsiderations on the Revolutionary War,* ed. Don Higginbotham (Westport, Conn., 1978), 14–31, 166–70; "The Anglo-American Military Tradition and the War of American Independence," *Against All Enemies: Interpretations of American Military History from Colonial Times to the Present,* ed. Kenneth J. Hagan and William R. Roberts (Westport, Conn., 1986), 21–47. J. A. Hould-

ing, *Fit for Service: The Training of the British Army, 1715–95* (Oxford, Eng., 1981), notes the absence of French works in earlier British reading habits. But he finds a "plethora of manual and platoon exercises . . . that appeared regularly from 1716 through 1746." See chap. 3, quotation on p. 187.

23. Fonblanque, *Political and Military Episodes,* 19.

24. Gruber, "Education of Sir Henry Clinton," 142–48, quotation on p. 143.

25. Washington to Boucher, July 9, 1771, *PGW: Col. Ser.* 3:50–51. Washington's supposed unappreciated interest in reading and books receives a firm corrective in Paul K. Longmore, *The Invention of George Washington* (Berkeley, Calif., 1988), 213–26.

26. *PWG: Col. Ser.* 2:208–9, 251, 4:344.

27. Ibid., 1:223, 6:355, 358, 400. Particularly helpful on Washington's military reading before the Revolution is Oliver L. Spaulding Jr., "The Military Studies of George Washington," *American Historical Review* 29 (1924): 675–80.

28. *PGW: Rev. War* 2:346–47.

29. I owe a huge debt to Ellen McCallister Clark, staff member at the Society of the Cincinnati Library in Washington, D.C., for sharing with me her excellent MS "George Washington's Reading List: Ten Books That Shaped the Continental Army." She not only compiled an important list but analyzed its contents.

30. Don Higginbotham, *Daniel Morgan: Revolutionary Rifleman* (Chapel Hill, N.C., 1961), quotation on p. 70; Robert K. Wright, *The Continental Army* (Washington, D.C., 1983), 149.

31. [Worth Bailey], *General Washington's Swords and Campaign Equipment* (Mount Vernon, Va., 1944), 10.

32. North Callahan, *Henry Knox: General Washington's General* (New York, 1958), 18–20, 29–30, 35–36; Theodore Thayer, *Nathanael Greene: Strategist of the American Revolution* (New York, 1960), 22–24, 44–45, 47–48, 61; J. Mark Thompson, "Citizens and Soldiers: Henry Knox and the Development of American Military Thought and practice" (Ph.D. diss., Univ. of North Carolina at Chapel Hill, 2000), 12–13, 62–63, 103–4; Robert J. Taylor et al., eds., *The Papers of John Adams,* ser. 3, *General Correspondence . . .* , 10 vols. to date (Cambridge, Mass., 1977–), 4:190; Houlding, *Fit for Service,* 252–53.

33. General Orders, May 8, 1777, *PGW: Rev. War Ser.* 9:368.

34. For examples, see ibid., 12:55, 56–57, 477–81, 532–33, 549, 552.

35. Greene to Washington, Dec. 1, 3, 1777, in Richard K. Showman et al., eds., *The Papers of General Nathanael Greene,* 11 vols. to date (Chapel Hill, N.C., 1976–), 2:225–29, 231–38.

36. Johann Ewald, *Diary of the American War: A Hessian Journal,* ed. and trans. Joseph P. Tustin (New Haven, 1979), 108.

37. Ibid. There are similar references and inferences about American military abilities elsewhere in Ewald's diary.

38. Johann Heinrichs, "Extracts from the Letter-Book of Captain Johann Heinrichs of the Hessian Jaeger Corps, 1778–1780," *Pennsylvania Magazine of History and Biography* 22 (1898): 137–40. That same year a French artillery officer serving with Washington, Louis de Recicourt de Ganot, saw Continental officers as possessed

of considerable potential. Durand Echeverria and Orville T. Murphy, eds., "The American Revolutionary Army: A French Estimate in 1777," *Military Affairs* 27 (1963): 1–7, 153–62.

39. *PGW: Rev. War. Ser.* 9:32.

40. Stanley J. Idzerda, Lloyd Kramer, et al., eds., *Lafayette in the American Revolution: Selected Letters and Papers, 1776–90,* 5 vols. to date (Ithaca, N.Y., 1977–), 1:11, 68–67.

41. John R. Alden, *General Charles Lee: Traitor or Patriot?* (Baton Rouge, La., 1951), chap. 2.

42. See, for example, Washington to Alexander McDougall, May 23, 1777, *PGW: Rev. War Ser.* 9:506.

43. Washington to Steuben, Feb. 26, March 11, 1779, to the President of Congress, March 11, 1779, *GW: Writings* 14:151–52, 227–28, 230.

44. Published by Styner and Cist in Philadelphia in 1779, seven other editions of the *Regulations* appeared by 1785. It was also used extensively by the state militias. For a facsimile of the first edition, as well as information on reprintings, see Joseph R. Riling, *Baron von Steuben and His Regulations* (Philadelphia, 1966).

45. Wright, *Continental Army,* 140.

46. For Lamb, see Isaac Q. Leake, *Memoirs of the Life and Times of John Lamb* (Albany, N.Y., 1858). Chastellux's praise of the Continental artillery is in Howard C. Rice, Jr., ed., *Travels in North America in the Years 1780, 1781, and 1782 by the Marquis de Chastellux,* 2 vols. (Chapel Hill, N.C., 1963), 1:282. See Evelyn M. Acomb, ed., *The Revolutionary Journal of Baron Ludwig von Clossen, 1780–83* (Chapel Hill, N.C., 1958), 156, for the comment on Rochambeau. Knox's role at Yorktown is examined in Thompson, "Citizens and Soldiers," 210–16.

47. Elizabeth S. Kite, *Brigadier-General Louis Lebègue Duportail, Commandant of Engineers in the Continental Army, 1777–1783* (Baltimore, 1933).

48. Paul K. Walker, ed., *Engineers of Independence: A Documentary History of the Army Engineers in the American Revolution, 1775–83* (Washington, D.C., 1981), is an invaluable source on the subject. Albert Heusser, *George Washington's Map Maker: A Biography of Robert Erskine,* ed. Hubert G. Schmidt (New Brunswick, N.J., 1966), is an antiquarian volume but useful for Erskine's correspondence.

49. Wright, *Continental Army,* 132.

50. Ibid., 152. See also Paul David Nelson, "Citizen Soldiers or Regulars: The Views of American General Officers on the Military Establishment," *Military Affairs* 43 (1979):126–32. In *The Age of Battles: The Quest for Decisive Warfare from Breitenfeld to Waterloo* (Bloomington, Ind., 1991), 234, Russell F. Weigley declares that the Continentals "made deep inroads into British tactical superiority" and that some American regiments, particularly Maryland and Delaware units, "attained parity with the British in soldierly skills."

51. Parker, *Military Revolution,* chap.5; Hew Strachan, *European Armies and the Conduct of War* (London, 1983), chap. 3; Weigley, *Age of Battles,* chap. 11.

52. *Maryland Journal,* Sept. 6, 1775.

53. John Adams to Henry Knox, June 2, Sept. 29, 1776, Paul H. Smith, ed., *Letters of*

Delegates to Congress, 26 vols. (Washington, D.C., 1976–99), 4:115, 5:261. For the tangled story of proposals for military education before Congress in late 1776, see Shaughnessy, "Beginnings of National Professional Military Education," 32–39.

54. Thompson, "Citizens and Soldiers," 88–91; Shaughnessy, "Beginnings of National Professional Military Education," 54–55.

55. Wright, *Continental Army,* 136–37; Shaughnessy, "Beginnings of National Professional Military Education," 39–48.

56. *GW: Writings* 34:59–60; Boyd, *Jefferson Papers* 8:15.

57. Hamilton to Washington, April 9, 1783, in Harold C. Syrett et al., eds., *The Papers of Alexander Hamilton,* 27 vols. (New York, 1962–87), 3:322. Washington asked for some time before replying so he could consult others before formulating his response. Washington to Hamilton, April 16, 1783, ibid., 331–32. In fact, two days earlier Washington had requested such opinions. For example, see Washington to Steuben, April 14, 1783, *GW: Writings* 26:315–16.

58. Shaughnessy, "Beginnings of National Professional Military Education," 71–72; Minor Myers Jr., *Liberty without Anarchy: A History of the Society of the Cincinnati* (Charlottesville, Va., 1983), 208.

59. Shaughnessy, "Beginnings of National Professional Military Education," 63–74; Lawrence Delbert Cress, *Citizens in Arms: The Army and the Militia in American Society to the War of 1812* (Chapel Hill, N.C., 1982), 78–84. Most originals of the letters from Washington's subordinates are in the Washington Papers, Library of Congress. See also some published versions in Jared Sparks, ed., *Correspondence of the Revolution: Being Letters of Eminent Men to George Washington,* 4 vols. (Boston, 1853), 4:27–31.

60. Richard H. Kohn, *Eagle and Sword: The Federalists and the Creation of the Military Establishment in America, 1783–1802* (New York, 1975), chap. 2; Myers, *Liberty without Anarchy,* chap. 1.

61. *GW: Writings* 26:374–98, esp. 396. Before Congress asked for Washington's views, it had received a detailed plan of military education from Secretary at War Benjamin Lincoln, which probably did not receive serious consideration. The lengthiest plan, thoughtful and comprehensive but hardly possible to adopt at the time, came from Major Jean Baptiste Obrey de Gouvion, a French professional soldier on Lafayette's staff. Shaughnessy, "Beginnings of National Professional Military Education," 59–60, 63–66.

62. Hamilton's congressional committee accepted Washington's "Sentiments" in somewhat modified form, but Congress failed to adopt any part of the Hamilton report. Shaughnessy, "Beginnings of National Professional Military Education," 77–83; Report on a Military Peace Establishment, [June 18, 1783], in Syrett, *Hamilton Papers* 3:378–97, esp. 382, 391, 396 for the committee's cautious approach to military schooling.

63. Memorandum of Matters to Be Communicated to Congress, [Nov. 1793], Fifth Annual Address to Congress, Dec. 3, 1793, *GW: Writings* 33:160–61, 166–67. The best treatment of efforts to put in place a program of military education in the 1790s is Theodore J. Crackel, *West Point: A Bicentennial History* (Lawrence, Kans., 2002),

chap. 2, which has significantly influenced my treatment of the decade. For Jefferson's thinking on a military academy in the 1790s, see his Notes of a Cabinet Meeting on the President's Address, Nov. 23, 1793, in Boyd, *Jefferson Papers* 27:428; David N. Mayer, *The Constitutional Thought of Thomas Jefferson* (Charlottesville, Va., 1994), 213–14.

64. Report to Military Committee, House of Representatives, Feb. 3, 1796, quoted in Crackel, *West Point,* 33.

65. Crackel, *West Point,* 34–35.

66. Alan C. Aimone, "Genesis of the U.S. Military Academy Library," MS by a member of the USMA Library staff, who is an authority on the early history of the institution.

67. Hamilton to Louis Duportail, July 23, 1798, Duportail to Hamilton, Dec. 9, 1798, in Syrett, *Hamilton Papers* 22:28–29, 339.

68. Shaughnessy, "Beginnings of National Professional Military Education," 103–10; Syrett, *Hamilton Papers* 24:69–75, 308–12; Crackel, *West Point,* 38–40.

69. Charles Francis Adams, ed., *Works of John Adams,* 10 vols. (Boston, 1850–56), 9:65–66; Crackel, *West Point,* 40–43.

70. No scholar has yet demonstrated that Federalist efforts to create a military school had a positive impact on Jefferson. Indeed, Hamilton's bold vision of several educational institutions would likely have shocked Jefferson. Even Washington, who received a copy of Hamilton's detailed measure, delicately declined to comment on its specifics, although he offered his general support. Hamilton to Washington, Nov. 28, 1799, Washington to Hamilton, Dec. 12, 1799, in Syrett, *Hamilton Papers* 24:79–80, 99–100. See also Crackel, *West Point,* 43–44.

71. Weigley, *Towards an American Army,* chaps. 1–2; William B. Skelton, *An American Profession of Arms: The Army Officer Corps, 1784–1861* (Lawrence, Kans., 1992), chaps. 1–3.

72. Aimone, "Genesis of the U.S. Military Academy," 12.

73. Skelton, *Profession of Arms,* 99–100, 102, 115, 123, 240–41, 249, and chap. 10; Weigley, *Towards an American Army,* chaps. 4–5.

74. Theodore J. Crackel, *Mr. Jefferson's Army: Political and Social Reform of the Military Establishment, 1801–1809* (New York, 1987), introduction, chaps. 1–4, and *West Point,* chap. 2.; Don Higginbotham, *War and Society in Revolutionary America: The Wider Dimensions of Conflict* (Columbia, S.C., 1988), chap. 9; Robert Gough, "Officering the American Army, 1798," *William and Mary Quarterly,* 3d ser., 43 (1986): 460–71. For a review of interpretations of the origins of the U.S. Military Academy that have appeared in print before 2001, see James W. Rainey, "Establishing the United States Military Academy: Motives and Objectives of Thomas Jefferson," *Assembly* 59 (2001): 42–44, 57.

75. Syrett, *Hamilton Papers* 20:311–12, 316, 318–19, 320; Farewell Address, Sept. 19, 1796, *GW: Writings* 35:230.

76. Washington introduced the matter in a short paragraph: "I have heretofore proposed to the consideration of Congress, the expediency of establishing a national University; and also a Military Academy. The desirableness of both the Institu-

tions, has . . . constantly increased with every new view I have taken of the subject."
Washington, as well as Presidents Jefferson, Madison, and Monroe, emphasized the
need for military education as a way to guarantee the future safety of the nation
against aggressive powers. All seemed at pains to advocate formal learning without
a suggestion that such an educational institution would lead to an enlarged professional army. Eighth Annual Address to Congress, Dec. 7, 1796, *GW: Writings*
35:316–17. As academy graduates left the military service, their knowledge would be
imparted to society at large by means of their serving later in their own state militias.
What Washington implied here some subsequent chief executives made explicit.
Washington himself had, at the conclusion of the War of Independence, recommended to state governors the appointment of veteran Continental army officers to
positions of leadership in the militias. *GW: Writings* 26:394; Harrison E. Ethridge,
"Patrick Henry and the Reorganization of the Virginia Militia, 1784–1786," *Virginia
Magazine of History and Biography* 85 (1977): 436. See also the splendid treatment
of the Farewell Address and Washington's Eighth Annual Message to Congress in
Joseph J. Ellis, *The Founding Brothers: The Revolutionary Generation* (New York,
2001), chap. 4.

Martial Spirit and Revolution

North and South

The Martial Spirit in the Antebellum South

SINCE I HAD BECOME president of the Southern Historical Association in 1990, it was my responsibility, and last act of my term, to deliver the presidential address the following year at the annual meeting in Fort Worth, Texas, on November 14. Fortunately presidential addresses are not vetted before publication. So without worrying about scholarly referees, one can be provocative, wide-ranging and freewheeling. In fact, that is the purpose of the presidential address: to speak on a subject that will catch the interest of the audience. This paper was not my first venture into comparative history; previous forays had compared the American Revolution with similar upheavals in Europe, Mexico, and Vietnam. It was, however, new for me to look at American regionalism in comparative terms. My fascination with the antebellum South may have had something to do with my own southern background, and it surely can be explained partly by my having taught the Antebellum South course for a half dozen years at Louisiana State University in the 1960s. If I learned a lot from this classroom experience, I probably gained even more insights into what eventually became the subject of my presidential address from my LSU colleague, friend, and neighbor T. Harry Williams, himself a former president of the Southern Historical Association. Williams taught at LSU from 1941 until his retirement in 1979 (he died later that year). He offered the United States Military History and Civil War courses and may well have been the most distinguished Civil War scholar of his generation. We had countless conversations about the Revolutionary War and the Civil War: how they were alike and how they were different.

This essay is something of an elaboration of North-South comparisons expressed by the late Marcus Cunliffe in his stimulating book *Soldiers and Civilians: The Martial Spirit in America, 1775–1865,* published in 1968. Cunliffe's northern comparisons start with the Revolution, whereas I maintain that they should begin with an examination of the militia and colonial wars in New England because I believe that there is really a continuous northern tradition, largely centered in the Puritan provinces, from the seventeenth century to the

Civil War. Moreover, I had the advantage of drawing on the literature that had appeared in the two decades after the publication of Cunliffe's monograph, along with some illuminating southern primary sources that he had not consulted. My work also looks at the question of whether a southern nationalism existed prior to the Civil War. I found no significant evidence for it, and I continue to take that position. For that matter, I also feel that American nationalism was not a factor in bringing on the American Revolution; that instead nationalism emerged a slow result of the Revolution. My presidential address is found in the *Journal of Southern History* 58 (February 1992): 3–26 and is reprinted with the permission of the editor.

————•·•————

MY PURPOSE IS to return to a very old question: Did the antebellum South have a distinct martial character? It has long been claimed that southerners were more enamored of soldiering, more warlike, and hence more willing to fight for their principles than Yankees were in 1861. Since we are speaking of military matters, let me, to use an appropriate metaphor, indicate my own strategy for entering this fray. First, let me give an overview of the historical debate in the thirty-five or so years after World War II, when several scholars directly addressed the martial tradition question. Second, I wish to throw comparative light on the subject by examining military thought and behavior in colonial New England, which, as I stress, had a considerable martial legacy of its own. Third, I must say some things based upon my own thinking and reading about the idea of a southern preoccupation with Mars. And finally, let me sketch broadly some preliminary conclusions about regional and national military configurations in 1861.

The case for a martial South is as follows. The continued existence of the frontier, the longtime duration of Indian dangers in that region, the presence of slavery, and the fear of black revolts all combined to make southerners attracted to things martial.[1] These tendencies were reinforced for the upper class by the very nature of plantation society. The gentry saw themselves as not unlike landed elites elsewhere, which invariably preached the centrality of honor, bravery, and physical prowess, including riding, shooting, and other field sports, in their system of values. The result of all the above was that southern gentlemen were hotheaded, sensitive to slights, ready to duel or cowhide an offender (whichever etiquette dictated), and enamored of fancy military raiment—be it that of a volunteer company, a West Point cadet, or a regular army officer.[2] If both northerners and southerners read Gothic novels, they internalized them in different ways. Southerners considered themselves not unlike the chivalrous knights and their ladies of old, as is evidenced by their enjoyment of ring tournaments and their characterization of themselves as descended from Normans and Cavaliers, while Yankees, with their plebeian lineages, could only find Saxon or Roundhead ancestry.

"Even Southerners without a claim to cavalier ancestry did not suffer from lack of fighting spirit." On the frontier and in thinly settled areas vigilantism and one-to-one confrontations in resolving personal problems were the rule and not the exception. In their own way the lower and middle orders were equally if not more prone to violence—kicking, gouging, and other forms of mutilation—than the cavalier planters. The backcountry Scots and Scotch-Irish maintained ancestral traditions "of pride, boastfulness, and vigor that found a congenial atmosphere in the frontier environment" that was much of the pre–Civil War South. "The habit of war was ingrained in the Scots; usually their heroes were warriors and their admiration for the qualities of courage, endurance, and loyalty to leaders was almost unbounded."[3] Indeed, some recent historians contend that all the Celtic peoples of the South, and not merely those of Scottish derivation, exhibited such physical and mental qualities.[4]

Southerners not only thought of themselves as more disposed to things military, but they acted on that belief as well. They contributed more men per capita to the War of 1812 and the Mexican War than the North; they had more than their share of secretaries of war and navy, of senior army officers, and of West Point cadets, not to mention prestigious faculty and administrators at that institution on the Hudson. The southern fascination for volunteer units (Charleston at one time had twenty-two); for military colleges (South Carolina had two, the Arsenal in Columbia and the Citadel in Charleston, patterned after the Virginia Military Institute); and for military academies (which offered secondary or college-preparatory curricula), have received, along with the West Point connection, particular attention.

These views had in reality offered much evidence in support of the broad contours of W. J. Cash's classic *The Mind of the South*,[5] with its focus on such themes as pride, bravery, impulsiveness, and violence. To be sure, academic historians wrote widely researched monographs, whereas Cash was a Charlotte journalist. Even so, one comes away from the secondary literature with the feeling that its authors would hardly cross swords with Cash over his judgment that North and South were truly divergent civilizations and that the "Southern world," in relative terms, had become "an extremely uncomplex, unvaried, and unchanging one."[6]

Although they avoided an attack on all fronts against the thesis of separate civilizations, Marcus Cunliffe in 1968 and his student Michael C. C. Adams a decade later took direct aim at the notion that the South's martial spirit was unique. And most reviewers felt they had scored several direct hits. These revisionists maintained that the subject of a warlike South had been studied without reference to the rest of the country. An examination of antebellum northern society would reveal similar tendencies that had hitherto been described as primarily southern phenomena. Cunliffe laid particular stress on the popularity of volunteer companies and the presence of military schools and academies above the Mason and Dixon Line, and he denied that West Point was a southern bastion. Moreover, the army's outstanding military theorist, Henry W. Halleck, was from the North, where most of the military periodicals were published.[7]

Neither Cunliffe nor Adams, however, denied that southerners perceived themselves as militarily superior. In fact, they might have quoted Cash when he said, with a touch of hyperbole, "that any Southerner at random" thought himself "equal to whipping a whole squad of Yankees" and that "nothing living could cross him and get away with it."[8] If, as Adams says, the notion was decidedly false, he goes on to explain why many influential northerners (including General George B. McClellan) believed the southern boast to be all too true and why it impeded the Union war effort in the East. Whether southerners were savage slavocrats or gentlemanly cavaliers, they were viewed as fearsome fighters, products of a healthy, outdoors rural environment, whereas the Northeast of the pallid, urban-dwelling factory worker produced only debilitated martial qualities in its citizenry. It took the arrival on the eastern front of the westerner Ulysses S. Grant, unfettered by self-defeating southern mythology, to destroy the stereotypes that had bedeviled Robert E. Lee's previous opposite numbers.[9]

Now I want to shift both time and space and telescope the martial scene in colonial New England. Two contentions may surprise you. First, New Englanders thought of themselves as a brave and warlike people; and second, they considered themselves in these respects superior to colonial southerners, and some southerners agreed with them. In short, we encounter a reversal of some regional images of a century or so later. What do we have here? Why does each region have a martial outlook at a particular time in its history, and why does it see the other region unfavorably? What is the linkage, and why?

We can best address these matters by reviewing aspects of New England military history. A harsh judgment of the Puritans would have it that they did not settle America but rather that they invaded America. They brought with them "guns and munitions to overpower Indian resistance and quantities of propaganda to overpower their countrymen's scruples."[10] A more charitable verdict would deny that the Puritans came to conquer like the Spanish conquistadors and would attribute white and red bloodlettings to more complex factors.[11] In any case, it can be said that the Puritan colonies lived with the fear of physical threats to their existence down to the American Revolution. Those threats, as the provincials perceived them, came first from the Indians, then from the French papists in Canada, and finally, after 1763, from Great Britain itself.

If, as advocates of a martial South assert, slavery and fears of black uprisings contributed greatly to a strain of southern violence and violence contributed to a martial spirit, it can surely be argued that the Indian had the same impact on New Englanders. After all, in their eyes, Native Americans too were heathens of an inferior race and culture. Unlike blacks in the South, Indians were not enslaved. They soon acquired muskets and used them lethally in King Philip's War. Half of all the towns in the region came under attack, and a dozen were burned to the ground. The result was the largest percentage of deaths out of the total population of any war in American history.[12] Puritan soldiers resorted to the most inhumane forms of torture and received cash bonuses for Indian scalps, including those of women and children. As for King Philip, his head was cut off and his body quartered. The Reverend Increase Mather defended such behavior in warfare, saying that Indians "act like wolves & are to be dealt withall as wolves."[13]

A New England concern with things martial is demonstrated by further evidence: heated militia elections, the popularity of military titles in everyday usage, and annual artillery sermons.[14] Furthermore, New Englanders produced a staggering quantity of military literature prior to 1776. Accounts of Indian wars and Indian captivity constituted a kind of popular history. Mary Rowlandson's *Narrative* of her captivity in King Philip's War, first printed in 1682, was republished three times just between 1771 and 1773. A sizable portion of Jeremy Belknap's *History of New Hampshire* re-creates skirmishes, raids, and massacres, themes also encountered in Thomas Hutchinson's *History of Massachusetts Bay.*[15]

Although New Englanders also published training manuals and reproduced British military treatises, a more revealing indication of their martial concerns appears in their sermon literature. The jeremiads of the various Mather clergymen, for example, stretching over several generations, articulated the idea of a just war, the responsibilities of citizens to bear arms, and the moral and physical benefits of soldiering. Whether in time of peace or in the midst of war, the themes were not forgotten. In 1737 the Reverend William Williams exhorted his listeners to develop "a warlike Genius, dextrous Skill and undaunted Courage." Over twenty years later, during the Seven Years' War, the Reverend Samuel

Cooper reminded his own flock that "the Soldier is as Necessary to a Community as the Magistrate."[16]

By any standard, the contributions of New England, particularly Massachusetts and Connecticut, to the Anglo-French imperial conflicts after 1688 were impressive. Massachusetts far outdistanced every colony except its neighbor in the taxation and recruitment of its citizens. During a four-year period in Queen Anne's War, 1707–11, Massachusetts mounted five expeditions against the French and had one-sixth or more of its service-eligible males under arms. In 1745 the Bay Colony provided a high percentage of the New England expeditionary army that seized Louisbourg, the Gallic citadel on Cape Breton Island. And in the Seven Years' War, the Puritan province mustered a third of its service-eligible men, a record no European nation of the time could match.[17]

What may be said of the military performance of the southern colonies? Information is sketchy for the period before the Seven Years' War, but assuredly their offerings in the post-1688 conflicts were meager compared with New England's—Virginia, for instance, raised only 136 men for King George's War in the 1740s.[18] That fact explains the Massachusetts General Court's prediction in 1754 that the southern colonies would not meet their commitments if Benjamin Franklin's Plan of Union was adopted. The court depicted the southern provinces as "but little disposed to and less acquainted with affairs of war."[19] Those judgments echoed in statements by Virginia's Governors Alexander Spotswood and Robert Dinwiddie and by Colonel George Washington. As the youthful Washington put it in 1757, "Virginia is a Country young in War" and prior to Braddock's defeat had enjoyed "Tranquil Peace; never studying War or Warfare."[20] In time it became clear to Dinwiddie and Washington that the Seven Years' War was decidedly unpopular in the Old Dominion, a condition that changed somewhat only after William Pitt's London government agreed to subsidize the American colonial war effort. Even so, the war concluded with the southern colonies having made a lamentable showing in the eyes of both British officials and New Englanders. In the South only one of eight free white males shouldered arms, whereas two of five of their counterparts north of Maryland did so, with New Englanders bearing a very disproportionate share of the burden compared with the middle colonies as well as the South.[21]

If we are mindful that the Seven Years' War and the War of Independence occurred within a single generation, we will hardly be astonished that New England's military heritage was alive and well in 1775, barely a dozen years after France lost its North American empire. New England's martial tradition was nurtured by Britain's aggressive new imperial policy, which Massachusetts opposed more vigorously than any other colony. Twice British troops were sent to Boston, with the consequence that violence erupted in the form of the Boston Massacre, the Boston Tea Party, Lexington and Concord, and the siege of Boston.

And the sermons and other forms of martial literature continued to flow from the New England printing presses. The annual "Massacre Day" orations reminded the people of their bravery and valor and of their soldierly superiority over redcoats, who were not upstanding citizens but the dregs of humanity who enlisted for pounds and pence, not principles.[22] Pamphleteers, comparing New England and British contributions in the Seven Years' War, all but excluded the island kingdom from any substantial role in the outcome. In several publications William Heath and Timothy Pickering, veteran militia officers, urged the public to read treatises on military preparedness; and Pickering proffered information on increasing the rapidity with which a soldier could fire and reload his musket.[23] Some essayists were explicit in their blunt warnings to the mother country. A sixty-two-year-old former colonial soldier announced his readiness to grab his flintlock as he had "in times past," but this time to "fly with double Fury" against British "Miscreants," not the French. One "Ranger" also pledged his willingness to "fight the enemies from Britain" as he previously had fought "Indians from Canada."[24]

Does any one person, in his writings if not his battlefield deeds, make the most eloquent case for a New England military way? The answer, hardly startling, is the ever-quotable John Adams. It is Adams who tells us that New England's culture was shaped by its schools, churches, town meetings, and militia; that the common people enjoyed things military far more than "Learning, Eloquence, and Genius; that the ideal of every young man was to "be Colonel of a Regiment of Militia." Nor, we might add parenthetically, did Adams during the Seven Years' War show disdain for British redcoats. He and his neighbors thrilled to see Lord Loudoun, Lord Howe, and General Jeffery Amherst and to hear the "delightfull" martial "Music" from a Scottish regimental band.[25]

Of course, attitudes about redcoats and Britain soured a few years later. It is Adams who also quite accurately informs us that from the Stamp Act onward New Englanders were ready to fight for their liberties; that, indeed in the First and Second Continental Congresses, Massachusetts was far in advance of the colonies below the Hudson in its advocacy of preparedness.[26]

While Adams, like most Americans of his generation, had reservations about ambitious generals, long-term enlistments, and unjust wars, the life of the soldier and war itself engendered no automatic hostility. Unlike his southern contemporary Thomas Jefferson, with whom he is so often compared,[27] Adams at times sounded like young Theodore Roosevelt in the 1890s—though Adams's perspective was Puritan and Roosevelt's Darwinian. To the New Englander wars and other "Calamities" were "catharticks of the body politick" and "aroused the soul," reviving "original virtues." Adams's writings are sprinkled with expressions such as "military pride" and "military Ardour." He stated that "Military Abilities and Experience, are a great Advantage to any Character." He believed that "boys from an early age should be accustomed to military activity." Adams called for an American military academy as early as 1776; Jefferson, who for years opposed the idea, came around to supporting it only in 1801.[28]

Adams, like some other New Englanders after the outbreak of hostilities in 1775, had doubts about the Spartan qualities of the southern colonies, not wholly different from those expressed by the Massachusetts General Court in 1754. "Military characters in the southern colonies are few," he complained in August 1776. "They have never known much of war, and it is not easy to make a people warlike who have never been so."[29] Although southern delegates in Congress were aware of these Yankee reservations, it is highly doubtful that southerners actually took seriously rumors then circulating that a New England army would, if necessary, "give law" to the South to whip it into line. But there is no question that Adams and other northern congressmen advocated Washington for the post of commander in chief of the Continental army partly as least in order to sound the war drums below the Mason and Dixon Line. If one wished to press the notion of Yankee military superiority into the Revolutionary War itself, it could be stated not only that both American general Charles Lee and British general Thomas Gage considered the South less war-minded than the North, a view shared by the London ministry throughout the struggle for independence, but also that royal armies overran much of the South, with South Carolinians surrendering Charleston without a fight. Moreover, the South was eventually "rescued" by Yankee generals Nathanael Greene and Anthony Wayne, both of whom became regional heroes and received plantations from grateful legislatures in the lower South.[30]

Just as Cunliffe and Michael Adams maintain that we have exaggerated the notion of antebellum southern military prowess, so there is evidence that John Adams and New Englanders generally made too much of their own martial background. The militia as an institution performed unevenly as the seventeenth century progressed, and Massachusetts and its sister colonies employed semiprofessional troops, lured by bounties and good wages, in the eighteenth-century Anglo-French wars. And as for the hawkish-sounding Adams, he declined to serve in the Seven Years' War (he may even have had a militia exemption since he was a schoolteacher), although he later said that had he possessed the necessary resources and connections, he would have accepted an officer's commission![31]

If both martial reputations are overblown, I consider New England's to have been more credible than that of its southern counterpart, which I reexamine later on. But for now let us see what they had in common. Both military traditions were seemingly necessary components of their own regional cultures. New England, because of its unique Puritan experiment, one that was threatened by external enemies, needed to feel that its sons were brave, even heroic and warlike. The South, increasingly defensive after 1830, also felt required to trumpet its distinctiveness in ways that contrasted favorably with the free states. Northerners could respect a fighting heritage in the South, and Michael Adams is convinced that many of them did.[32]

Myth and agrarianism also contributed to the respective martial traditions of the two regions. Military prowess is a subject that has always lent itself to myth. How many men will deny to themselves characteristics that historically have been the very essence of manliness? Moreover, the claim of martial ardor, from ancient times onward, has been most closely associated with agrarian peoples, who in their everyday lives supposedly displayed qualities synonymous with the necessary defense of the homeland—qualities of virtue, strength, and endurance. Thus it was that colonial New Englanders, steeped in the history of England as interpreted by radical Whigs, believed that the mother country's "golden age" had been in Saxon times when a militia system of alodial landholders had been the safeguard of liberty. Boston lawyer Josiah Quincy depicted those agrarian warriors as the "ornament of the realm."[33] Thus, too, we find antebellum southern editor and publisher J. D. B. De Bow linking agrarian attributes and soldierly qualities: "Hardy independence, sterling patriotism, enthusiastic devotion to liberty, and love of country, and all the [other] noble virtues will be found in the agricultural classes."[34]

While New England was changing significantly in the nineteenth century, we should be wary of contending that its early military character had become extinct. As late as the Missouri crisis of 1819–21, a southern senator, Freeman Walker of Georgia, acknowledged that New Englanders were "brave, virtuous, moral, religious, and patriotic." A decade later southern literary figure William Gilmore Simms conceded that "the Yankee is the man, who first hung out the banner of liberty . . . and determined to be free."[35] And in 1846, during the congressional debates over Manifest Destiny concerning Texas and Oregon, Jeffer-

son Davis of Mississippi eulogized Joseph Warren and other New England heroes of Bunker Hill, where their commemorative monument stands on "the
ground made sacred by the blood of Warren."[36]

Such martial proclivities, with 130 years of history already behind them in
1776, would have been hard to erase in one or two generations. George Wilson
Pierson goes so far as to argue that New England's old ideals and values remained intact between 1800 and 1860; they included "sense of duty," "extraordinary moral devotion," "fortitude," and "Will."[37] The claim is not diminished
by New England's opposition to the War of 1812 and the indifference and even
hostility of some of its sons to the Mexican War, conflicts that were deemed either unjust or hardly touching vital interests.[38] During the antebellum period all
the New England states, save one, submitted annual militia returns in 65 percent
or more of those years, whereas only three southern states issued reports at least
50 percent of the time, and ten other states from Dixie did so not quite a third of
the time.[39]

The emphasis on retaining a viable militia in New England, when that institution was rapidly atrophying elsewhere, is to be found in the fact that it was still
seen as reflective of the communal and localist values of the region. Dr. Thomas
Nichols, writing about regimental training days of the 1820s in New Hampshire,
declared that militia addresses invariably included references to New England's
heroes in earlier wars and to how his own generation of militiamen continued
their glorious traditions as the present-day "pillars of the State."[40] Even J. D. B.
De Bow, the strong southern apologist, praised the Maine militia in 1850 for
standing ready to repel any British effort to redefine with force the northeastern
American-Canadian boundary ("militia bayonets . . . bustled along the Maine
frontier").[41]

The South's martial self-awareness, in contrast, had a relatively brief history
prior to the Civil War. Surely it was nonexistent in the Revolutionary era, which
John R. Alden has termed "The First South."[42] Furthermore, no historian to my
knowledge has found any evidence of it between 1789 and 1830, a period of
southern history yet to be labeled but one in which American nationalism took
precedence over sectionalism, as is illustrated in the career of the young John C.
Calhoun. Now the customary view is that 1830 marks an approximate turning
point toward still another phase of southern history, the rise of southern sectionalism and then nationalism. Though not unmindful of its minority status
within the Union in the 1820s, the South had been severely shaken by the nullification crisis of the early 1830s and by the appearance of militant abolitionist
William Lloyd Garrison's newspaper the *Liberator*. Certainly in the years there-

after southerners engaged in a torrential outpouring of writings in support of their way of life. If much of that literature was defensive, a great deal of it countered with positive information on southern distinctiveness, which the authors also described as proof of their region's cultural dominance over the civilization of the North.

One thing is astounding, however, given the durability and force of the martial South idea among historians. It is the almost total neglect, in these southern effusions, of the theme of comparative military talents, a theme that would be so passionately enunciated immediately before and during the secession crisis of 1860–61 and during the early stages of the Civil War itself. One encounters it only occasionally, as in Nathaniel Beverley Tucker's novel *The Partisan Leader* (1836), a tale of Virginia's effort to secede from the Union and join an already existing southern nation; but even here the issue of North-South martial proclivities is not clear-cut. Virginians themselves are deeply divided, and the novel ends before the war's outcome is known.[43] For many years the martial topic is almost wholly missing from the South's major literary publications—the *Southern Literary Messenger*, the *Southern Quarterly Review*, and *De Bow's Review*—although in other respects those journals were ever ready to draw North-South comparisons in the 1840s and 1850s and to display what scholars have called "southern literary nationalism."[44]

Yet the martial expressions we do encounter came mainly from intellectual figures who repeated their claims as the clouds of disunion formed and then burst over the nation—Edmund Ruffin, William Gilmore Simms, De Bow, and Daniel R. Hundley. At first, several authors charged that the South's military gifts in former wars had not been appreciated because American historians, notably George Bancroft, were mostly from the North and showed a Yankee bias. This was the line taken by Simms as well as by Griffith J. McRee and Francis L. Hawks, two North Carolina historians. That concern itself prompted Simms to aver that in the Revolution, New Englanders had fought to protect their property, and southerners had battled for principles.[45] And De Bow, who between 1857 and 1861 pulled out all the stops to prepare his section for the war that might result from secession, could assure his readers that southerners were "mainly the descendants of those who fought the battles of the Revolution."[46]

During the secession upheaval southern filiopietism was rampant in magazines and newspapers, and never more so than in *De Bow's Review*, which vowed, much as John Adams had done years earlier, that war brought out the best in men, though the magazine's exemplary heroes were southerners, not New Englanders. The latter region was noted for its pacifism and partly for that reason at least lacked the southern "military spirit." But it was not just the South's Revolutionary heritage that provided inspiration, for the South was "a warrior race" that would demonstrate its "Cavalier blood to be still worthy of its Norman origin."[47]

In my own examination of the martial South idea, I have stressed that the literary evidence—the spoken and written word as it has come down to us—is remarkably thin before the late 1850s. But as we have seen in discussing the scholarship of the last generation or so, proponents of the idea have also endeavored to erect much of the edifice with institutional evidence—from the militia, military schools, and the army itself. There is reason to question the use of some of this evidence and to provide some further information that carries us beyond that presented by Cunliffe and Adams.

As for the militia, it was certainly related to the institution of the slave patrol, although the connection seems to have varied from state to state and even from county to county. In 1849 James Cathcart Johnston of Edenton, North Carolina, boasted that the patrol was unnecessary in the Roanoke River valley. A planter did not even need to bolt his door at night, although blacks outnumbered whites many times over. He also expressed his doubts about the necessity of a city watch in Charleston, South Carolina; but the presence of the patrol was "perfectly characteristic of a city whose inhabitants are all Knight Errants."[48]

In any case, the patrol is a subject that needs renewed study, for no historian has yet been able to demonstrate that it operated effectively for lengthy periods or that it gave southerners valuable military experience. Some southern states endeavored to shore up their militias before 1860,[49] but their efforts were more often than not spasmodic and halfhearted prior to the secession crisis. There is every reason to believe that Augustus B. Longstreet's hilarious account of a "Militia Company Drill" in Georgia—a comedy of disorganization and mass confusion—was hardly atypical of such gatherings elsewhere before 1860.[50]

Moreover, the southern states' infrequent militia returns to the War Department in the antebellum years could well be interpreted to mean that some of the northern states had done a better job of keeping up their own militias. That is the position of the leading authority on the American militia, John K. Mahon, who singles out three New England states: Massachusetts, Connecticut, and Rhode Island. Above all others, North and South, these states "had throughout the years attended to their militias."[51] True, Rollin G. Osterweis sees it as highly revealing of a southern military disposition that Charleston, South Carolina, at one time had twenty-two volunteer companies. But whatever those numbers

mean, South Carolina was not the South in microcosm. A close reading of studies adhering to the martial South thesis will show that a high percentage of their
data comes from one state, South Carolina.[52]

Even the previous treatment of the Palmetto State requires further examination, especially as to the militia and to military education. In an essay published
in March 1860 in *Russell's Magazine,* James Johnston Pettigrew, a former militia
officer, an officer in the Washington Light Infantry, and a future Confederate
general, articulated grave reservations about the state's military system, including the Charleston volunteer companies that Osterweis described as exemplify-
ing a fighting spirit. To Pettigrew, the volunteer units were elitist and social in
nature, hardly a source of state security; nor, for that matter, was Charleston's organized militia, now "almost defunct."

Even though fearful of abolitionists' intrusions and slave insurrections, Pettigrew did not at that late juncture in the sectional confrontation advocate a regular military establishment for the state. As he explained, "A standing army is out
of the question. The traditions of our country condemn such an idea, as treason
against the first principles of free government." His solution was to upgrade the
militia, which had "become defective and inapplicable to . . . changing necessi-
ties," a charge he also leveled at the militia of Virginia, a state that had suffered
the indignity of having to rely on federal marines to thwart "the threatened invasion of John Brown." Were the South Carolina militia required to turn out sud-
denly, it would surely perform dismally, not only for want of soldierly knowledge
but also because the state's young men had grown soft and lazy, "incapable of
standing ordinary fatigue."[53] Had Pettigrew the information at hand, he could
have been just as harsh concerning the North Carolina militia, which had virtually ceased to exist. From 1859 to 1861 the state militia had no adjutant general,
and only after the state seceded were there meaningful efforts to revive it.[54]

Although Cunliffe has already alerted us to the existence of more military
schools in the North than we knew, it is still quite likely that a greater concentra-
tion of military schools was to be found in the South; and we have observed that
at one time South Carolina had two military colleges, the Arsenal and the
Citadel. If they were modeled after the Virginia Military Institute, it is also noteworthy that an organizing principle connected with the establishment of all
three of these Virginia and South Carolina institutions had come from Captain
Alden Partridge, a Vermonter, a West Point graduate, and former superintendent there. Partridge had pointed out that states could save money at the same
time they provided military training for future militia leaders. That could be

accomplished by turning existing arsenals over to students—instead of paying guards and caretakers—who would receive both regular academic and military training while they took care of the state's arms and ammunition.[55]

When we keep in mind the cadets' custodial and maintenance duties, we need not accept the common assertion that the state's exempting them from tuition and other fees was a sign of its determination to create a reservoir of military talent, or the statement that these schools should be viewed within the context of "the rising tide of Southern nationalism."[56] Actually, a professor at the Citadel informed Partridge in 1843 that military training was not popular with young South Carolinians, that it might be abolished altogether, and that a branch of the Citadel that had recently opened on Sullivan's Island threatened to eclipse the mother institution in Charleston. The reason: it did not require military study or exercises. Eleven years later the state issued a report showing that none of the eighty-seven graduates of the two South Carolina military academies had become a professional soldier, a career choice that seems to have been equally unattractive to graduates of the Virginia Military Institute.[57]

Because the South lagged behind the North in the number and quality of its schools at all levels, the energetic, peripatetic Partridge considered Dixie his most fertile field. For roughly thirty years he and his former students labored in the southern vineyards; but some of their academies and seminaries failed, and others succeeded only because, as the captain admitted, southerners were more interested in what they called New England forms of classical education than in the curriculum he himself favored, which emphasized the mechanical and military arts. The fact is, declares Dean Baker, Partridge's biographer, that neither North nor South displayed great support for military schools. "Historians have generally overrated Southern enthusiasm for the purely military aspects of his system."[58]

While at this time a logical transition might draw us to the debate over the southernness of West Point, the nation's premier military college, let me first bring up some matters concerning army enlisted men before we shift to the United States Military Academy and, more generally, to the officer corps in the late antebellum years. Daniel Hundley, an Alabama lawyer, in his *Social Relations in Our Southern States* waxed eloquent about the love of the outdoors and the shooting skills of the "yeomanry of our Southern States"—there was not "a more reliable citizen soldiery" in the world.[59] Some historians would seemingly have no difficulty with that statement. One writes that "some type of military experience—indeed, any type—presented an exciting prospect to young Southerners. Recruiters for the United States Army seldom experienced difficulty in filling their quotas in Southern communities."[60] Unfortunately, only one piece of evidence is cited: Philip St. George Cooke's account of his successful recruiting foray into western Tennessee in 1833. The proposed unit was to be an elite dragoon regiment, which made it much more attractive than the infantry. Not only did Cooke meet his quota with ease, but so did recruiters for the regiment who worked the northern states. And what company in the regiment had the highest desertion rate during its three-year enlistment? It was Cooke's Tennesseans. And what company demonstrated the best completion rate? One from upstate New York![61]

The safest thing we can say about northern and southern enlisted men prior to the Civil War is that the evidence for the primacy of one or the other, in any category, is inconclusive. That judgment seems particularly warranted when we return to Cooke's account of his southern recruiting. Five years previously he had offered, in speaking of a body of Mississippi enlistees, "a spice of their quality." He denounced these "drunken and mutinous" men as being "as precious a set of scoundrels as were perhaps ever collected. . . . One of them, whom I had tied up with a half-inch rope, repeatedly gnawed himself loose!" A militant southerner was not necessarily a soldierly southerner.[62]

When we look at West Point, its alumni, and army officers collectively, we discover that Cunliffe's interpretations have come under sharp attack from James M. McPherson. For example: although McPherson accepts Cunliffe's assertion that approximately 60 percent of both the school's alumni and regular army officers were northerners and only about 40 percent were southerners in the immediate pre–Civil War decades, he accuses Cunliffe of failing to acknowledge that southerners constituted only about 30 percent of the nation's white population.[63] In any event, two very recent books back Cunliffe's major conclusions with revealing new material.

In *"The Best School in the World": West Point, the Pre–Civil War Years, 1833–1866,* James L. Morrison Jr. would seem to have the latest word on several matters. He states bluntly that "the statistical evidence refutes any contention that the South dominated antebellum West Point." On the basis of white population, the South was not overrepresented on the faculty and staff, and in just three of the academic departments did southerners exceed one-third of the total. Only slightly under 15 percent of all the officers who served at West Point in those years joined the Confederacy, and none of those holding permanent professorships did. Although Dennis Hart Mahan, the most distinguished faculty member, is normally classified as a southerner, it is misleading to do so since he was born in New York, the son of Irish immigrants who later moved to Norfolk, Virginia. In his teens Mahan matriculated at West Point, not because he was a southerner, not because at that time he even wanted to be a soldier; he did so because he wanted to study drawing.[64] (Here is a good opportunity to make explicit a point that must be apparent by now: it is wonderful how we can make statistics march to our own drumbeat. What do we make of the fact that twenty-three of the first one hundred West Point graduates were Vermonters, including Alden Partridge, class of 1806, who founded the first military college at the state level, in his own Vermont?[65] Should we speak of a martial Vermont?)

Even so, at times it is necessary to crunch numbers to confute entrenched error. Concerning West Point cadets, states Morrison,

> it is true that in comparison with the total white male population between fifteen and twenty years of age, 4.7 percent more cadets were admitted from the future Confederate states than their proportion of the total population warranted, but this was because more Southern students failed academically or were dismissed for misconduct, necessitating additional appointments to fill the vacancies which resulted from departures. With respect to graduates, the data reveal that a grand total of seven (0.5 percent) more Southerners graduated than the population of that region merited.[66]

Perhaps a more intriguing question is whether southerners, both West Point cadets and officers throughout the army, saw themselves as a breed separate from and superior to their northern counterparts. Though assuredly the military was not isolated from the sectional tensions that were on the rise throughout American society, it revealed more solidarity and less particularism than was exhibited by such institutions as the churches and the political parties. Ironically, as late as the 1850s Jefferson Davis as secretary of war rejected the suggestion of creating in the South a second federal military school, and later as a United States senator he boasted of West Pointers as men who knew no sectional prejudice and thought of themselves first as Americans. If regional clannishness and occasional acrimony were visible at the academy in the decade before the Civil War, Morrison assures us that few southerners resigned their appointments before they received word that their states were seceding, and some agonized over their decision before doing so.[67]

Just as Morrison finds that accounts of pernicious southern self-awareness at West Point have been exaggerated, so Edward M. Coffman's *The Old Army,* a social history of the nineteenth-century military establishment, also discerns an absence of extreme sectional tensions and acute regional fissures within the officer cadre. Quarreling itself was almost a part of the fabric of army life, however, for promotional opportunities were limited and men might spend most of their careers at small, remote posts. Boredom, isolation, and neglect provoked altercations, even duels, but they were usually devoid of sectional implications. Actually, strong ties existed between countless northern and southern officers who had attended West Point together, served in the same Mexican War campaigns, and seen their families grow up side by side in the same garrison communities. Officers tended toward political moderation and respect for different outlooks on the issues that threatened to tear the country apart after 1848. That was the opinion of northerner Oliver Otis Howard and southerner James Longstreet, the latter of whom, though doubtless exaggerating, may not have been far off the mark when he claimed that "there were probably" no southern offices "in the Summer and Autumn of 1860 who were known as secessionists." Coffman, who uncovers no sign of a southern military caste within the army's officer corps, informs us that most of the officers favored "conciliation and hoped that they would not have to face the hard choice."[68]

Now for some final reflections. First, the connection between regionalism and military prowess initially revealed itself in New England, where feelings of defensiveness and the linking of agrarianism and heroic values contributed to notions of military self-confidence, even to the point of mythmaking, all of which in time were also true of the South.

Second, New England had developed before Lexington and Concord both a military ethos and a military tradition, terms that are not always interchangeable. It was an ethos that extolled the bravery and fighting qualities of a people who saw themselves as unique in terms of their culture and their need to defend themselves against outside enemies alien to all that their Puritan experience stood for. It was also a tradition in that New Englanders had in fact time and again over many years turned out their sons in large numbers, not only to defend New England but to carry fire and sword to their enemies' own lands.

Third, within the northern states it may well be that between the Revolution and the Civil War a martial spirit was stronger in New England than in other areas above the Mason and Dixon Line. This third point is advanced quite tentatively, but some of the evidence presented tilts in that direction, such as the endeavors of Alden Partridge and the condition of the New England militia, as well as the fact that the highest percentage of army officers (based on the white male population) from the northern states were New Englanders.[69] A sampling of some of the secondary literature covering the 1850s and the secession crisis in particular seems to reveal a spirit and zeal for war on the part of numerous New England intellectuals that surely must have rivaled that of their Puritan ancestors, to say nothing of the De Bows, the Ruffins, and the Simmses in the South.[70]

And the same may be said of most of New England's governors, who were led by Massachusetts governor John A. Andrew, "a model of energy, efficiency, and enthusiasm" for war, which he felt should be pursued relentlessly until the South was so totally devastated that it could never rise again to threaten the nation.[71]

Indeed, Senator Andrew Johnson, the Tennessee Unionist, declared that more than any of the other states, South Carolina and Massachusetts were itching for a sectional showdown. "I do not intend to be invidious," he asserted on February 5, 1861, "but I have sometimes thought it would be a comfort if Massachusetts and South Carolina could be chained together as the Siamese twins, separated from the continent, and taken out to some remote and secluded part of the ocean, and there fast anchored, to be washed by waves, and to be cooled by the winds; and after they had been kept there a sufficient length of time, the people of the United States might entertain the proposition of taking them back."[72] If subsequent investigators should bolster this hypothesis of a martial New England, it should hardly be astounding since that region had more cultural and geographic cohesion in 1861 than, for instance, the middle Atlantic states or the midwestern states.[73]

Fourth, the martial South idea came later than most authorities have acknowledged, received its most vigorous enunciation from literary figures and other civilian intellectuals, and exerted less influence on state and federal military institutions than has been claimed.

Finally, if the picture of a vibrant, distinctive southern military character has been overdrawn, it should encourage us to continue our pursuit of the elusive question of whether there existed separate northern and southern civilizations, to say nothing of southern nationalism, on the eve of the Civil War.[74] In so doing, we might discover a common military heritage that was more powerful than any regional ones—in the South, in New England, or in the North generally. A reading of certain works that focus on the northern home front come particularly to mind, especially the scholarship of Kenneth M. Stampp, George M. Fredrickson, and Earl J. Hess, all indicating as deep a commitment to a test of arms as existed in the South.[75] Some of the latest investigations of Civil War enlisted men may be equally instructive as to sectional mental configurations. Most insightful is Gerald F. Linderman's highly regarded *Embattled Courage*, a thoughtful, sensitive rendering of the mentalities of the common soldiers on both sides in the Civil War, young men who, early in the struggle, seemed to reveal identical motives and values; who spoke in their letters and journals of honor, duty, courage, and valor; who internalized moral values in ways foreign to twentieth-century soldiers' cynicism and obsession with survival.[76]

It is hardly ahistorical to speculate that it may be as easy for peoples with shared values to fight each other as it is for peoples of different values to do so. In any case, I would posit the notion that one reason the Civil War occurred was that each side was certain it would win. After all, Americans had a winning habit. When had Americans ever lost a war? And how could they do so given the values they attributed to themselves? It was in part at least that shared understanding of their history and character that led them to Bull Run, Gettysburg, and so on. But something had to give when Americans squared off; the winning way could not survive.

Or could it? In less than a generation, with the rise of the Lost Cause—the rituals and writings that kept alive the memory of the Confederacy—there were no losers, only winners: both North and South had covered themselves with honor and glory; both had prevailed in ways that seemed important to Americans in the Gilded Age and onward into the new century. "Rather than looking at the war as a tragic failure and trying to understand it, or even condemn it," explains Gaines M. Foster, "Americans, North and South, chose to view it as a glorious time to be celebrated."[77]

The idea of American exceptionalism, so far as its martial heritage went, was still intact. But what the 1860s failed to do for American exceptionalism, the 1960s did resoundingly in the distant jungles of Vietnam.

Notes

1. The most detailed and persuasive arguments for a martial South appear in Rollin G. Osterweis, *Romanticism and Nationalism in the Old South* (New Haven, 1949), and John Hope Franklin, *The Militant South* (Cambridge, Mass., 1956). Both authors cite much of the earlier scholarship on the subject.
2. The idea of a distinct southern moral code is examined in exhaustive detail in Bertram Wyatt-Brown, *Southern Honor: Ethics and Behavior in the Old South* (New York, 1982), although it does not investigate the concept of a southern military disposition.
3. Franklin, *Militant South*, 4. A recent account of southern frontier violence maintains that the antebellum northwestern frontier displayed fewer signs of social turbulence. Elliott J. Gorn, "'Gouge and Bite, Pull Hair and Scratch': The Social Significance of Fighting in the Southern Backcountry," *American Historical Review* 90 (1985): 18–43.
4. Grady McWhiney and Perry D. Jamieson, *Attack and Die: Civil War Military Tactics and the Southern Heritage* (University, Ala., 1982). The authors draw on several recent studies that contend Celtic numbers and cultural influences in the South have been inadequately recognized. Forrest McDonald and Grady McWhiney,

"The Antebellum Southern Herdsman: A Reinterpretation," *Journal of Southern History* 41 (1975): 147–66; Forrest McDonald and Ellen Shapiro McDonald, "The Ethnic Origins of the American People, 1790," *William and Mary Quarterly,* 3d ser., 37 (1980): 179–99; McDonald and McWhiney, "The South from Self-Sufficiency to Peonage: An Interpretation," *American Historical Review* 85 (1980): 1095–1118. See also McWhiney, "Ethnic Roots of Southern Violence," in *A Master's Due: Essays in Honor of David Herbert Donald,* ed. William J. Cooper Jr., Michael F. Holt, and John McCardell (Baton Rouge, La., 1985), 112–37; McWhiney, *Cracker Culture: Celtic Ways in the Old South* (Tuscaloosa, Ala., 1988).

5. W. J. Cash, *The Mind of the South* (New York, 1941).

6. Ibid., 99. See also in general John Temple Graves, *The Fighting South* (New York, 1943); Clement Eaton, *The Mind of the Old South,* rev. ed. (Baton Rouge, La., 1967). Though not unaware of societal complexities, Eaton follows Osterweis and Franklin in his treatment of the "Romantic Mind." He writes of "a devotion to the military tradition" that was a part "of the Romantic movement as it developed in the Old South." *Mind of the Old South,* 249. Eaton's chap. 12 is entitled "The Romantic Mind."

7. Marcus Cunliffe, *Soldiers and Civilians: The Martial Spirit in America, 1775–1865* (Boston, 1968), esp. chap. 10; Michael C. C. Adams, *Our Masters the Rebels: A Speculation on Union Military Failure in the East, 1861–65* (Cambridge, Mass., 1978). Other scholars have called for a modification of the martial South idea: Dickson B. Bruce Jr., *Violence and Culture in the Antebellum South* (Austin Tex., 1979), chap. 7; Robert E. May, "Dixie's Martial Image: A Continuing Historiographical Enigma," *Historian* 60 (1978): 213–34, and "John A. Quitman and the Southern Martial Spirit," *Journal of Mississippi History* 41 (1979): 155–81.

8. Cash, *Mind of the South,* 82, 46.

9. Adams, *Our Masters the Rebels.* In dealing with northern images of the South, Adams draws considerably on William R. Taylor, *Cavalier and Yankee: The Old South and American National Character* (New York, 1961).

10. Francis Jennings, *The Invasion of America: Indians, Colonialism, and the Cant of Conquest* (Chapel Hill, N.C., 1975), vii.

11. Alden T. Vaughan, *The New England Frontier: Puritans and Indians, 1620–1675* (Boston, 1965); Wilcomb E. Washburn, "Seventeenth-Century Indian Wars," in *Northeast,* ed. Bruce G. Trigger, vol. 15 of *Handbook of North American Indians,* William C. Sturtevant, general ed., 9 vols. published out of sequence (Washington, D.C., 1978–), 89–100.

12. Douglas Edward Leach, *Flintlock and Tomahawk: New England in King Philip's War* (New York, 1958), 243.

13. Quoted in John E. Ferling, *A Wilderness of Miseries: War and Warriors in Early America* (Westport, Conn., 1980), 45.

14. Military forms of address are discussed in Norman H. Dawes, "Titles as Symbols of Prestige in Seventeenth-Century New England," *William and Mary Quarterly,* 3d ser., 6 (1949): 69–83.

15. *The Sovereignty of Goodness of GOD, together with the Faithfulness of His Promises*

Displayed; Being a Narrative of the Captivity and Restoration of Mrs. Mary Rowlandson (Cambridge, Mass., 1682); Jeremy Belknap, *The History of New-Hampshire*, 3 vols. (Philadelphia and Boston, 1784–92); Thomas Hutchinson, *The History of the Colony and Province of Massachusetts-Bay*, ed. Lawrence Shaw Mayo, 3 vols. (1764–1828; rpt., Cambridge, Mass., 1936).

16. Ferling, *Wilderness of Miseries*, 68, 55. A superb account of military concerns in sermon literature is Harry S. Stout, *The New England Soul: Preaching and Religious Culture in Colonial New England* (New York, 1986), esp. chap. 12. Also useful but less satisfactory is Marie L. Ahearn, *The Rhetoric of War: Training Day, the Militia, and the Military Sermon* (Westport, Conn., 1989).

17. John M. Murrin, "Anglicizing an American Colony: The Transformation of Provincial Massachusetts" (Ph.D. diss., Yale Univ., 1966); William Pencak, *War, Politics, and Revolution in Provincial Massachusetts* (Boston, 1981); Fred Anderson, *A People's Army: Massachusetts Soldiers and Society in the Seven Years' War* (Chapel Hill, N. C., 1984); Harold E. Selesky, *War and Society in Colonial Connecticut* (New Haven, 1990).

18. Richard L. Morton, *Colonial Virginia*, 2 vols. (Chapel Hill, N.C., 1960), 2:534–35.

19. Quoted in Albert Bushnell Hart, ed., *Commonwealth History of Massachusetts*, 5 vols. (New York, 1927–30), 2:461.

20. R. A. Brock, ed., *The Official Letters of Alexander Spotswood . . .*, 10 vols. (Richmond, 1882–85), 2:212, and *The Official Records of Robert Dinwiddie . . .*, 2 vols. (Richmond, 1883–84), 2:344; *PGW: Col. Ser.* 4:90.

21. James Titus, *The Old Dominion at War: Society, Politics, and Warfare in Late Colonial Virginia* (Columbia, S.C., 1991); Thomas L. Purvis, "Colonial Participation in the Seven Years' War, 1755–63" (paper presented at the General Brown Conference at the University of Alabama, Tuscaloosa, 1983), as well as more recent information provided me by the author.

22. The "Massacre Day" orations, which continued through the Revolutionary War, are in Hezekiah Niles, *Principles and Acts of the Revolution in America* (Baltimore, 1822), 15–79.

23. Rufus R. Wilson, ed., *Heath's Memoirs of the American War . . .* (New York, 1904), 15–17; Boston *Gazette*, Jan. 27, Feb. 24, Sept. 21, 1772, Nov. 15, 1773, Oct. 10, 1774; Timothy Pickering, *East Plan of Discipline for a Militia* (Salem, Mass., 1775).

24. Hartford *Connecticut Courant*, Jan. 19, Dec. 14, 1773.

25. L. H. Butterfield, ed., *The Adams Papers: The Diary and Autobiography of John Adams*, 4 vols. (Cambridge, Mass., 1961), 2:53, 3:195, 266–67; Lester J. Cappon, ed., *The Adams-Jefferson Letters: The Complete Correspondence between Thomas Jefferson and Abigail and John Adams*, 2 vols. (Chapel Hill, N.C., 1959), 2:402.

26. On January 2, 1766, Adams wrote: if the "great Men" of the London ministry persisted, "they will find it a more obstinate War, than the Conquest of Canada and Louisiana." Butterfield, *Adams Diary and Autobiography* 2:284. In his "Novanglus" essays, published in the Boston *Gazette* in the three months prior to the outbreak of the Revolutionary War, Adams not only encouraged provincial preparedness but also warned Britain that America could prevail in a military struggle. The essays are

conveniently found in Bernard Mason, ed., *The American Colonial Crisis: The Daniel Leonard–John Adams Letters to the Press, 1774–75* (New York, 1972), 98–266.

27. Reginald C. Stuart, *The Half-War Pacifist: Thomas Jefferson's View of War* (Toronto, 1978).

28. Robert J. Taylor et al., eds., *The Adams Papers: Papers of John Adams,* 11 vols. to date (Cambridge, Mass., 1977–), 1:192 (first four quotations); Butterfield, *Adams Diary and Autobiography* 3:442–43 (fifth quotation), 2:160 (seventh quotation); Lyman H. Butterfield et al., eds., *The Adams Papers: Family Correspondence,* 4 vols. (Cambridge, Mass., 1963–73), 2:166 (sixth quotation); John A. Schutz and Douglass Adair, eds., *The Spur of Fame: Dialogues of John Adams and Benjamin Rush, 1805–13* (San Marino, Calif., 1966), 137; David W. Hazen, "John Adams and the Foundation of American Military Policy" (M.A. thesis, Univ. of North Carolina at Chapel Hill, 1978), 166–68.

29. Charles Francis Adams, ed., *The Works of John Adams . . . ,* 10 vols. (Boston, 1850–56), 1:252.

30. On Washington's appointment and sources divulging sectional considerations, see Don Higginbotham, *The War of American Independence: Military Attitudes, Policies, and Practice, 1763–89* (New York, 1971), 8, 22, 84, 95–96. British attitudes toward the South are treated in Paul H. Smith, *Loyalists and Redcoats: A Study in British Revolutionary Policy* (Chapel Hill, N.C., 1965).

31. Adams went on to say, "Could I have obtained a troop of horse or a company of foot, I should infallibly have been a soldier." Adams to Charles Cushing, March 13, 1817, in Charles Francis Adams, *Works of John Adams* 2:38.

32. For an earlier examination of the cavalier ideal in both North and South, see Taylor, *Cavalier and Yankee.*

33. Josiah Quincy, *Memoir of the Life of Josiah Quincy, Jun., of Massachusetts* (Boston, 1825), 413. The theme of the agrarian warrior is prominent in the writings of James Harrington. In fact, J. G. A. Peacock believes that Harrington's uniting of landed "proprietorship and the control of the sword probably did more than anything else to preserve Harringtonian doctrine" into the eighteenth century. Pocock, ed., *The Political Works of James Harrington* (Cambridge, Eng., 1977), 130–44, quotation on p. 131.

34. *De Bow's Review* 2 (1846): 116.

35. *Annals of Congress,* 16th Cong., 1st sess., 35:162 (Senate debate of Jan. 18, 1820); John W. Higham, "The Changing Loyalties of William Gilmore Simms," *Journal of Southern History* 9 (1943): 211.

36. *Congressional Globe* 29th Cong., 1st sess., 86:320 (House debate of Feb. 6, 1846).

37. George Wilson Pierson, "The Obstinate Concept of New England: A Study in Denudation," *New England Quarterly* 28 (1955): 3–17, quotations on p. 13. Anne Norton maintains that Puritan religious and cultural beliefs were consciously reinvigorated in response to Catholic immigration and other changes in American life. A belief in organized "collective violence," she writes, "was a powerful and deeply meaningful reaffirmation" of age-old values. Norton, *Alternative Americas:*

A Reading of Antebellum Political Culture (Chicago, 1986), 31–32, 74, 82, quotation on p. 122. See also Hal S. Barron, *Those Who Stayed Behind: Rural Society in Nineteenth-Century New England* (Cambridge, Eng., 1984); Tamara Plakins Thornton, *Cultivating Gentlemen: The Meaning of Country Life among the Boston Elite, 1785–1860* (New Haven, 1989); Paul A. Varg, *New England and Foreign Relations, 1789–1850* (Hanover, N.H., 1983).

38. Several articles by Donald R. Hickey show the New England Federalists to have been fairly generous in their support of defensive military measures and naval appropriations before and during the War of 1812: "New England's Defense Problem and the Genesis of the Hartford Convention," *New England Quarterly* 50 (1977): 587–604; "Federalist Party Unity and the War of 1812," *Journal of American Studies* 12 (1978): 23–39; "The Federalist and the Coming of War, 1811–1812," *Indiana Magazine of History* 75 (1979): 70–88; and "Federalists Defense Policy in the Age of Jefferson, 1801–1812," *Military Affairs* 45 (1981): 63–70. There appears to be no good study of New England and the Mexican War, but certainly there was considerable support for the war, and most opponents were hardly pacifists. The ambivalence of New England antiwar critics in 1846–48 and of the peace movement generally are illuminated in Robert W. Johannsen, *To the Halls of the Montezumas: The Mexican War in the American Imagination* (New York, 1985), 214–18, 270–79.

39. William H. Riker, *Soldiers of the States: The Role of the National Guard in American Democracy* (Washington, D.C., 1957), 27.

40. Thomas Low Nichols, *Forty Years of an American Life, 1821–1861,* 2 vols. (1864; rpt. New York, 1937), 1:29–30.

41. *De Bow's Review* 9 (1850): 166.

42. Alden, *The First South* (Baton Rouge, La., 1961).

43. Tucker, the half brother of John Randolph of Roanoke, was as committed to political conservatism and states' rights as his sibling and may well have been the South's first avowed secessionist. Robert J. Brugger, *Beverley Tucker: Heart over Head in the Old South* (Baltimore, 1978). Both northerners and southerners considered Tucker's *Partisan Leader* (Washington, D.C., 1836) to be timely reading after the outbreak of the Civil War. It was reprinted in New York (1861) and in Richmond (1862).

44. David Kelly Jackson, *The Contributors and Contributions to the Southern Literary Messenger (1834–64)* (Charlottesville, Va., 1936); Frank Winkler Ryan Jr., *"The Southern Quarterly Review, 1842–1857:* A Study in Thought and Opinion in the Old South" (Ph.D. diss., Univ. of North Carolina at Chapel Hill, 1956); Ottis Clark Skipper, *J. D. B. De Bow: Magazinist of the Old South* (Athens, Ga., 1958); Jay B. Hubbell, "Literary Nationalism in the Old South," in *American Studies in Honor of William K. Boyd,* ed. David Kelly Jackson (Durham, N.C., 1940), 175–220.

45. Griffith J. McRee to David L. Swain, Oct. 21, 1855, Aug. 27, [1857], Francis L. Hawks to Swain, Dec. 18, 1857, David Lowry Swain Papers, Southern Historical Collection, University of North Carolina at Chapel Hill; William Gilmore Simms, "South Carolina in the Revolution," *Southern Quarterly Review* 14 (1848): 37–77, esp. 49; Higham, "The Changing Loyalties of William Gilmore Simms," 210–23. On the use of the Revolution generally by sectional partisans, see John Hope

Franklin, "The North, the South, and the American Revolution," *Journal of American History* 62 (1975): 5–23.

46. *De Bow's Review* 30 (1861): 73.

47. Ibid., 31 (1861): 36 (first quotation), 70–77 (last two quotations on p. 72). De Bow, however, had not always been consistent. A decade earlier he had written that a martial spirit was a national phenomenon, not a regional one. Ibid., 9 (1850): 165–66. See also Adams, *Our Masters the Rebels,* 68–69; Donald E. Reynolds, *Editors Make War: Southern Newspapers in the Secession Crisis* (Nashville, Tenn., 1970), 174; Frank Moore, ed., *The Rebellion Record,* 12 vols. (New York, 1861–68), 1:59, 114; Dwight Lowell Dumond, ed., *Southern Editorials on Secession* (New York, 1931); Daniel R. Hundley, *Social Relations in Our Southern States,* ed. William J. Cooper Jr. (Baton Rouge, La., 1979).

48. James Cathcart Johnston to James Johnston Pettigrew, June 16, 1849, Pettigrew Family Papers, Southern Historical Collection.

49. Franklin, *Militant South,* 188–89, chap. 12.

50. Augustus B. Longstreet, *Georgia Scenes* (1835; rpt. New York, 1852), 145–51. Just over a decade later another Georgian echoed Longstreet when he complained that the state's militia was "synonymous with epithets of contempt and reproach." "The State of Georgia," *De Bow's Review* 10 (1851): 245.

51. John K. Mahon, *History of the Militia and the National Guard* (New York, 1983), 97–98, quotation on p. 98. In fact, the Massachusetts militia, in a high state of readiness in 1861, had steadily improved its effectiveness and morale during the twenty years before the outbreak of the Civil War. Robert F. McGraw, "Minutemen of '61: The Pre–Civil War Massachusetts Militia," *Civil War History* 15 (1969): 101–15.

52. The statement is particularly true of Osterweis's *Romanticism and Nationalism,* which also draws heavily on evidence from Virginia and Louisiana.

53. [James Johnston Pettigrew], "The Necessity for Improved Military Defences Considered," *Russell's Magazine* 6 (1860): 529–40, quotations on pp. 530, 532. About this same time Pettigrew declared in a letter to a relative that "the Militia and Patrol system are dying out everywhere." Pettigrew to W. S. Pettigrew, Nov. 20, 1859, Pettigrew Family Papers, Southern Historical Collection. Even in South Carolina during most of 1860, no one was quite certain what that state or other southern states would do about their status in the Union. The point is well illustrated in Pettigrew's case; he sought and received assistance from the federal garrison in Charleston in reorganizing and upgrading the local militia. Clyde N. Wilson, *Carolina Cavalier: The Life and Mind of James Johnston Pettigrew* (Athens, Ga., 1990), 122–23. For a detailed examination of events within the state, see Steven A. Channing, *Crisis of Fear: Secession in South Carolina* (New York, 1970). Virginia's deficiencies are detailed in "Military Defenses of Virginia," *De Bow's Review* 19 (1855): 445–50; Moreau B. C. Chambers, "The Militia Crisis," *Virginia Cavalcade* 16 (1967): 10–14. In 1860 Nathaniel Francis Cabell of Virginia vowed that "we must arm & discipline our people, nor must the Military Spirit ever again be allowed to become dormant as in time past." Quoted in Bruce, *Southern Violence,* 163.

54. *Report as to Organization and Condition of the Militia of the State* (Raleigh, N.C.,

1859); Raymond A. Heath Jr., "The North Carolina Militia on the Eve of the Civil War" (M.A. thesis, Univ. of North Carolina at Chapel Hill, 1974).

55. Dean Paul Baker, "The Partridge Connection: Alden Partridge and Southern Military Education" (Ph.D. diss., Univ. of North Carolina at Chapel Hill, 1986), 311; [William Hume], "Military Schools of South-Carolina," *Southern Quarterly Review,* new ser., 2 (1850): 527–34.

56. Osterweis, *Romanticism and Nationalism,* 126.

57. Baker, "Partridge Connection," 424–25. Approximately ten years after their conversion to educational institutions, however, the Arsenal and the Citadel were reported to be making significant progress in the quality of both their academic and military programs. [Charles Courtney Tew], "South-Carolina Military Academies," *Southern Quarterly Review,* new ser., 2 (1854): 191–204, which also contains a statistical breakdown of the graduates' professions. Tew's contention about improvements would seem to be borne out by Thomas Hart Law, *Citadel Cadets: The Journal of Cadet Tom Law . . .* (Clinton, S.C., [1941]). But as late as December 1858, a lengthy unsigned article about South Carolina's two military schools dealt almost entirely with their academic subjects and gave no hint that their cadets and recent graduates might be needed to defend the state from northern aggression. "Origin of the State Military Academies," *Russell's Magazine* 4 (1858): 219–26. For Virginia Military Institute, see B. J. Barbour, "Address Delivered before the Literary Societies of the Virginia Military Institute, July 4th, 1854," *Southern Literary Messenger* 20 (1854): 513. See also the series of articles on the "Progress of Education in Virginia," comparing Virginia Military Institute with the state's public and private colleges and the University of Virginia, in vols. 24 and 25 of the *Southern Literary Messenger* between March and August 1857.

58. Baker, "Partridge Connection," 424.

59. Hundley, *Social Relations,* 198–203, quotation on p. 200.

60. Franklin, *Militant South,* 15.

61. Philip St. George Cooke, *Scenes and Adventures in the Army, or, Romance of Military Life* (1856; rpt. New York, 1973), 197–201. That New Yorkers in the regiment were proud of their military record is demonstrated in the memoirs of Brooklyn-born James Hildreth. See his *Dragoon Campaigns to the Rocky Mountains . . .* (New York, 1836). Statistical information on the composition and performance of the dragoon regiment is from Dale E. Steinhauer, "Enlisted Men in the U.S. Army, 1815–1860" (Ph.D. diss., Univ. of North Carolina at Chapel Hill, 1992).

62. Cooke, *Scenes and Adventures,* 24–25. Steinhauer informs me that in the antebellum years the army did most of its recruiting in the northeastern cities, where concentrations of manpower reduced the time and cost of the General Recruiting Service. Therefore, it will be difficult ever to reach definitive conclusions about northern and southern attitudes toward military enlistments.

63. James M. McPherson, "Antebellum Southern Exceptionalism: A New Look at an Old Question," *Civil War History* 29 (1983): 230–44.

64. James L. Morrison Jr., *"The Best School in the World": West Point, the Pre-Civil War Years, 1833–66* (Kent, Ohio, 1986), 47, 131.

65. Dale E. Steinhauer, "West Point's First One Hundred Graduates by State of Birth and State of Appointment," MS in the author's possession.

66. Morrison, *"The Best School in the World,"* 132, app. 7.

67. Ibid., 126–31.

68. Edward M. Coffman, *The Old Army: A Portrait of the American Army in Peacetime, 1784–1898* (New York, 1986), 66–70, 81, 89–96, quotations on pp. 92, 95. On accounts of equally agonizing decisions in the maritime branch, see William S. Dudley, *Going South: U.S. Naval Officer Resignations and Dismissals on the Eve of the Civil War* (Washington, D.C., 1981). An examination of what he calls core values of Civil War soldiers, based on a content analysis of their diaries, leads Michael Barton to the conclusion that southern officers were mainstream Americans in their strong adherence to "Achievement, Humanitarianism, Efficiency, Materialism, Freedom, Equality, Science, and Democracy." Barton, *Goodmen: The Character of Civil War Soldiers* (University Park, Pa., 1981), 25–26. Southerners undoubtedly held a larger proportion of high-ranking posts in the army between 1848 and 1861, but the scholar who has investigated the southern presence during those years finds career concerns and economic opportunities to be the paramount explanation for the disproportionate numbers of southerners in the upper levels of the army. Regional bias was not a significant factor in accounting for southern influence. See David Kenneth Bowden, "The South and the American Army, 1848–1860: A Search for Southern Dominance" (Ph.D. diss., Univ. of South Carolina, 1980).

69. Bowden, "South and the American Army," 50–51.

70. For example, Theodore Parker, the Massachusetts clergyman and radical abolitionist, took inspiration from his grandfather who fought at Lexington in 1775 and from Massachusetts's leadership in the Revolution. To Parker, New England men were still upright and virile and ready to spill their blood to end slavery in the South. Michael Fellman, "Theodore Parker and the Abolitionist Role in the 1850s," *Journal of American History* 61 (1974): 666–84. For a second example, see Richard Bridgman, *Dark Thoreau* (Lincoln, Nebr., 1982), which stresses Henry David Thoreau's admiration of John Brown and Brown's New England antecedents, particularly his grandfather's part in the War of Independence. More generally see Norton, *Alternative Americas,* and sources cited in note 75, below.

71. William B. Hesseltine, *Lincoln and the War Governors* (New York, 1948), 112–14, 115, 128–30, 148–50, quotation on p. 148.

72. Leroy P. Graf et al, eds., *The Papers of Andrew Johnson,* 16 vols. (Knoxville, Tenn., 1967–2000), 4:220.

73. On northern perceptions of New England's economic and cultural differences from the other free states, see Howard Cecil Perkins, ed., *Northern Editorials on Secession,* 2 vols. (New York, 1942), 1:384–88, 391, 401–2, 405–8, 414, 2:563, 572, 589–91, 731–32.

74. Among the most recent and thoughtful discussions of southern nationalism are David M. Potter, *The South and the Sectional Conflict* (Baton Rouge, La., 1968); John McCardell, *The Idea of a Southern Nation: Southern Nationalists and Southern Nationalism, 1830–1860* (New York, 1979); Richard E. Beringer, Herman Hatta-

way, Archer Jones, and William N. Still Jr., *Why the South Lost the Civil War* (Athens, Ga., 1986); Drew Gilpin Faust, *The Creation of Confederate Nationalism: Ideology and Identity in the Civil War South* (Baton Rouge, La., 1988).

75. George M. Fredrickson, *The Inner Civil War: Northern Intellectuals and the Crisis of the Union* (New York, 1965), 36–37, 43, 48, 50, 61, 67, 71–75, 86, 176–80, 217, 219–20, 227–28; Kenneth M. Stampp, *And the War Came: The North and the Secession Crisis, 1860–61* (Baton Rouge, La., 1950), chaps. 6, 12; Earl J. Hess, *Liberty, Virtue, and Progress: Northerners and Their War for the Union* (New York, 1988).

76. Gerald F. Linderman, *Embattled Courage: The Experience of Combat in the American Civil War* (New York, 1987). The late Bell Irvin Wiley, author of the most detailed and comprehensive studies of Union and Confederate soldiers, once observed to Edward Pessen that (as the latter paraphrased it), "if the thousands of letters written home by the youngsters on both sides were thrown in the air and then fell to earth with all identifying characteristics removed, it would be impossible to know which were written by Rebs, which by Yanks." Pessen, "How Different from Each Other Were the Antebellum North and South," *American Historical Review* 85 (1980): 1166. Two other recent accounts of Civil War soldiers give more weight to northern and southern common values than to their differences. See Reid Mitchell, *Civil War Soldiers* (New York, 1988), and James I. Robertson Jr., *Soldiers Blue and Gray* (Columbia, S.C., 1988).

77. Gaines M. Foster, *Ghosts of the Confederacy: Defeat, the Lost Cause, and the Emergence of the New South, 1865 to 1913* (New York, 1987), 196. See also Linderman, *Embattled Courage;* Thomas C. Leonard, *Above the Battle: War Making in America from Appomattox to Versailles* (New York, 1978); Rollin G. Osterweis, *The Myth of the Lost Cause, 1865–1900* (Hamden, Conn., 1973). On treatments of the martial South idea for the New South period, see May, "Dixie's Martial Image," 227–34; John Hawkins Napier III, "The Militant South Revisited: Myths and Realities," *Alabama Review* 33 (1980): 243–65; James C. Bonner, "The Historical Basis of Southern Military Tradition," *Georgia Review* 9 (1955): 74–85.

8 ⋮ *Fomenters of Revolution*

I RECEIVED THE OPPORTUNITY of giving a second presidential address (fortunately there are no others!), this time to the Society for Historians of the Early American Republic in Chapel Hill, North Carolina, on July 24, 1993. There was no deal, no quid pro quo, attached to my presidency and the annual meeting being held at the University of North Carolina, my academic institution. Unlike most historical association gatherings, this one is always held in midsummer on a college or university campus, and the site was set before my selection. The fact that the organization is relatively small makes this kind of location ideal. It brings a closeness and collegiality impossible to create in a large urban atmosphere. A few hundred historians at most show up for the Society for Historians of the Early American Republic meetings. Several thousand regularly turn out annually for the Organization of American Historians and the American Historical Association.

The society defines its interests chronologically from the Revolutionary era to the eve of the Civil War, and my presentation literally spans those years. Whereas in chapter 7 I compared New England and the South in terms of regional attitudes toward war and other things military, here in chapter 8 I look at parallels between Massachusetts's role in the coming of the American Revolution and South Carolina's part in bringing on the Confederate Revolution. I try to show why each of these polities was out in front—leading the charge—in these respective upheavals.

Implicitly, the search for answers really creates another question, one I might explore at another time. It too is critical to understanding the rise of secessionist impulses: why did some colonies or states lag behind, behave more conservatively in terms of a willingness to engage in revolution and war? In 1776 certain colonies hung back until almost the last moment for fairly obvious reasons, but they were not the same reasons for every colony. New York and Pennsylvania, and the Middle Colonies in general, lacked societies that were culturally cohesive, characterized rather by ethnic and religious diversity. South Carolina's hesitancy to accept independence surely had something to do with fear about the prospect of unsettling a population made up of more blacks—slaves—than whites. It would be hard to argue that political thought divided Massachusetts and other aggressive polities such as Virginia from their neighbors who responded to British threats more slowly. Whig thought about representation, sovereignty, and constitutionalism hardly separated them. The point about political ideas also holds true for southerners in 1861. For example, the Border State leaders shared with Deep South chieftains a belief in states' rights and the legality of secession. But slavery itself was less an overriding issue in the upper South, where the black population, relatively speaking, had been declining for years. South Carolina's large slave population casts significant light on why the state's secession convention voted unanimously to separate from the Union. The state's leaders believed the election of a Republican, Abraham Lincoln, posed a direct threat to their social order. The lower South, with its substantial black population, quickly followed, but the upper South seceded only after the firing on Fort Sumter and Lincoln's call for troops. My presidential address appeared in the *Journal of the Early Republic* 14 (Spring 1994): 1–33 and is reprinted with the permission of the coeditors.

———◆———

OCCUPYING ARMIES rarely respect enemy cities. Witness the British troops of Generals Thomas Gage and William Howe in Boston, Massachusetts, in 1775–76 and the Union forces of General William T. Sherman in Columbia, South Carolina, in 1865. Both armies marauded for understandable reasons. Redcoats swore that without Massachusetts no American rebellion would have occurred. Bluecoats cursed that had not South Carolina sown the seeds of secession, no southern rebellion would have transpired. Both Boston and Columbia paid a high price for their disunionist leadership.

General Hugh, Earl Percy drew a menacing parallel between Massachusetts's insurgency and the Scottish "Rebellion of Forty-five."[1] Many other royal army officers sought to replicate the bloody retribution that the duke of Cumberland had inflicted upon the Highlanders after the Battle of Culloden. Boston's churches, repositories of what one Briton called the colony's "cursed Puritanick spirit," were singled out for harsh treatment. Soldiers gutted or all but destroyed Old North and West. They ripped out the pews of Old South and covered the floor with gravel to make a riding school for the king's army. They demolished two hundred houses to provide firewood for the royal garrison. Before giving up the city, redcoats "plundered every unprotected shop and house in town."[2] These British depredations would have been worse had not hun-

dreds of loyalists taken refuge there, and any effort to burn the town prior to English evacuation on March 17, 1776, would have brought an attack by Washington's army on the British rear guard.

During the Civil War things were much worse for South Carolina in general
and Columbia in particular. It seems as though all the diarists in Sherman's
army eagerly anticipated invading the Palmetto State, which they almost univer-
sally blamed for the war. Carolinians, hysterical with fear, knew that Sherman's
men held them in special contempt. As advance parties of the Fourteenth Corps
crossed over a bridge into the state, one veteran looked back and yelled, "Boys,
this is old South Carolina, lets give her hell." South Carolina "cried out the first
for war," exclaimed an Iowan, "and she shall have it to her hearts content. She
sowed the Wind. She will soon reap the Whirlwind." Another Union soldier
vowed that "nearly every man in Sherman's army Say they are in for disstroying
every thing in South Carolina." Though Sherman and his staff maintained they
had nothing to do with the torching of Columbia, and though one Ohio lieutenant insisted that "*whisky done it* and *not the* soldiers," the capital was left as
"nothing but a pile of ruins, a warning to future generations to beware of treason," as one bluecoat phrased it.[3]

This undertaking seeks to cast light on the above-mentioned perceptions of
Massachusetts and South Carolina. It is a reflection of my continuing efforts in
recent years to examine the American Revolution in certain comparative ways;[4]
but only now am I looking at an aspect of the Confederate Revolution in relation
to the American Revolution.[5] Even though a presidential address may give one
license for boldness, I venture forth with even more trepidation than was displayed by the revolutionists of either 1776 or 1861. I begin with the admission
that no two revolutions are really alike, and I agree with Crane Brinton's cautionary reminder that it takes all kinds of people to make a revolution. I also concede the danger of making too much of some kinds of comparisons—of suc-
cumbing to the "so what" pitfall. Even so, the role of Massachusetts and South
Carolina in their respective revolutions reveals enough similarities as well as
contrasts to make this excursion worthwhile. First, I investigate why Massachusetts and South Carolina could successfully engage in threats and acts of defiance for so long, emphasizing the decentralized nature of the federal system in
which each operated and the growing homogeneity of each society. Second, I
examine the similarity of views held by both the friends and the enemies of the
Bay Colony and the Palmetto State—notably the ambivalence of friends and the
hostility of enemies. Third, I point to the reluctance of both Massachusetts and
South Carolina to go it alone or to press their allies to extreme lengths in behalf

of independence. Finally, I conclude that Massachusetts came around to separation more reluctantly than did South Carolina. Massachusetts and South Carolina were each a part of a political system that had maintained rather little authority over its constituent components. That is to say, neither the Hanoverian
British Empire nor the antebellum United States government exercised very
many internal controls. The generality of provincial inhabitants in Massachusetts never encountered a crown customs officer or redcoated soldier. Even after
the adoption of the Constitution of 1787, the United States Post Office was the
only national agency or department with which most citizens had meaningful
contact. Any act of defiance, short of armed rebellion, might well find the peripheries prevailing over the center before 1774 in the old empire and before 1861
in the federal Union.

For example, one can note colonial Massachusetts's circumvention of the
White Pines Act and the Molasses Act, at the same time pointing to nineteenth-
century Charlestonians' removal of abolitionist literature from the federal mails
and their city officials' flouting of the Seamen's Act, which granted shore privileges to crews—including blacks—of foreign vessels in American ports. It is
hard for present-day Americans, mindful of the forced exiles of such recent
revolutionaries as Vladimir Lenin, Ho Chi Minh, and Yasser Arafat, to understand why the metropolitan establishments failed to imprison or exile preindependence radicals or presecession fire-eaters. Even most modern Western
democracies today would likely have arrested some Massachusetts and South
Carolina incendiaries under their sedition and treason statutes. No doubt Andrew C. McLaughlin had, in effect, the answer why such incarcerations did not
take place when he declared, many years ago, that both the eighteenth-century
British Empire and the later American Union were loosely structured federal
systems. The centers, London and Washington, showed considerable reluctance to employ even the power that they legitimately possessed or might ar-
guably claim under broad interpretations of their constitutional prerogatives.[6]

Friends and foes of both Massachusetts and South Carolina had at least one
thing in common. They recognized that those two polities were different from
all others, for each had played a larger part than any of its neighbors in bringing
about a revolution. This had been possible—according to outside observers of
various political persuasions—partly because each seemed to be something of a
monolith, as much if not more socially, culturally, and politically united than the
other colonies/states. Contributing to that cohesion was the fact that each occupied a relatively small geographic area, lacking formidable mountains and waterways that otherwise might have served to divide its inhabitants in significant

ways. Hence, neither had internal fissures that might take on the ferocity of fratricide, severely weakening its public stands. To put it another way, both lacked the pluralism so often described as the essence of America.

Continuity and internal stability had prevailed in Massachusetts, especially after the collapse of the Dominion of New England and after the colony acclimated itself to the royal charter of 1691. Its people were overwhelmingly English, and its Congregational Church was the strongest in the colonies. Its House of Representatives was one of the most powerful lower houses in America. Completely dominant in the area of finance, it had prevailed over the crown in refusing to grant its royal governors a fixed salary from permanent revenues.[7] There were from time to time loose, amorphous political factions, so-called court and country parties that revolved largely around personalities and quests for office, with the major players known to shift sides as easily as Colonel James Otis Sr., who, like other powerful men, took his town with him as he angled for preferment, be it the speakership of the House of Representatives or the post of chief justice of the Superior Court.[8]

Massachusetts's bold stand during the imperial crisis owed much to the absence of the kinds of religious divisions and east-west controversies that fueled factionalism in the middle colonies and certain of the southern colonies, making internal unity against Britain impossible to achieve. The pragmatic character of Massachusetts politics explains why earlier controversies receded and past enemies came together in the face of a common threat. There were influential exceptions, particularly crown officeholders and provincial placemen who depended upon the royal governor—most noteworthy were the friends and family of Thomas Hutchinson and the western "river gods," power brokers in Hampshire and Berkshire Counties. Yet by 1766 the court party was on the defensive and would never recover as its adversaries, now called the popular party or liberty party, made crown officeholders impotent. And, as Benjamin Labaree has observed, "with this change a difference in ideology would appear for the first time in the politics of Massachusetts Bay."[9] Contrary to the long-standard interpretation, the Boston committee of correspondence did not manipulate and pressure the interior towns into joining the resistance. Instead, as Richard D. Brown has shown, the Boston committee tactfully encouraged the inland communities to express similar views, which included a staunch adherence to inviolable constitutional rights first carried to Massachusetts Bay by their Puritan ancestors. Townspeople everywhere realized that they shared the same political values and faced the same threat. These conditions and circumstances made loyalism in the Revolution probably weakest of all in Massachusetts.[10]

South Carolina in the middle of the nineteenth century appeared every bit as homogeneous as had the Bay Colony nearly a century earlier. But the Palmetto State had not always been that way, whereas Massachusetts had never strayed fundamentally from the Puritan values of John Winthrop's founding generation.[11] Prior to the American Revolution, South Carolina revealed religious and ethnic divisions, as well as political discontent, that separated the up-country from the low country, manifesting themselves in the frontier Regulator movement and in sizable pockets of inland loyalism during the War of Independence.[12]

South Carolina's subsequent uniqueness—its special peculiarities—has attracted far more scholarly attention than the commonalities of preindependence Massachusetts, probably because historians have made greater efforts to link South Carolina to the Civil War than they have made to connect Massachusetts to the Revolution.[13] Moreover, historians of South Carolina have found only limited agreement concerning the peculiarities of their subject. By the 1830s, however, it is generally acknowledged, South Carolina was eschewing the emerging two-party system in America; its politics could be characterized as factional in character, with disagreements more on tactical than philosophical matters; and except for universal manhood suffrage, its political institutions were the most undemocratic in the nation.

John C. Calhoun, the state's political colossus, hardly created this political system. It therefore exaggerates to say, as did some of his contemporaries, that "when Calhoun took snuff, South Carolina sneezed," or that "South Carolina and Mr. Calhoun are the same," or that his was a "political despotism" like that of "Henry the Eighth."[14] But he eloquently defended the state's political culture and worked hard and successfully to keep it resistant to change. Many of its citizens, while nominally Democrats, scantily identified with the national Democracy, as was the case with Calhoun himself, who only flirted with the national party and only when it suited his personal ambitions or the interests of his state. The weakness of the Democratic Party and the virtual absence of the Whig Party are explained in large part by South Carolinians' obsession with defending slavery in a state that had the highest ratio of slaves to whites in the Union, a state that saw permanent servitude and the cotton plantation system moved steadily into the up-country, so that eventually slavery was more evenly distributed territorially in South Carolina than anywhere else in America. Assuredly ideas inimical to its system of race relations did not often come from any segment of the white population, which in 1860 was 96.6 percent South Carolina born.[15]

A man with the genteel values of Charleston and the low country, but one who hailed from the upcountry, Calhoun personified the coming together of the sections in social and economic terms and in presenting to the nation a common front in protecting slavery. In fact, that process had begun in the generation of Calhoun's father Patrick, who accumulated land, slaves, and political influence. And it continued in the decade after John C. Calhoun's death in 1850, years that witnessed a dramatic growth in the state's market economy, highlighted by significant advances in railroading and banking that resembled those of the cotton South.[16]

Whether South Carolina should be viewed as an aristocratic backwater, controlled by elites in both sections, or as a state with strong yeomen influences in a political system more democratic than is usually conceded remains a topic of debate.[17] This much is certain: contemporaries, admirers, and adversaries, to say nothing of South Carolinians themselves and later historians, have all agreed that South Carolina was different from the rest of the South. Just as loyalism was weakest in Revolutionary Massachusetts, so visible Unionism was almost wholly absent in South Carolina after secession. Of all the states of the Confederacy, South Carolina contributed the fewest men to the Union cause and was the only southern state not to have at least one organized unit of white troops in the United States Army.[18]

Even allies of Massachusetts in 1776 and South Carolina in 1860 had viewed them with ambivalence in the years of mounting tension between the centers and the peripheries: steadfast and principled in their resistance to external intrusions, they were also extremists, threatening to pull their compatriots into violent upheaval. To their opponents, the Bay Colony and the Palmetto State were the rotten apples threatening to contaminate the barrel.

The historical record largely supports such judgments. Openly defiant in the seventeenth century, Massachusetts accepted the Restoration monarchy after 1660 only under duress and later led the way in the overthrow of the Dominion of New England in 1688–89. Its "merchants and shipmasters were second to none in discovering ways to avoid the payment of customs duties on importations."[19] Naval officials would never forget that the most violent anti-impressment riot in colonial annals had taken place in Boston in 1747. Lord Loudoun and other British commanders saw Massachusetts soldiers in the Seven Years' War as undisciplined and irresponsible, literally leaving the service the day their enlistments in the provincial service expired, regardless of the military situation.[20]

To Britons and American loyalists, the post-1760 events that took Massachusetts down the road to independence were consistent with its earlier behavior.

Massachusetts added to its notoriety in the writs of assistance controversy, in its violent reaction to the Stamp Act, in its circular letter to the other colonies during the Townshend crisis, in its hostile reaction to the creation of an American Board of Customs, in its response to the crown's decision to pay the salaries of certain royally appointed provincial officials, in its initiating a network of local committees of correspondence, in its publication of the Hutchinson letters, in its destruction of 90,000 pounds of taxed tea, and in its taking its militia away from its governor and creating a provincial army responsible to an extralegal provincial congress—all these occurrences before Lexington and Concord.[21] Everywhere in America and England, people knew the names of three Massachusetts radicals, if they knew those of no other incendiaries in the thirteen provinces: James Otis, Joseph Warren, and especially Samuel Adams. Indeed, Adams became a benchmark by which one measured unremitting, inflammatory opposition to Britain. Charles Thomson of Pennsylvania, Cornelius Harnett of North Carolina, and Christopher Gadsden of South Carolina all invited depiction as the Samuel Adams of their respective colonies.

Some moderate leaders of the American resistance voiced not one but two concerns about the Boston-led firebrands: they sought independence and a revolutionized political order. Suspicions mounted after the Boston Tea Party in December 1773. However much provoked by the tea ships' presence, the townspeople had supposedly overreacted in the destruction of the duticed brew. The violence in Boston Harbor contrasted sharply with the usual legal-constitutional reaction that had characterized most forms of American resistance prior to that time. Clearly, republican political ideas motivated those agitators who fostered such violent crowd behavior, declared Edward Rutledge of South Carolina. He dreaded "their low cunning, and those . . . principles which men without character, and without fortune in general possess, which are so captivating to the lower classes of mankind, and will occasion such fluctuation of property as to introduce the greatest disorder." Rutledge's perception of Massachusetts mirrored that of all his province's delegates in the Continental Congress except Christopher Gadsden, who later reminded Samuel Adams that many in that body had looked upon Adams and like-minded members "with a kind of Horror . . . artful and designing Men altogether pursuing selfish purpose."[22]

Maryland, like South Carolina, hardly stood in the forefront for independence, and between 1774 and 1776 its conservative leadership gravely mistrusted Samuel Adams and his Bay Colony allies.[23] Pennsylvania's John Dickinson warned Josiah Quincy Jr. of Massachusetts against "one colony's breaking the line of opposition, by advancing too hastily before the rest." Such sentiments even resonated with some of Massachusetts's near neighbors. Silas Deane of Connecticut complained that the Bay Colony's adventurism contravened "every principle of good reason and sound policy." James Duane of New York spoke darkly of Massachusetts's ambitious designs in the First Continental Congress, which had adopted the Bay Colony's Suffolk Resolves, calling for stiff resistance to the Coercive Acts. Ironically, moderates had engineered the calling of the Congress to stall the Boston radicals' proposal for an immediate and total stoppage of all trade with Britain, a proposal backed by no other colony at the time.[24]

British attitudes toward Massachusetts revealed anger, not ambivalence. The king's friends in America fine-tuned old English resentments toward the Bay Colony. These loyalists, like some conservative Whigs, envisioned Adams and fellow radicals as intent on creating an independent America, a nation dominated by New England. To Jonathan Sewall their machinations unmasked the "ancient republican independent spirit" that the Puritans had carried to New England a century and a half ago. Boston's political agitators had powerful support from the always influential Congregational clergy, who "hoodwinked, inflamed, and goaded on" the citizenry. The loyalists might disagree among themselves on some matters, but all considered Massachusetts the main culprit and its suppression the key to cracking the rebellion.[25]

Was it the case that, as the Reverend Joseph Bellamy explained to his congregation, the London ministers "are angry with us, more than with any part of America, because we are puritans and particularly of the old puritans"?[26] Assuredly, British perceptions of Massachusetts's past, including its Calvinist heritage, combined with its post-1760 resistance, brought exceedingly harsher punishment than any imposed on Virginia, another major leader in the opposition, or on any other colony. Twice, in 1768 and in 1774, sizable British army contingents were sent to Boston. In the first instance the reason for doing so was flimsy: undocumented complaints from royal customs collectors that they needed outside protection. In the second instance the provocation—the Boston Tea Party—while admittedly greater, did not warrant, along with the redcoats, the Coercive Acts and the combining of the civil and military power with the appointment of General Thomas Gage, army commander in chief in North America, as governor of the province.

Here a counterfactual question better illuminates Massachusetts's center-stage performance in the imperial drama. What if the tea party had occurred somewhere else? Would Britain then have responded with such severity? The answer is undoubtedly no; Massachusetts already stood condemned as the principal American troublemaker. The several destructive acts elsewhere against British tea in subsequent months attracted relatively minor notice at Whitehall. The burning of the revenue cutter *Gaspee* in Narragansett Bay in 1772 posed a more direct challenge to London than the dumping of privately owned tea: a government vessel was attacked while performing its official duties. But despite the ministry's threats and fulminations, nothing came of this episode involving Rhode Islanders.[27]

Just as Britain had fewer grievances against Rhode Island, so too did London officialdom believe that it could single out and chastise Massachusetts in isolation, because, far more so than Rhode Island or any other province, Americans in general considered that colony to be rash and extremist in its behavior. But Britons grossly exaggerated Massachusetts's unpopularity in America when they equated it with Britain's disdain for the Bay Colony. It resulted in "a fatal misunderstanding, for it led the Parliament to believe that the town [of Boston] could be punished without arousing the sympathy of the other colonists."[28] Without the explosive combination of Massachusetts's extreme defiance of Britain and the mother country's extreme reaction to the Bay Colony's tea party, American independence would hardly have come when it did and the way it did.

Much was also similar about the admirers and detractors of South Carolina before the Civil War. Although Massachusetts had always suffered from an unsavory reputation in Britain, South Carolina had not projected an image harmful to the Union prior to the Jacksonian era. Rhode Island has been castigated for its unwillingness to send delegates to the Constitutional Convention and for its failure to ratify the new national charter until 1790. Pennsylvania had been criticized for its defiance of the federal government on two occasions, prompting strong responses from two southern presidents, George Washington and James Madison. Massachusetts and Connecticut had been censured for endeavoring to throw constitutional roadblocks in the path of the national administration in the War of 1812. At the time of Andrew Jackson's election, Georgia was already embroiled in what became a long-running dispute, first with Congress and later with the Supreme Court, concerning federal recognition of Indian land titles within the state.

The idea of using nullification or state interposition in response to a federal law had first received wide publicity through the efforts of two Virginians, James Madison and Thomas Jefferson, authors of the Virginia and Kentucky Resolutions. That idea, increasingly interpreted to mean that the nation originated as a compact of sovereign states that continued to retain their sovereignty after the adoption of the Constitution, was periodically refurbished and amplified by conservative Jeffersonians—Old Republicans, as they styled themselves, true to the "principles of '98." Previous to the nullification crisis, Virginians led in the defense of southern interests.[29] But South Carolina seized the limelight from nullification onward. It declared the tariffs of 1828 and 1832 and President Jackson's Force Bill null and void within its borders and prepared for armed resistance. Nullification evoked high drama, with Vice President Calhoun resigning to take a seat in the United States Senate and with the end of the federal-state confrontation coming only as a result of Henry Clay's compromise tariff in 1833.[30]

The nullification controversy denoted the most serious constitutional crisis in America between 1787 and the Civil War. The truly alarming concern went beyond nullification itself, beyond South Carolina's contest with Andrew Jackson. The more ominous idea linked nullification with secession, going well beyond the political and constitutional objectives of the Virginia and Kentucky Resolutions.[31] Secession as a theory, like nullification, had been expressed only rarely and even then in abstract or rhetorical ways before the Ordinance of Nullification in 1832. But, significantly, South Carolina had fervently articulated it as a final solution to any seemingly insoluble federal problems even prior to the nullification crisis. In the 1820s Charles Pinckney threatened secession if the state's political, economic, or slavery interests were attacked. Louis T. Wigfall, a future extremist, remembered that South Carolina College's oratorical societies had been debating secession for more than a half dozen years before his arrival there in 1836, with the pivotal points of disagreement being only when and how it might take place. The youthful debaters reflected the influence of Dr. Thomas Cooper, president of the school, who continued for years to dispute the desirability of South Carolina's remaining in the Union, a sentiment he conveyed bluntly to President Martin Van Buren in 1837.[32]

Not until the passage of the Coercive Acts in 1774 did Massachusetts and its sister colonies begin to take positions comparable to nullification and secession, developing elaborate reasons for denying any binding parliamentary authority over the colonies and expressing a commonwealth interpretation of the empire. For years the colonists' only strategy for combating measures considered unconstitutional, such as the Stamp Act and the Townshend duties—besides trade boycotts, infrequent physical intimidation of royal officials, and simply going about their business as if certain laws did not exist—was to write pamphlets and draft memorials addressed to the king and Parliament. These stated that American liberties under the British constitution had been violated and that there were suitable precedents in English constitutional history for their positions.

That is, their focus was on showing Parliament the error of its ways rather than acting on a doctrine that led them literally to disallow a British statute or to justify withdrawal from the empire.[33]

In contrast, not only did antebellum South Carolinians articulate theories threatening to the Union, but the state's most vocal spokesmen had a resolute and uncompromising position on slavery issues. In fact, from the time of the nullification crisis, nullification, secession, and slavery "became fatefully entwined."[34] According to William W. Freehling, the defense of slavery as a perpetual blessing received early expression in the Palmetto State, and no other part of Dixie matched its strident voice in behalf of the peculiar institution before the 1850s. The first defenses of slavery as a moral good to be delivered in the national political arena, apart from a brief, bitter debate in the First Congress, came from South Carolinians—from Senator William R. Smith and Congressman Charles Pinckney during the Missouri crisis. Congressman James Henry Hammond echoed the argument in 1836 during the Gag Rule debate in the House of Representatives.[35] State representative Whitemarsh Seabrook introduced a resolution warning that enactment of the Wilmot Proviso or elimination of slavery in the nation's capital would constitute reason to dissolve the Union. Shortly thereafter Lawrence M. Keitt, another extremist, vowed that no South Carolina congressman should support any candidate for Speaker of the United States House of Representatives "in the slightest degree tainted with unsoundness on the slavery question."[36]

John C. Calhoun became in the public mind the spokesman for South Carolina as he defended nullification, secession, and slavery. No other antebellum politician was so viewed as synonymous with all his state stood for—not even Daniel Webster of Massachusetts or Henry Clay of Kentucky, the other members of the midcentury great triumvirate.[37] As Lacy K. Ford states, Calhoun's "prominence undoubtedly focused an unusual amount of national attention on events in South Carolina, and, at the same time, national issues always loomed large in South Carolina politics because of Calhoun's influence."[38] Perhaps Calhoun's ultimate legacy to his state and to the South—and his final one in time as well—was his chilling speech in the Senate debates leading to the Compromise of 1850. Pale and feeble, his death imminent, he listened as Senator James M. Mason of Virginia read his prepared peroration. Calhoun proclaimed that southerners would never compromise on their right to take slave property into the Mexican cession territories. His solution, to save the Union, was a constitutional guarantee of maintaining permanently a balance of sectional rights and interests, an impossible dream.[39]

South Carolinians, with their national legislators casting "only one of a possible 34 congressional votes . . . for the moderates' settlement, outside the fugitive slave part,"[40] and claiming their section had been sold out, continued to be the hotspurs of the South in the 1850s. Seven of the eight most visible southern fire-eaters, as defined by Eric H. Walther, either hailed from South Carolina or had direct links to the state.[41] These extremists, as well as lesser-known ones, often pressed for conventions of southern states. South Carolina played a major hand in the lower South convention activity between 1849 and 1851, and it alone took serious, if eventually aborted, secessionist steps during the midcentury crisis.[42] Its reputation for recklessness gained reinforcement from Congressman Preston Brooks's caning of Senator Charles Sumner of Massachusetts and from the inflamed rhetoric of Robert Barnwell Rhett's Charleston *Mercury*. And of course in 1860, a month after the election of Lincoln, South Carolina withdrew from the Union. The first state to nullify became the first to secede. The state then dispatched commissioners to other southern states to encourage them to take the same step. It was appropriate and gratifying to southern zealots everywhere that South Carolinians fired on *The Star of the West* as it endeavored to supply the federal garrison in Charleston Harbor and that the Civil War began there a short time later with the firing on Fort Sumter.[43]

And how was South Carolina perceived by southern moderates—advocates of states' rights constitutionalism? However troubled they were by secessionist mouthing, they at least did not have one fear that gripped some American resistance leaders in the 1770s: that Massachusetts radicals sought a new leveling political order. South Carolina planters, with their huge slave population and tradition of political dominance, would never shred their internal fabric. But southern moderates were likely ambivalent or negative about nullification and secession, either for constitutional or practical reasons. One can hazard two further generalizations for what was a thirty-year period—the period between South Carolina's "crazy fit[s]" of the 1830s and 1860s, as one of its native sons put it later. First, many moderates believed that South Carolina was waging the good fight for the entire South, but that it should be steady and temperate.[44] Second, because of its early and persistent visibility on sectional issues, some concluded in subsequent years that it should let southern states with more judicious or restrained reputations take the lead.

Some southern moderates who eventually went along with secession, as well as others from the region who were Unionist to the end, roundly denounced the Palmetto State. The similarity of opinions of southern moderates-turned-reluctant-secessionists and unflinching Dixie Unionists not infrequently appeared remarkable. Both William Heth, an army officer from Virginia who finally threw in his lot with the Confederacy, and Senator Andrew Johnson, the Tennessee Unionist, had a watery solution to the problem of South Carolina. Heth would "dig South Carolina up and throw her into the ocean"; Johnson would tow the state out to sea in the hope that the Atlantic breezes would cool its irrational passions.[45] Few critics of the state were as sharp-tongued as two of its native sons who painfully parted company in 1860–61, the reluctant secessionist Benjamin F. Perry, an up-country newspaper editor, and the Charleston lawyer and steadfast old Federalist James L. Petigru. The latter's desire for an ordered society governed by natural elites echoed the sentiments of such blue-blooded Boston loyalists as Thomas Hutchinson. Petigru, alarmed at separatist tendencies since nullification, swore that the state had gone mad. He described its mental condition shortly before the election of 1860: "My own countrymen here in South Carolina are distempered to a degree that makes them . . . real objects of pity. They believe anything that flatters their delusions or their vanity; and at the same time are credulous to every whisper or suspicion about insurgents or incendiaries." But his most memorable and often quoted characterization is more pithy: "South Carolina is too small to be a Republic, and too large to be an insane asylum."[46]

Other southerners pronounced equally unflattering judgments of South Carolina. People said that it had been Tory since the Revolution, its fire-eaters being lineal descendants of low-country royalists, never comfortable with independence or the Union; that it wished to deflect attention from its undemocratic political institutions by fomenting sectional strife—a charge of Senator Sam Houston of Texas, who branded its seditionists "more culpable . . . than Benedict Arnold"; that it sought to dominate the South—in or out of the American republic. Others asserted that the state's politicians sought to inflame the country as a way of advancing their own ambitions. Some felt that since the nullification crisis the state's hotbloods had conspired with like-minded regional fanatics to make any excuse for splitting off the South. In short, there was no pleasing it under any circumstances. It was averred that its paranoia would make it equally unhappy in a southern confederacy, prompting it soon to secede from such a nation. One writer suggested that if its sons were so hyperthyroid, so revolutionary-minded, then let them join Garibaldi. Mary Boykin Chesnut, wife of a recently resigned United States senator from South Carolina, acknowledged in February 1861 that her state "had been . . . rampant for years. She was the torment of herself and everybody else. Nobody could live in this state unless he were a fire-eater."[47]

Just as I earlier raised counterfactual questions about Britain's reaction to the Boston Tea Party, asking if the London government's response would have been more temperate had the taxed drink been destroyed elsewhere, if Parliament would have passed Lord North's Coercive Acts by such lopsided majorities, so now let us consider whether the Lincoln administration would have been as determined to push for a showdown with the Confederacy when it did if Fort Sumter had been located elsewhere, say, in Georgia or Texas. Perhaps it would not have mattered to Lincoln, who felt great pressure to take decisive measures. But that is unlikely. The garrison at Fort Sumter had become "in northern eyes the defenders of a modern Thermopylae."[48] It was common knowledge that South Carolinians from the moment of secession were eager to clear Charleston Harbor of federal troops. Newspapers in Columbia and Charleston railed at state officials for their failure to storm the federal outpost. With the creation of the Confederacy, state leaders finally took a much tougher line. They urged that unless the new government in Montgomery ordered an assault on Fort Sumter, then the state should immediately attack on its own.[49]

Lincoln, aware of the heated atmosphere in the Palmetto State, having sent agents to Charleston in late March, believed that only in South Carolina were a majority of southerners committed secessionists. Secretary of State William H. Seward, opposed to supplying Fort Sumter, said that doing so would be viewed as partisan and provocative, as a Republican, antislavery act; he favored instead the reinforcement of Fort Pickens in Florida and the evacuation of Fort Sumter. To some degree the president himself, though rejecting Seward's advice, saw the confrontation as much with South Carolina as he did with the Confederate government. He communicated his intentions concerning the fort to Governor Francis W. Pickens, not with Confederate executives in Montgomery (whom he did not recognize); and Lincoln's emissary to Pickens, State Department clerk R. S. Chew, refused on orders from the chief executive to accept a reply from the governor.[50] Whatever the president's thinking, it is hard to escape the conclusion—from sampling northern press reaction to the secession of South Carolina and to the firing on Fort Sumter—that Lincoln could not have picked a better location for a confrontation that would rally northern support for the war that followed.[51]

Although Massachusetts and South Carolina stand out as the two political entities most critical and defiant of constituted authority in their respective prerevolutionary eras, their attitudes about secession and independence can easily be oversimplified. For the radical camps in each polity the future held uncertainties. The extremists had no master plan and felt apprehensive about what lay ahead. No Lenin or Ho Chi Minh guided either radical party. The leaders were in both cases mainly hesitant, sometimes reluctant revolutionaries. This is particularly true of Massachusetts.

Yet the idea that Massachusetts had designs for independence early on—the contention of the loyalists and the ministry in London—has had great currency with historians. It forms the centerpiece of most biographies of Samuel Adams, who is depicted as almost single-handedly driving Massachusetts and, in time, America to revolution. If countless revolutionaries in modern history have been described as mentally unstable—having agendas that owed much to their various peculiarities stemming from cultural alienation, dysfunctional families, narcissism, and so on—so too has Samuel Adams. Pictured as neurotic, possibly psychotic, he stands convicted of being a subversive, a rabble-rousing demagogue. Two of Adams's most scholarly biographers assign subtitles that vividly portray their approaches to the man. To the first, he served as the "Promoter of the American Revolution"; and to the second, he stood out as the "Pioneer in Propaganda."[52]

If occasional scholars have also singled out specific fire-eaters from South Carolina and elsewhere as requiring psychological explanations of their behavior, no historian has endeavored to provide us with a collective assessment of such phenomena for the Palmetto State's political chieftains the way James H. Hutson has done for the Bay Colony radicals.[53] Hutson, a highly respected historian, claims mental instability may well have been rampant among the "anything but reasonable" leadership of Massachusetts. Hutson placed with Samuel Adams such notables as James Otis (his troubled psyche is hardly in dispute), John Adams, and Joseph Hawley, the most prominent Whig in western Massachusetts. Rather than depicting their fears of a British conspiracy to rob them of their liberties as a part of age-old concerns about corruption and misuse of power—the influential thesis of Bernard Bailyn—Hutson denies that Massachusetts's reaction to British acts and policies had tenacious roots in the colonists' intellectual past. Instead, these insecure and paranoid men saw British measures aimed at their colony as assaults on their personal esteem. Their delusions about the London ministry's motives projected "unacceptable feelings" about themselves.[54]

Although Hutson believes the Massachusetts impetus for independence began with deep resentments against England during the Seven Years' War, owing to imperious treatment on the part of loyal military officers and administrators, the burden of proof rests with those who share that opinion. In sharp contrast, John Murrin writes convincingly that the middle colonies were most disgruntled and resistant to imperial integration in 1760, whereas they would be the "least rebellious part of America in 1775." On the other hand, Massachusetts— along with Virginia—was the "most loyal" province in the Seven Years' War, and it would lead the resistance movement from the time of the Stamp Act.[55]

The record bears out Murrin's claim of the Bay Colony's fidelity in the 1750s and even earlier. William Pencak points out that in the post-1688 imperial wars, "Massachusetts mustered and taxed its inhabitants to a degree unduplicated in any other British colony." These wartime offerings emanated from a province that "had not been directly attacked since the early days of the eighteenth century." Its monetary gifts in the Seven Years' War were especially impressive: net, nonreimbursed expenditures of $466,006, 31 percent of the total from the North American colonies, with Virginia a distant second, contributing $286,142, 19.1 percent of the total.[56]

Massachusetts, proud of its wartime contributions, looked for an even better relationship with the mother country. Francis Bernard, on assuming the governorship in 1760, called the colony politically tranquil and predicted a smooth course at the helm of the ship of state. The Reverend Thomas Barnard of Salem, delivering one of the numerous victory sermons in the early 1760s, spoke in raptures not unlike his fellow clergymen: "Safe from the Enemy of the Wilderness, safe from the gripping Hand of arbitrary Sway and cruel Superstition; Here shall be the late founded Seat of Peace and Freedom. Here shall our indulgent Mother, who has most generously rescued and protected us, be served and honoured by growing Numbers, with all Duty, Love and Gratitude, till time shall be no more."[57]

Massachusetts's visceral reaction to British post-1763 measures grew in part out of a sense of betrayal—of being bled in return for all it had contributed to the imperial war machine, exclaimed James Otis in his *Rights of the British Colonists Asserted and Proved*,[58] but the province's response had little effect on the colonists' feeling for the king and for what Richard L. Bushman terms "monarchical culture" before 1774 and sometimes even later.[59] John Adams, himself no moderate, predicted just prior to learning of the Boston Port Act that any final crisis between England and the colonies lay years in the future: "Our Children" would more likely "see Revolutions."[60] Despite the suspicions about Samuel Adams, then and now, and despite the fact the Bay Colony radicals urged others to take the lead in the First Continental Congress, there is no reason to assume that Massachusetts pushed that body further than it wanted to go. It unanimously ratified Massachusetts's Suffolk Resolves, which were not as belligerent as has been claimed, speaking as they did of the colony's continued "affection" for George III and of the need "to act merely upon the defensive."[61]

While Massachusetts's delegates would have gone beyond the actions of the First Continental Congress, that fails to demonstrate they were pressing for independence; it does show their concern about the Coercive Acts and their anger about General Gage's occupying army. Although the Continental Congress served as a check on Massachusetts, it also played a beneficial role for the colony that more than offset its restraining influence. The existence of the Congress meant that Massachusetts was not alone. The Adamses and their allies knew that they had the support of all the other colonies represented in Philadelphia— a form of backing and encouragement that South Carolina's later would-be revolutionaries never had. Time and again after the nullification crisis their extremist flank had been exposed by fair-weather friends in Mississippi and Alabama.

If Massachusetts paid a price for Congress's support—that body's unwillingness to be led by the Bay Colony—most Massachusetts leaders recognized that their own citizens were not yet ready for independence. Monarchical culture proved tenacious, though it had been severely battered. There may have been "less loyalty to the king" than "loyalty to the idea of a king." Whatever the case, it manifested itself in county conventions draping their resolves in declarations of allegiance to their sovereign and in a willingness of the Provincial Congress to reinstate the king's representative, Governor and General Gage, under certain conditions, a possibility renounced following the outbreak of hostilities in April 1775.[62]

In the end, Massachusetts cautiously embarked on the unknown sea of independence firmly setting its course behind that of the Continental Congress. At its almost frantic insistence, the intercolonial tribunal had taken control of the New England provincial army and had responded to the Bay Colony's urgent request for instructions about setting up a provincial government. (Massachusetts's motives were not to expand the war and launch a drive for independence, with radically new political forms, but rather to contain the situation, to keep its own forces from acting rashly or from getting out of control, and to restore legitimate civil authority.)[63] Nearly a year after the guns first sounded, Abigail Adams, skirting the name of the king, still spoke of the enemy as the "Ministerial Troops" besieged in Boston.[64] As late as May 1776, the House of Representatives equivocated on the matter of separation, and so did most of the towns. The war itself had generated political factionalism that included concerns about the character of the future government of Massachusetts, combining with whatever remained of ties with the king to slow the process of separation. The inhabitants of Barnstable, home of the Otis family, reflected the effects of this turmoil, voting narrowly against independence on June 25, 1776, with exactly half the assembled citizens abstaining. But even most of those who questioned independence in the spring and summer of 1776 in Barnstable and elsewhere were likely to have been as critical of Britain's treatment of the Bay Colony as were the fervent advocates of immediate disunion.[65]

Uncertainties also persisted within the province's delegation in the Second Continental Congress. John Adams deplored their "unfortunate and fatal divisions."[66] He and his cousin Samuel frequently clashed with Thomas Cushing, Robert Treat Paine, and John Hancock. Not until February 1776 did a majority of the Bay Colony men favor a total break, and John Hancock, the president of Congress, seems to have held out until May. Such hesitancy reflected the attitude of their constituents. Compared with its bold defiance of royal authority on countless occasions in its history, Massachusetts approached its exodus from the empire with a whimper: the legislature agreed to appoint a committee! That committee was authorized to draft a letter to its delegates in Philadelphia stating that if the Congress "should think it proper to declare the colonies independent of the kingdom of Great Britain, this house will approve of the measure."[67] The date was July 3; the day before, Congress had in fact declared independence, with Massachusetts's irresolution enormously embarrassing to two most fiery congressmen, John and Samuel Adams.

South Carolina's position within southern councils was profoundly different. It could not, except for the quite distant events of the American Revolution, legitimately claim to have made great sacrifices for the nation as Massachusetts had been able to do in the previous century for the old empire.[68] And, unlike the Bay Colony, it could not claim to have been betrayed. The federal government was too broad, amorphous, and impersonal to arouse and sustain great anger over a span of years, even in South Carolina. Besides, through much of the country's history southerners had dominated the political machinery in Washington. Countless proslavery men had held high elective and appointive office and continued to do so. And at times the state had been notably honored. The revered Calhoun had been confirmed as secretary of state by the Senate's unanimous vote in 1844, at a time when the question of admitting Texas to the Union as a slave state revived old sectional tensions and created new ones. Charles M. Wiltse, writing of Calhoun's death six years later, states: "Not since the death of Washington had the passing of any public figure so profoundly affected the country."[69] Even the nullification crisis, in the persuasive argument of Richard

E. Ellis, was more of a victory for South Carolina than most historians have recognized.[70] The tariff, such a bone of contention in the late 1820s and early 1830s,
never surfaced again as a fruitful issue for hot-blooded disunionists.

Of course, some South Carolinians blustered, fulminated, and threatened
over slavery issues as they related to Texas and the lands obtained from Mexico,
to fugitive bondsmen and the peculiar institution in the District of Columbia;
but the state hardly led the South during the congressional wars over the
Kansas-Nebraska Act or Kansas statehood. The Louisiana Purchase lands were
too distant, as were the Mexican cession areas, to pose any direct threat to the immediate interests of South Carolina.[71] And only a handful of fugitive slaves from
South Carolina had escaped to the North between 1840 and 1860, a smaller percentage than from any other state. Indeed, after the passage of the Fugitive Slave
Act in 1850, the number of successful runaways actually decreased in the South
as a whole in the next ten years. To James Henry Hammond, elected to the
United States Senate in 1857, a self-styled Calhoun disciple who hoped to succeed the great man as the dominant influence in state politics, preserving slavery
within its current boundaries always ranked far above questions about its exten-
sion westward, which really seems to have been of small interest to him.[72]

Several things slowed disunionist impulses after the state rejected secession
in the early 1850s. Political factionalism increased, partly the inevitable result
of Calhoun's death and partly because of disagreements over South Carolina's
proper position regarding the Union. On the ends of the political spectrum
stood uncompromising secessionists and uncompromising Unionists, the latter distinctly the smaller group. The middle belonged to the cooperationists,
who agreed on vigorously preserving states' rights and forcefully articulating the
constitutionality of secession. But the secessionists and various shades of
secessionist-leaning cooperationists disagreed sharply on strategy, "on the practical wisdom of seceding at a particular moment."[73] If South Carolina committed itself to secession, then should it travel that road alone, period—whatever
the consequences? Should it set out by itself, predicated on some reasonable
assumption that its forthright behavior would cause other states to follow?
Should it persuade one of the cotton states to secede first, either Mississippi or
Alabama, and could Virginia be counted on to follow suit? Or should it revive
the thus far unsuccessful approach of acting through a southern convention, a
safer if less spectacular course pursued by Massachusetts in the first American
Revolution? The state that had been left high and dry by its southern neighbors
in 1832–33 and in 1851–52 did not relish being in that position again.

For years South Carolina's fire-eaters revealed a striking propensity to let their words outweigh their actions. Though assuredly a malcontent, the state created a reputation as a threat to the Union that has probably been exaggerated, then and now, prior to 1859 or 1860. "Our planters," sighed Mrs. Chesnut, are "impulsive but hard to keep moving. They are wonderful for a sport." After that they "like to rest."[74] These inconsistencies constitute a major theme of William W. Freehling's *Road to Disunion.* "Seldom has so geographically concentrated a revolutionary fringe group been so early committed to revolution," he writes. "Seldom have such committed revolutionaries been so chary about rebellion."[75]

Ironically, as the 1850s wore on, a flock of South Carolina's political chieftains displayed more willingness to protect the state's interests by working through the national Democratic Party than they had done in years. This change in course can be seen in the state's breaking precedent by sending a delegation to the Democratic national convention in 1856, in its congressman James L. Orr's election as Speaker of the United States House of Representatives, in its hosting the Democratic national convention in Charleston in 1860, and in the composition of what was actually a moderate state delegation at the convention. That delegation, it should be added, was not of one mind about walking out of the convention over the issue of guarantees for slavery in the territories—it was preceded by delegates from three other states—and it elected not to take any formal action after it did depart. W. W. Holden, the Raleigh newspaper editor, still a Unionist after returning to North Carolina from Charleston, blamed Alabamians—"Yanceites," he called them—with their Alabama platform, for doing most of the damage to the Democracy.[76] Furthermore, the maneuverings of South Carolinians in subsequent efforts that spring to reunite the national party or unite the southern wing of the Democracy do not signal a clear sense of purpose.[77]

Simply put, South Carolina did not know where it was going before the election of Lincoln. It was a state that had allowed its militia to so deteriorate that it existed more on paper than in reality by 1860.[78] Well into the Buchanan administration, Robert Barnwell Rhett, the preeminent fire-eater, lobbied for the appointment of a friend for a post in the federal government. If Rhett did not know what lay ahead, then who did? During the winter of 1859–60, Rhett and his Charleston *Mercury* blew hot and cold on the prospects for South Carolina independence, much of the time evincing deep doubts.[79] Rhett's uncertainty matched that of the supposedly dedicated secessionist William H. Trescot, who accepted appointment as assistant secretary of state in the summer of 1860. Francis W. Pickens, who presided over the secession of South Carolina as its governor, had earlier in 1860 positioned himself as a moderate interested in the presidential nomination of the Democratic Party. Even after the adoption of the state's secession ordinance, Pickens proposed that South Carolina not withdraw until Lincoln's inauguration. After that, he conceded, it would take a miracle to save the nation.[80]

Assuredly James Henry Hammond had no precise reading of the Fates, nor did the state's other United States senator, James Chesnut. Both moderates in the 1850s, they privately in 1860 expressed their fear of the consequences of separate state secession if Lincoln was elected.[81] Though both Chesnut and Hammond resigned their Senate seats following Lincoln's victory, neither was a certain irreconcilable at that moment. Hammond, who left the Senate in part because Chesnut resigned ahead of him and in part because he wearied of being pressured by different factions within the state, contemplated the future with gloom and apprehension. He composed a thirty-page address to the state legislature (which was suppressed by the man Hammond asked to read it publicly) declaring that Lincoln's election offered no constitutional grounds for state secession; that if the state insisted on leaving the Union at that time, then at least two other states should actually depart ahead of South Carolina; and that internal social upheaval might be the long-term result of separation for the Palmetto State. He concluded, "I fear our own demagogues at home, more than all our enemies abroad." Secession, to Hammond, meant a revolution, and revolutions brewed the unpredictable. He quietly advised his brother not to resign his commission in the United States Navy! It is questionable, of course, whether many South Carolinians shared Hammond's reservations, which stemmed more from his concern over the unknown than his feeling for the old flag.[82]

In the final analysis, how do we distinguish between the ultimate decisions of Massachusetts and South Carolina, which in both cases were more difficult and complex than they have usually been pictured? The homogeneity of both the colony and the state enabled them to stake out the strongest positions, among the peripheries, in their conflicts with the centers in London and Washington. In doing so, they lived up to their reputations with friend and foe alike until faced with the prospect of actually leaping over the hedge, the expression of Colonel James Otis Sr.[83] Massachusetts was angered and then sobered by the Coercive Acts and their consequences. South Carolina, having gone to the brink of secession in 1851–52, slowly drew back over the remainder of the decade.

Massachusetts, for so long a leader of the provincial resistance, fell into line behind the Continental Congress. And it was Congress, not Massachusetts, that made the decision for independence. No Massachusetts radical, either in the colony or in Congress, pulled the strings. That is only to say that Samuel Adams's influence in his colony and later in Congress has been exaggerated. He was no more "the dictator of Massachusetts" than was Robert Barnwell Rhett or any other single South Carolina fire-eater the guiding hand of a revolution. The truth is, as two scholars stress, we do not thus far have conclusive evidence of a tightly knit independence party in either Massachusetts or South Carolina.[84]

The ability of Massachusetts to sidestep a full-blown debate over withdrawing from the empire—at the very time that political factionalism heightened[85]— meant that the Bay Colony would escape the ill effects of such wrenching deliberations that transpired in 1861 in some southern state secession conventions. Their results often left substantial minorities disgruntled, sometimes coerced into reluctantly signing secession ordinances—all of which cast light on the subsequent apathy, disaffection, and Unionism that would contribute to the internal erosion that plagued parts of the Confederacy.

South Carolina determined its own course of action, a decision slow in coming. And for that reason its behavior requires more attention here. Many of her radicals had favored collective activity but had never been able to bring it about, nor had they persuaded their own citizens to lead the South in an act of separate state secession. Would Lincoln's election have finally produced a convention movement supported by all or most of the slave states? South Carolina did not wait to find out. Would any of its Deep South neighbors have seceded ahead of the Palmetto State had it waited a few months? One again, South Carolina did not wait to find out. The dominant force in state politics in the late 1850s, the cooperationist movement simply collapsed in the aftermath of the Republican capture of the White House.

Although the full story of what happened in South Carolina between Lincoln's election and the state's secession remains to be written, some further speculations, however tentative, seem worthwhile. First, the position of James L. Orr and other influential moderates had been weakened by their strategy that might be described as a trade-off in dealing with the fire-eaters and secessionist-leaning cooperationists. They had bargained for support of the state's going slow and giving the national Democrats more time to protect South Carolina's interests. In return, they had said or implied—some as early as the 1856 presidential election—that they too would back secession if a Republican won the chief executive's office. If some merely hoped it would not occur, others likely believed it virtually impossible for the new sectional party to prevail—until they were jolted by the disintegration of the Democratic Party in the spring and summer of 1860. Thus, when Lincoln defeated John C. Breckinridge, the southern

Democratic candidate, Stephen A. Douglas, and John Bell in the contest for the White House, the moderates, having boxed themselves in, had no alternative to secession to offer the state. They suffered the double loss of Lincoln's winning and, not emphasized enough, the total discrediting of the national Democracy, which was no longer strong enough to shield the South, then or in the future.

Second, although it may well be that neither Mississippi nor Alabama would have seceded before South Carolina, it is probable that the South Carolina fire-eaters felt more confident than ever before that this time one or both of those two states would follow soon after, and indeed both promptly seceded. Interesting enough, however, cooperationism still asserted itself in the Mississippi, Alabama, and Georgia secession conventions, and in Alabama moderates came close to derailing secession, at least for the time being.[86]

Massachusetts, a follower rather than a leader in 1776, accepted independence, justifying it on the basis of what had happened—its mistreatment for over a decade, mistreatment that worsened appreciably with the Coercive Acts and subsequent British measures. South Carolina, without a demonstrable record of suffering abuse at the hands of the federal government, responded from fear of what might happen at the hands of Abraham Lincoln and his party. In any case, it seems that monarchical culture was more adhesive in Massachusetts in 1775–76 than Unionism was persistent in South Carolina in 1860. Ironically, the polity with the greater list of grievances found the break more painful than the polity that had never been singled out for punishment.

Notes

1. Charles Knowles, ed., *Letters of Hugh, Earl Percy from Boston and New York, 1774–76* (Boston, 1902), 37, 44.
2. G. B. Warden, *Boston, 1689–1776* (Boston, 1970), 319.
3. Quotations in Joseph T. Glatthaar, *The March to the Sea and Beyond: Sherman's Troops in the Savannah and Carolinas Campaigns* (New York, 1986), 140, 79, 143, 146. Sherman in later years conceded that his army had a particular antipathy for South Carolinians, based both on the view that they were "the cause of all our troubles" and that in 1865 they were "less passive" than Georgians and "would fight us to the bitter end, daring us to come over, etc.; so that I saw and felt that we would not be able longer to restrain our men as we had done in Georgia." *Memoirs of General William T. Sherman*, 2 vols. (New York, 1891), 2:254.
4. Don Higginbotham, "The Relevance of the American Revolution," *Anglican Theological Review* 1 (1973): 21–37; Higginbotham, "The Uses and Abuses of Compara-

tive History," *Latin American Research Review* 13 (1978): 238–45; Higginbotham, *War and Society in Revolutionary America: The Wider Dimensions of Conflict* (Columbia, S.C., 1988), chaps. 1, 8.

5. Five decades ago I did write an M.A. thesis, under the direction of Frank E. Vandiver, at Washington University on a Civil War topic. It appeared in revised and abbreviated form in Don Higginbotham, "A Raider Refuels: Diplomatic Repercussions" *Civil War History* 4 (1958): 129–42.

6. Andrew C. McLaughlin, "The Background of American Federalism," *American Political Science Review* 12 (1918): 215–40. See also John M. Murrin, "A Roof without Walls: The Dilemma of American National Identity," in *Beyond Confederation: Origins of the Constitution and American National Identity,* ed. Richard Beeman, Stephen Botein, and Edward C. Carter II (Chapel Hill, N.C., 1987), 333–48, who shrewdly analyzes the problems of creating both an imperial nationalism before independence and an American nationalism after the ratification of the Constitution. "Americans," declares Murrin, "would accept a central government only if it seldom acted like one." Ibid., 346. British problems of employing coercive power in Massachusetts are attributed to the strength of local law and local courts and the restraints upon the exercise of imperial law in John Phillip Reid, *In a Defiant Stance: The Conditions of Law in Massachusetts Bay, the Irish Comparison, and the Coming of the American Revolution* (University Park, Pa., 1977).

7. Jack P. Greene, "The Role of the Lower Houses of Assembly in Eighteenth-Century Politics," in Greene, *The Reinterpretation of the American Revolution, 1763–89* (New York, 1968), 89–90.

8. John J. Waters Jr., *The Otis Family in Provincial and Revolutionary Massachusetts* (Chapel Hill, N.C., 1968); William Pencak, *War, Politics, and Revolution in Provincial Massachusetts* (Boston, 1981).

9. Benjamin W. Labaree, *Colonial Massachusetts: A History* (Millwood, N.Y., 1979), 144.

10. Richard D. Brown, *Revolutionary Politics in Massachusetts: The Boston Committee of Correspondence and the Towns, 1772–74* (Cambridge, Mass., 1970); Labaree, *Colonial Massachusetts,* 277, 300; Robert J. Taylor, *Western Massachusetts in the American Revolution* (Providence, 1954), 62–69; Wallace Brown, *The King's Friends: The Composition and Motives of the American Loyalist Claimants* (Providence, 1968), 19–44, 294–98. One investigator identifies 1,423 adult male loyalists, 2 percent of the population in Massachusetts. See Robert M. Calhoon, "The Reintegration of the Loyalists and the Disaffected," in *The American Revolution: Its Character and Its Limits,* ed. Jack P. Greene (Baltimore, 1987), citing an MS by David E. Mass, 64, 72.

11. The idea of Puritan declension, once powerfully argued by Perry Miller and others, has now been modified or rejected in various ways. Most pertinent to this essay is the new emphasis on greater continuity in religious thought and practice, including piety and church attendance. Harry S. Stout contends, "Israel remained as crucial to New England's self-identity in 1760 as it had been a century earlier," in *The New England Soul: Preaching and Religious Culture in Colonial New England* (New

York, 1986), 252. See David D. Hall, "On Common Ground: The Coherence of American Puritan Studies," *William and Mary Quarterly,* 3d ser., 44 (1987): 193–229.

12. Richard Maxwell Brown, *The South Carolina Regulators* (Chapel Hill, N.C., 1963); Jerome J. Nadelhaft, *The Disorders of War: The Revolution in South Carolina* (Orono, Maine, 1981); Robert Stansbury Lambert, *South Carolina Loyalists in the American Revolution* (Columbia, S.C., 1987); Rachel N. Klein, *Unification of a Slave State: The Rise of the Planter Class in the South Carolina Backcountry, 1760–1808* (Chapel Hill, N.C., 1990).

13. Two of the most stimulating interpretations of the political character of antebellum South Carolinians are Robert M. Weir, "The South Carolinian as Extremist," *South Atlantic Quarterly* 74 (1975): 86–103, and James M. Banner Jr., "The Problem of South Carolina," in *The Hofstadter Aegis: A Memorial,* ed. Stanley Elkins and Eric McKitrick (New York, 1974), 60–93. The best comprehensive analysis of the literature on antebellum South Carolina is David Moltke-Hansen, "Protecting Interests, Asserting Rights, Emulating Ancestors: U.S. Constitutional Bicentennial Reflections on 'The Problem of South Carolina,' 1787–1860," *South Carolina Historical Magazine* 89 (1988): 160–82.

14. Lacy K. Ford Jr., *Origins of Southern Radicalism: The South Carolina Upcountry, 1800–1860* (New York, 1988), 146, 172, 192. A recent essay argues that Charles Pinckney anticipated Calhoun's fears and concerns as early as the Missouri controversy and that his influence on the state's political behavior has been neglected. Mark D. Kaplanoff, "Charles Pinckney and the American Republican Tradition," in *Intellectual Life in Antebellum Charleston,* ed. Michael O'Brien and David Moltke-Hansen (Knoxville, Tenn., 1986), 85–122.

15. Tommy W. Rogers, "The Great Population Exodus from South Carolina, 1850–1860," *South Carolina Historical Magazine* 68 (1967): 14–21, which examines place-of-birth information in the federal censuses of 1850 and 1860. If, as has been estimated, almost half of all whites born in the state after 1800 migrated elsewhere, overwhelmingly to parts of the lower South, then one wonders what influences concerning slavery and states' rights they carried with them and imparted to others. Ibid., 14–15, 20.

16. Klein, *Unification of a Slave State,* 1–2, 6, 14, 15, 135, 144; Ford, *Origins of Southern Radicalism.*

17. Certainly most of Calhoun's biographers emphasize the conservative, elitist interpretation of state politics, and so do two important recent works: Klein, *Unification of a Slave State,* esp. 303–5, and William W. Freehling, *The Road to Disunion: Secessionists at Bay, 1776–1854* (New York, 1990). By far the fullest account of the coming together of up-country and low country sees South Carolina, whatever its outmoded political machinery, as affected positively by democratic political tides elsewhere and plays down the image of Calhoun as the state's sole political arbiter. See Ford, *Origins of Southern Radicalism.*

18. Richard N. Current, *Lincoln's Loyalists: Union Soldiers from the Confederacy* (Boston, 1992), 107, 217, 218.

19. Labaree, *Colonial Massachusetts,* 197.

20. Studies that examine aspects of Massachusetts's relationships with the mother country prior to 1763 include ibid.; Michael Garibaldi Hall, *Edward Randolph and the American Colonies, 1676–1703* (Chapel Hill, N.C., 1960); Pencak, *War, Politics, and Revolution;* Fred Anderson, *A People's Army: Massachusetts Soldiers and Society in the Seven Years' War* (Chapel Hill, N.C., 1984).

21. There is a substantial literature on Massachusettts's controversies with Britain in the dozen years before independence. See esp. Pencak, *War, Politics, and Revolution;* Richard L. Bushman, *King and People in Provincial Massachusetts* (Chapel Hill, N.C., 1985); Hiller B. Zobel, *The Boston Massacre* (New York, 1970); Benjamin Woods Labaree, *The Boston Tea Party* (New York,1964); Brown, *Revolutionary Politics in Massachusetts;* John Cary, *Joseph Warren: Physician, Politician, Patriot* (Urbana, Ill., 1961); Bernard Bailyn, *The Ordeal of Thomas Hutchinson* (Cambridge, Mass., 1974), and their bibliographies, as well as sources cited subsequently in this essay.

22. Edward Rutledge quoted in John M. Head, *A Time to Rend: An Essay on the Decision for American Independence* (Madison, Wis., 1968), 127–28; Christopher Gadsden to Samuel Adams, Apr. 4, 1779, in Richard Walsh, ed., *Writings of Christopher Gadsden* (Columbia S.C., 1966), 163; E. Stanley Godbold Jr. and Robert H. Woody, *Christopher Gadsden and the American Revolution* (Knoxville, Tenn., 1982), chaps. 6–8.

23. Keith Mason, "Localism, Evangelicalism, and Loyalism: The Sources of Oppression in the Revolutionary Chesapeake," *Journal of Southern History* 56 (1990): 30–31.

24. John Dickinson to Josiah Quincy Jr., June 20, 1774, in Josiah Quincy, *Memoir of the Life of Josiah Quincy, Jun. of Massachusetts* (Boston, 1825), 169; Silas Deane to Samuel H. Parsons, April 13 [June], 1774, "Correspondence of Silas Deane, 1774–1776," Connecticut Historical Society, *Collections* 2 (1870): 130; Jack N. Rakove, *The Beginnings of National Politics: An Interpretive History of the Continental Congress* (Baltimore, 1979), 68–69.

25. Robert McLuer Calhoon, *The Loyalists in Revolutionary America, 1760–81* (New York, 1973), 73, 74; Pauline Maier, *The Old Revolutionaries: Political Lives in the Age of Samuel Adams* (New York, 1980), 275; William H. Nelson, *The American Tory* (New York, 1961), 178–82.

26. Mark Valeri, "The New Divinity and the American Revolution," *William and Mary Quarterly,* 3d ser., 46 (1989): 741. Bellamy in fact spoke of New England in general, for often hostile Englishmen used the term *New England;* but after reading on in their diatribes in the press, in Parliament, or in their personal correspondence, it is transparent that New England was normally a synonym for Massachusetts.

27. Labaree, *Boston Tea Party,* chaps. 8–13; Lawrence J. De Varo Jr., "The Gaspee Affair as Conspiracy," *Rhode Island History* 32 (1973): 107–21; Neil L. York, "The Uses of Law and the *Gaspee* Affair," ibid., 50 (1992): 3–22.

28. Labaree, *Boston Tea Party,* 260.

29. Norman K. Risjord, *The Old Republicans: Southern Conservatism in the Age of Jefferson* (New York, 1965).

30. Two superb books on the nullification controversy differ somewhat as to interpretation and emphases. See William W. Freehling, *Prelude to Civil War: The Nullification Controversy in South Carolina, 1816–36* (New York, 1966), and Richard E. Ellis, *The Union at Risk: Jacksonian Democracy, States' Rights, and the Nullification Crisis* (New York, 1987). Freehling puts the subject in a larger context and responds to his most important critics in *Road to Disunion*, chaps. 14–15 and notes.

31. See Dumas Malone, *Thomas Jefferson as Political Leader* (Berkeley, Calif., 1963), 61–67; Drew R. McCoy, *The Last of the Fathers: James Madison and the Republican Legacy* (Cambridge, Eng., 1989), 119–70.

32. Kaplanoff, "Charles Pinckney and the American Republican Tradition," 85–87, 121–22; Daniel Walker Hollis, *South Carolina College* (Columbia, S.C., 1951), 104–5, 240–41; Alvy L. King, *Louis T. Wigfall: Southern Fire-Eater* (Baton Rouge, La., 1970), 13; Dumas Malone, *The Public Life of Thomas Cooper, 1783–1839* (New Haven, 1926), 307–11, 325, 389.

33. Jack P. Greene, "From the Perspective of Law: Context and Legitimacy in the Origins of the American Revolution," *South Atlantic Quarterly* 85 (1986): 56–75; Greene, *Peripheries and Center: Constitutional Development in the Extended Politics of the British Empire and the United States, 1607–1788* (Athens, Ga., 1986), chaps. 4–7; Bernard Bailyn, *The Ideological Origins of the American Revolution* (Cambridge, Mass., 1882), chap. 5.

34. Ellis, *Union at Risk*, ix.

35. Freehling, *Road to Disunion*, 150, 319; Kaplanoff, "Charles Pinckney and the American Republican Tradition," 85–89; Hollis, *South Carolina College*, 268–69.

36. Eric H. Walther, *The Fire-Eaters* (Baton Rouge, La., 1992), 166.

37. For an engaging study of the trio of political giants, see Merrill D. Peterson, *The Great Triumvirate: Webster, Clay, and Calhoun* (New York, 1987).

38. Ford, *Origins of Southern Radicalism*, 190.

39. This is not to say that Calhoun had given up every last shred of realistic hope. He was, in fact, ambivalent and made contradictory statements in his conversation and correspondence to the very end. But certainly his final, dramatic public statements were decidedly negative as to sectional reconciliation. John Niven, *John C. Calhoun and the Price of Union: A Biography* (Baton Rouge, La., 1988), 342–45.

40. Freehling, *Road to Disunion*, 510.

41. Walther, *The Fire-Eaters*.

42. John Barnwell, *Love of Order: South Carolina's First Secession Crisis* (Chapel Hill, N.C., 1982); Ford, *Origins of Southern Radicalism*, chap. 5.

43. Harold S. Schultz, *Nationalism and Sectionalism in South Carolina, 1852–1860: A Study of the Movement for Southern Independence* (Durham, N.C., 1950); Steven A. Channing, *Crisis of Fear: Secession in South Carolina* (New York, 1970); Ford, *Origins of Southern Radicalism*, chap. 10. It must have appeared to some southerners during the dawning days of the Confederate nation that South Carolina would re-

tain its hotspur reputation. Its leaders complained about the Confederate Constitution's failure to acknowledge expressly the right of state secession, as well as the
document's lack of a prohibition on the admission of nonslaveholding states and
the continuation of the three-fifths language in congressional apportionment.
Don E. Fehrenbacher, *Constitutions and Constitutionalism in the Slaveholding
South* (Athens, Ga., 1989), 66–67, 102.

44. There is an excellent discussion of the complexities of states' rights thought and
southern support for South Carolina during the nullification crisis in Ellis, *Union
at Risk*. See also Freehling, *Prelude to Civil War*. The "folk wisdom" about thirty-
year convulsions, including the Tillman movement in the 1890s, is in Ford, *Origins
of Southern Radicalism*, 99.

45. James L. Morrison Jr., ed., *The Memoirs of Henry Heth* (Westport, Conn., 1974),
149; Leroy P. Graf et al., eds., *The Papers of Andrew Johnson*, 10 vols. (Knoxville,
Tenn., 1967–92), 4:220.

46. James L. Petigru to Edward Everett, Aug. 28, 1860, in James Petigru Carson, *Life,
Letters, and Speeches of James Louis Petigru: The Union Man of South Carolina*
(Washington, D.C., 1920), 359–60. An excellent analysis of Petrigru's political con-
servatism and Unionism is Lacy Ford, "James Louis Petigru: The Last South Car-
olina Federalist," in O'Brien and Moltke-Hansen, *Intellectual Life in Antebellum
Charleston*, 152–85. See also Lillian Kibler, *Benjamin F. Perry: South Carolina
Unionist* (Durham, N.C., 1946), and "Unionist Sentiment in South Carolina in
1860," *Journal of Southern History* 4 (1938): 346–66.

47. The following contain examples of the opinions expressed in the above paragraph
as well as other indictments of the state. Ulrich Bonnell Phillips, ed., "The Correspondence of Robert Toombs, Alexander H. Stephens, and Howell Cobb," *Annual
Report of the American Historical Association for the Year 1911*, 2 vols. (Washington,
D.C., 1913), 2:195, 217, 228, 235, 236, 238, 240; Richard L. Zuber, *Jonathan Worth:
A Biography of a Southern Unionist* (Chapel Hill, N.C., 1965), 109–10, 119; W[il-
liam] G. Brownlow, *Sketches of the Rise, Progress, and Decline of Secession . . .*
(Philadelphia, 1862), 63, 81–82, 109–10, 116; James W. McKee Jr., ed., "Reflections
of a Tennessee Unionist," *Tennessee Historical Quarterly* 33 (1974): 435; Oliver P.
Temple, *East Tennessee and the Civil War* (1899; rpt. New York, 1971), 334, 338;
John Minor Botts, *Great Rebellion: Its Secret History, Rise, Progress, and Disas-
trous Failure* (New York, 1866), 244, 273–74; Donald E. Reynolds, *Editors Make
War: Southern Newspapers in the Secession Crisis* (Nashville, 1970), 135–36, 163–66;
Dwight L. Dumond, ed., *Southern Editorials on Secession* (New York, 1931), 327–
28; Howard K. Beale, ed., *The Diary of Edward Bates, 1859–1866* (Washington,
D.C., 1933), 168. Sam Houston's expressions are in Amelia W. Williams and Eugene C. Barker, eds., *The Writings of Sam Houston, 1813–1863*, 8 vols. (Austin,
Tex., 1938–43), 2:250–51, 265, 293–97, quotation on p. 251. For Mrs. Chesnut's comment, see *Mary Chesnut's Civil War*, ed. C. Vann Woodward (New Haven, 1981), 4.
Chesnut herself heard a report in 1861 that "South Carolina apparently was going to
secede from the new Confederacy." Ibid., 11. Much more information on the topic is
in Carl N. Degler, *The Other South: Southern Dissenters in the Nineteenth Century*

(New York, 1974), chaps. 5–7; William C. Harris, "The Southern Unionist Critique of the Civil War," *Civil War History* 31 (1985): 39–56, which stresses the conspiracy theme in Unionist writings.

48. James M. McPherson, *Battle Cry of Freedom: The Civil War Era* (New York, 1988), 267.

49. John B. Edmunds Jr., *Francis W. Pickens and the Politics of Destruction* (Chapel Hill, N.C., 1986), 154–63.

50. In his message to Congress of July 4, 1861, Lincoln declared, "There is much reason to believe that the Union men are the majority in many, if not every other one [except South Carolina], of the so-called seceded States." Roy P. Basler, ed., *The Collected Works of Abraham Lincoln,* 8 vols., 2 supplements (New Brunswick, N.J., 1953–55), 4:437. For Lincoln's correspondence concerning Fort Sumter with Seward, Chew, and Pickens, see ibid., 316–18, 323–24.

51. Howard Cecil Perkins, ed., *Northern Editorials on Secession,* 2 vols. (New York, 1942), 1:97, 104–5, 124, 157, 331, 352, 2:516, 517, 672, 739–40, 845, 862, 875. The standard accounts of the issues and events associated with Fort Sumter are William A. Swanberg, *First Blood: The Story of Sumter* (New York, 1957); Richard N. Current, *Lincoln and the First Shot* (Philadelphia, 1963). The most convincing analysis of Lincoln's motives and behavior is Kenneth M. Stampp, *The Imperiled Union: Essays on the Background of the Civil War* (New York, 1980), chap. 6.

52. Ralph Volney Harlow, *Samuel Adams: Promotor of the American Revolution* (New York, 1923); John C. Miller, *San Adams: Pioneer in Propaganda* (Stanford, Calif., 1936).

53. Studies with psychological themes stress status anxiety on the part of various fire-eaters and other strong proslavery advocates. This literature is summarized and generally criticized as overly simplistic in Robert E. May, "Psychobiography and Secession: The Southern Radical as Maladjusted 'Outsider,'" *Civil War History* 34 (1988): 46–69.

54. James H. Hutson, "The American Revolution: The Triumph of a Delusion," in *New Wine in Old Skins: A Comparative View of Socio-Political Structures and Values Affecting the American Revolution,* ed. Erich Angermann et al. (Stuttgart, Germany, 1976), 177–94. Hutson continues his examination of the psychological dimensions of early American political behavior in "The Origins of 'The Paranoid Style in American Politics': Public Jealousy from the Age of Walpole to the Age of Jackson," in *Saints and Revolutionaries: Essays on Early American History,* ed. David D. Hall, John M. Murrin, and Thad W. Tate (New York, 1984), 332–72. Hutson's portrayal of the Massachusetts leaders does not vary appreciably from their unflattering characterization in Douglass Adair and John A. Schutz, eds., *Peter Oliver's Origins and Progress of the American Rebellion: A Tory View* (San Marino, Calif., 1961), 39–45, 83–84. A compelling revisionist interpretation of Samuel Adams, showing him to be somewhat cautious in pressing the case of Massachusetts in the Continental Congress and arriving relatively late to an advocacy of independence—perhaps not before November 1775—appears in Maier, *Old Revolutionaries,* 3–50, esp. 21–26. See also, for another judicious treatment of Adams,

Charles W. Akers, "Sam Adams—and Much More," *New England Quarterly* 47 (1974): 120–31. Otis's mental difficulties are analyzed in John J. Waters, "James Otis, Jr.: An Ambivalent Revolutionary," *History of Childhood Quarterly* 1 (1973): 142–50.

55. John M. Murrin, "Political Development," in *Colonial British America: Essays in the New History of the Early Modern Era*, ed. Jack P. Greene and J. R. Pole (Baltimore, 1984), 445.

56. Pencak, *War, Politics, and Revolution*, xi, xii; Jack P. Greene, "The Seven Years' War and the American Revolution: The Causal Relationship Reconsidered," *Journal of Imperial and Commonwealth History* 8 (1980): 97–98; John M. Murrin, "The French and Indian War, the American Revolution, and the Counterfactual Hypothesis: Reflections on Lawrence Henry Gipson and John Shy," *Reviews in American History* 1 (1973): 314–15.

57. Thomas Barnard, *A Sermon Preached before His Excellency Francis Bernard, Esq., . . . May 25, 1763* (Boston, 1763), 44.

58. Bernard Bailyn, ed., *Pamphlets of the American Revolution, 1750–1765* (Cambridge, Mass., 1965), 455, 481. Similar expressions by other Massachusetts writers appear in Pencak, *War, Politics, and Revolution*, 237–38.

59. Bushman, *King and People*, chap. 6.

60. John Adams to James Warren, Apr. 9, 1774, in Robert J. Taylor et al., eds., *The Adams Papers: Papers of John Adams*, 11 vols. to date (Cambridge, Mass., 1977–), 2:83.

61. Worthington C. Ford, et al., eds., *Journals of the Continental Congress*, 34 vols. (Washington, D.C., 1904–27), 2:35.

62. Bushman, *King and People*, 213.

63. Don Higginbotham, *The War of American Independence: Military Attitudes, Policies, and Practice, 1763–89* (New York, 1971), 82–83; Cary, *Warren*, 196, 199–200; Jerrilyn Greene Marston, *King and Congress: The Transfer of Political Legitimacy, 1774–76* (Princeton, N.J., 1987), 143–49, 253–61.

64. Abigail Adams to John Adams, Mar. 16, 1776, in Lyman H. Butterfield et al., eds., *The Adams Papers: Adams Family Correspondence*, 4 vols. (Cambridge, Mass., 1963–73), 2:357. For the reluctance of Americans everywhere to give up on the king, see William D. Liddle, " 'A Patriot King, or None': Lord Bolingbroke and the American Renunciation of George III," *Journal of American History* 65 (1979): 951–70.

65. Calhoon, *Loyalists in Revolutionary America*, chap. 30; Waters, *Otis Family*, 184–88; Stephen E. Patterson, *Political Parties in Revolutionary Massachusetts* (Madison, Wis., 1973), chap. 5.

66. Quoted in Merrill Jensen, *The Founding of a Nation: A History of the American Revolution, 1763–76* (New York, 1968), 652.

67. Massachusetts House *Journals*, quoted in ibid., 677.

68. Some South Carolinians did feel in the late antebellum period that their state's contributions to the Revolution were not fully appreciated, partly because such Yankee historians as George Bancroft had deliberately slighted the state. William Gilmore Simms led the state's efforts on behalf of its Revolutionary past, not only in his his-

tories and novels but also by making a northern speaking tour. John Hope Franklin, "The North, the South, and the American Revolution," *Journal of American History* 62 (1975): 5–23.

69. Charles M. Wiltse, *John C. Calhoun, Sectionalist, 1840–1850* (Indianapolis, 1951), 476. Calhoun retained the great respect of his most distinguished colleagues to the end of his life. Old opponents such as Webster and Clay visited him during his final days and later delivered eulogies in the Senate. One is also reminded today of Calhoun's national standing by visiting such places as Calhoun County, Illinois, and Lake Calhoun in Minnesota.

70. Ellis, *Union at Risk*, chap. 9.

71. Ernest McPherson Lander Jr., *Reluctant Imperialists: Calhoun, the South Carolinians, and the Mexican War* (Baton Rouge, La., 1980), shows that substantial sentiment in the state opposed territorial acquisitions in the Southwest and saw revived sectional discord as a result of such additions to the Union.

72. *House Executive Documents,* 37th Cong., 3d sess., 116, 137; Drew Gilpin Faust, *James Henry Hammond and the Old South: A Design for Mastery* (Baton Rouge, La., 1982), 344–45. Exaggerated notions in both North and South of successful slave escapes to freedom are detailed in Larry Gara, *The Liberty Line: The Legend of the Underground Railroad* (Lexington, Ky., 1961).

73. Don E. Fehrenbacher, *Constitutions and Constitutionalism in the Slaveholding South* (Athens, Ga., 1989), 51.

74. Woodward, *Mary Chesnut's Civil War, 366.*

75. Freehling, *Road to Disunion,* esp. 213–14, 252, 277–78, 286, 333, 519, 520, 528–29, 530–32, 536, quotation on p. 213.

76. William C. Harris, *William Woods Holden: Firebrand of North Carolina Politics* (Baton Rouge, La., 1987), 87–89, 91, 104.

77. South Carolina's political maneuverings in 1860 prior to the election of Lincoln are treated in Channing, *Crisis of Fear,* chaps. 4–7; Schultz, *Nationalism and Sectionalism,* 200–224; Charles Edward Cauthen, *South Carolina Goes to War, 1860–1865* (Chapel Hill, N.C., 1950), 14–30; Roy F. Nichols, *The Disruption of American Democracy* (New York, 1948), 288–367.

78. Don Higginbotham, "The Martial Spirit in the Antebellum South: Some Further Speculations in a National Context," *Journal of Southern History* 58 (1992): 17–18; Jean Martin Flynn, *The Militia in Antebellum South Carolina Society* (Spartanburg, S.C., 1991). The chief advocate of reviving and reforming the militia in 1860 was James Johnston Pettigrew, who as late as October of that year did not fully sense the likelihood of secession anytime soon. He corresponded with northerners about revitalizing the militia and had an excellent personal and professional relationship with the officers of the federal garrison in the Charleston area. Clyde N. Wilson, *Carolina Cavalier: The Life and Mind of James Johnston Pettigrew* (Athens, Ga., 1990), chap. 10, esp. 129–30. As to the military posture of the state in December 1860, Governor Pickens declared that "I found everything in utter confusion, when I came into office, and really no military supplies." Quoted in Edmunds, *Pickens,* 160. Similar comments on the state's unpreparedness came from Captain Abner

Doubleday of the Fort Sumter garrison and William Howard Russell, a war correspondent of the *Times* of London. Abner Doubleday, *Reminiscences of Forts Sumter and Moultrie in 1860–'61* (New York, 1876), 71; Martin Crawford, ed., *William Howard Russell's Civil War: Private Diary and Letters, 1861–1862* (Athens, Ga., 1992), 42–43.

79. Fehrenbacher, *Constitutions and Constitutionalism,* 55; Laura A. White, *Robert Barnwell Rhett: Father of Secession* (New York, 1931), chaps. 8–9; Charleston *Mercury.*

80. Edmunds, *Pickens,* 144–45, 148, 150. Mary Chesnut reported that, according to former United States senator Louis T. Wigfall of Texas, "before he left Washington, Pickens, our governor, and Trescot were openly against secession. Trescot does not pretend to like it now. He grumbles all the time. But Governor Pickens is fire-eater down to the ground." *Mary Chesnut's Civil War,* 40.

81. Schultz, *Nationalism and Sectionalism,* 34, 176, 181, 206, 223.

82. Lawrence T. McDonnell, "Struggle against Suicide: James Henry Hammond and the Secession of South Carolina," *Southern Studies* 22 (1983): 109–37, quotation on p. 118; Foust, *Hammond,* 349–63.

83. Waters, *Otis Family,* 186, 188.

84. McDonnell, "Struggle against Suicide," 118; Akers, "Sam Adams—and Much More," 127–30.

85. Patterson, *Political Parties,* chap. 5.

86. For a carefully detailed study, see William L. Barney, *The Secessionist Impulse: Alabama and Mississippi in 1860* (Princeton, N.J., 1974); Ralph A. Wooster, *The Secession Conventions of the South* (Princeton, N.J., 1962), chaps. 3–4. Barney, my colleague, remains convinced that Alabama and Mississippi would not have seceded first. William W. Freehling, in a forthcoming volume, will examine the question of whether a conspiracy existed between certain Deep South extremist leaders and South Carolina fire-eaters, involving assurances that if South Carolina withdrew from the Union, their states would immediately follow suit.

Index